Running on a Dream
The Pat Farmer Story

Ian Eckersley

ALLEN & UNWIN

First published in 2000

Copyright © Ian Eckersley 2000

Allen & Unwin
9 Atchison Street
St Leonards NSW 2065
Australia
Phone: (61 2) 8425 0100
Fax: (61 2) 9906 2218
Email: frontdesk@allen-unwin.com.au
Web: http://www.allenandunwin.com

National Library of Australia
Cataloguing-in-Publication entry:

Eckersley, Ian.
Running on a dream: the Pat Farmer story.

 ISBN 1 86508 411 5
 Includes index.

 1. Farmer, Pat, 1962– . 2. Marathon running—Australia—Biography.
 3. Runners (Sports)—Australia—Biography. I. Title.

796.4252092

Set in 12.5/15 pt Adobe Garamond by DOCUPRO, Sydney
Printed and bound by Griffin Press Pty Ltd, South Australia

10 9 8 7 6 5 4 3 2 1

Contents

Acknowledgments

Heroes and inspiration. They may be different things to different people, but we all need someone or something to believe in and admire. The burgeoning world of professional sport is brimming with stars and celebrities who are worshipped by children and adults alike. Ultra marathon running has not tossed up too many national heroes—it is a sport that lacks glamour, hype and that all-important ingredient, sponsorship. But what Pat Farmer and these extraordinary men and women possess is courage that defies common sense; mind power that defies science; and an iron will that is the envy of many. They rarely receive the plaudits of other higher-profile sportspeople but their achievements deserve to be ranked up there with the greatest triumphs of the human spirit. They shun conventional wisdom and physical limits and prove that 'impossible' is merely a word that exists in the confines of our minds.

In the circle of life heroes come and go, while inspiration is sometimes fleeting. Originally, Pat Farmer did not seek to motivate people and stir patriotism among Australians. But amidst a sea of pain and loneliness, it helped him make sense of why he pushes himself to the absolute limit of mental and physical endurance. He does not seek to create a nation of ultra marathon runners—another one or two might be more competition than he needs if he ever decides to emerge from retirement. Pat merely hopes to inspire people to be the best they can be at whatever they want, and not to be cramped or bounded by what convention, upbringing or society says is possible or impossible.

First and foremost, my thanks to my loving and devoted wife Angie who amazes and humbles me with her endless supply of patience, support and belief in me. This book is dedicated to her and to our children Dominic, Lucas and Claudia. I trust I am always a hero to them in every possible way—there could be no greater reward for any parent. Special thanks to my parents Vilma and the late Ian senior, who provided my three siblings and me with a wonderful example of sacrifice, service and a strong work ethic.

To my second family—Dominic, Tricia and Maria—a thousand thanks for nourishing and supporting us in every way. Thanks also to James and Shirine for upgrading my computer skills, and to my sister Sharyn and brother Mark for their eternal love and support.

Finally, thanks to Pat Farmer and his family for their inspiration, cooperation and honesty during the preparation of this, my first book. I had the pleasure of meeting Lisa Farmer before her untimely death and could see from just one encounter that she was indeed a unique person. I could easily appreciate why she and Pat shared such a special bond.

To part-time mentor Adrian McGregor and Patrick Gallagher of Allen & Unwin—thank you for your faith in the project and me. There were many who doubted it—the world will always have more knockers than believers—but the support of positive thinkers goes a long way. My thanks to senior editor Emma Cotter who expertly guided me through the creative process and gave me positive feedback when I needed it most. I am also indebted to Mark Gladwell for his constant supply of help and information and the Austin family for their friendship and hospitality.

I hope everyone who reads this story derives just a little bit of inspiration to follow their dreams.

Prelude

The scenery was breathtaking. When summer lit up the Rocky Mountains, it exposed the full majesty of one of Nature's wondrous creations. The remnants of spring snow lay by the side of the mountain pass. Below, icy water gushed through gorges as part of the regular cleansing cycle. But in the midst of such beauty, Pat Farmer's leg felt like it was on fire. The swelling around his shin was now the size of a tennis ball and it throbbed through his skin and tendons, back deep into his bone. The pain was excruciating. He couldn't imagine it could have intensified, but this was now the third day of debilitating pain and it felt as if someone were thrusting a knife into his left leg with each faltering step.

Pat looked longingly at the never-ending trail of snow on either side of the road. The urge to stop and sink his leg into the ice was almost overwhelming at times. But he feared that, if he stopped, the temptation to stay might be too great. Pain had a strange way of messing with his mind. His thoughts were a jumble of frustration, self-pity and regret, balanced by an underlying tenacity and determination to work through this calamity.

The injury, which had been diagnosed as a stress fracture of the tibia, could not have come at a worse time. Pat was the lone

Australian in the toughest foot race in the world, the 4675 kilometre Trans-America road race. His dream—indeed, he hoped his destiny—was to win and prove he was the best ultra marathon runner on earth. When the pain first surfaced he was running three hours behind one of the most ruthless competitors in the sport, Dusan Mravlje, a soldier in the Slovenian army. Pat wasn't sure what the time lag was now, but his quest was becoming increasingly difficult with each passing hour. He knew the concept of justice held no sway in this most gruelling of sports. But he had sacrificed so much—too much at times—to have the prize snatched from his grasp now.

This dream had obsessed and driven him. But it seemed that Pat's aggression and fierce competitive streak had in fact been his downfall. In hindsight he could see how his reluctance to concede even one second to his rival during each of the gruelling daily stages had been self-destructive. The human body wasn't designed to be pushed like that for an average of 70 kilometres a day for 64 days. Dusan knew it; Pat should have known it. Maybe he should have accepted the Slovenian's offer of a deal—run together to New York and make it easy on themselves. But to settle for second place would be treachery—to himself, to his cherished principles and to all those who believed in him. The notion of surrender, to anyone or anything, was something he despised.

After more than three weeks, he was tired of the pain, tired of his heart aching for his devoted wife and newborn baby, tired of the tough lifestyle, tired of being tired. Why go on, and fight what was probably a losing battle against serious injury? The obvious questions were posed by *Sixty Minutes* reporter Tracy Curro in the middle of his worst crisis. Why not quit? What was he afraid of?

Before a national audience, a vulnerable and tearful Pat Farmer spoke openly of one of his greatest fears:

'I'm scared of being normal. I'm scared of being like everybody else. I just want to be somebody and do something. I've got a gift to be able to run long distances and I'd be foolish if I didn't do it.'

Pat Farmer, the Aussie battler, was at war with his own body. He had endured three of the hardest days of his life. But there were still 40 days of extreme exertion to go. How many more could he endure? He had always wondered what his limits were. Maybe now he had his answer.

Pat's inspiration flowed from many springs. But none was deeper or more sustaining than his wife and soulmate Lisa. He challenged his body to achieve extraordinary things, often so he could say to her: 'Look, I did it. I told you I would!' Not that she ever doubted him. Her unconditional love and support knew no bounds. For the first time in his life, Pat faced the terrifying prospect of not rising to a challenge. This was his greatest test ever, yet still Lisa believed, telling every television, radio and newspaper reporter who inquired back in Sydney: 'Pat is the most determined person you'll ever meet in your whole life. He's going to get to New York whatever happens, if he has to crawl across the finish line Pat will be there.'

'She gave me so much strength because of her total belief in me. I couldn't fathom how she could have so much faith. Lisa was only ever a phone call away and I drew motivation from her words. It wasn't just what she said but the way she said them, her reassuring tone. That's what got me through every day.'

He couldn't let the most important person in his life down. He wouldn't let himself, family and friends down. 'Gambatte!'— 'Fight on!' That's what the Japanese runners and crew would say to Pat whenever they passed. I have to believe I can still win this, he told himself. If I can conquer this injury, nothing will stop me finishing. If I can suffer a serious injury, why not the others? Could they endure the humiliation of going from first to last? Do they have the courage and strength to fight on?

1

The worst day of my life

The sweet, unmistakeable sound of children's laughter echoed through the house. Unbridled and unstoppable, it filled the rooms and halls of the rambling low-set residence adding life and vitality to bricks, mortar, timber and plaster. Dillon's delighted squeals when Lisa tickled him made her laugh in turn. The baby—nurtured and nursed by his mother since conception—now fed off one of the most natural of emotions. Three-year-old Brooke appeared bleary-eyed at the door. She immediately sensed there was fun to be had. She ran and jumped into her parents' bed. The scene was getting out of control for an athlete in training who had to snatch sleep whenever and wherever he could.

A house which only months earlier was very much a construction site was rapidly becoming a home. It was a testament to the strongest of work ethics and a couple's obsession with a dream. Walls had been brought to life with the proud display of photos, prints and memorabilia; even the bedroom floors had been given a lift by the installation of commercial-grade carpet. This dwelling would provide shelter from the approaching winter with greater comfort than they had known for several years—it was certainly a progression from the Spartan existence in the garage that they had previously endured. Pat and Lisa had lived and breathed the creation of their dream home, and like all of their goals and rewards, it didn't happen without considerable effort. It was steadily filling with the moments and memories that make a house a haven. This night was one to be savoured now and treasured later for a lifetime.

Pat decided these times were too precious to miss. Never mind the fact that he had to get up in two hours to launch himself into another eighteen-hour day. Tears from the pain of teething still stained Dillon's cheeks. His distress upset his parents, so they were happy to help trigger a transformation. 'Better laughing than crying,' thought Pat. 'Either way I'm not going to get back to sleep.' The distraction worked. When the moment had passed they all huddled in a state of near-exhaustion under the doona.

The taxi headlights pierced the morning gloom as the cab signalled its arrival with the crunching of rubber on dirt and gravel. Pat scrambled the last of his possessions and did a mental checklist—keys, suit, tie, shirt, dress shoes, mobile phone. He mused on his life as the car wended its way through the darkness. A smile creased his face as his mind drifted back in time several hours. 'How blessed am I,' he thought. 'I have two precious bundles of joy—a girl and a boy—perfect, just perfect. A beautiful loving wife who is forever my rock of Gibraltar and the life-blood of my hopes and dreams. Training for the world record for vertical running up the AMP Tower in two months is going well; a few other events are flowing nicely through in the pipeline; and my Mount Everest looms in the distance: the 14 500 kilometre run around Australia. The daily grind of running 300 kilometres a week and working a nine-hour day as a landscaper [with his brother, Tony], coupled with the usual financial stress, has been somewhat wearying for us. But hey, the house is really starting to take shape and we're all in good health. Yes, life is good, thought Pat. Life is very good.'

Never give up and finish at all costs. It was a motto that Pat had shared with his running friend Valerie Warren. Despite a 30-year age gap, the pair had a connection and identified closely with the creed in both training and life. Val's courageous attitude was a prominent theme at her funeral, as friends and family reflected on her life. Known as the 'female Cliff Young', she had only begun running in her forties, and was continuing to set age records in her sixties. The service had been a mixture of sadness for the passing of such a generous, warm person, yet joy that Val had lived long enough to fulfil her passion for running and died doing what she loved best. A casualty of an unpredictable heart attack while on the road for her morning 10 kilometre run, it was the abruptness of it that shocked everyone. 'She was so healthy—you don't expect people like Val to die suddenly,' they said. 'You think people like that will go on and on.' Indeed she had, over many years of ultra marathon running, culminating in a world veteran's record, at the age of 56, for six-day running—an amazing 571.5 kilometres in 1990. Transformed from mourner back to labourer, Pat was returning to work when he was jolted from his thoughts by the piercing ring of his mobile phone.

'Pat, it's Camden police. Where are you?'

'I'm driving back to a job site at Turramurra. I've been to a funeral at Castlebrook.'

'We want you to pull over and wait for us.'

'I can't. I'm driving someone else's car and I've got to return it.'

'We don't care. We want you to pull over and wait for us at the nearest train station.'

'What for? What's the matter? What's going on?' Pat inquired with a growing sense of urgency.

His persistent questions failed to elicit further information, so Pat agreed to the police request. The 'weirdest phone call of his life' had enveloped Pat with a feeling of fear and alarm he had rarely felt. He immediately rang his brother Tony and recounted the conversation. 'Look, I don't know what this is all about, but you better get up to Turramurra station and meet me there. I'm not sure what's happened, but I know this much: they don't come and pick you up when you've got a speeding fine.'

Pat's mind went into panic mode. His immediate concern was for his 65-year-old mother Mary. With Pat and Lisa booked for a fund-raising event for the Paralympics, she was scheduled to travel to their home that day to baby-sit. He called his mother but when the phone rang out without answer, he felt an odd sense of reassurance, convincing himself she was in transit and was all right.

His next phone call was to Camden Credit Union where Lisa had been working for over a year. Client Services Manager Colleen Chittendon was a lifelong family friend of the Farmer family and a friend to Lisa. She had helped her secure a job with the Credit Union when she was looking for work closer to home while pregnant with Dillon.

'Colleen, do you know what's going on?'

'I don't know, Pat. All I can tell you is that Lisa's not here,' she said.

Almost reading his mind, she added, 'I've already rung the child-care centre and the kids are all right, they're fine. I just don't know about Lisa. All I know is that she's not at work. The detectives rang looking for contact details for the next of kin. They wouldn't tell me anything else.'

Deep down Colleen felt something was terribly wrong. Lisa had sounded her normal bright and bubbly self when they had spoken by telephone earlier that morning. No hint of any problem. But Lisa's lateness this morning—even by one hour— was completely out of character for a woman regarded as one of the most dedicated and efficient workers in the office. Sensing her friend was in trouble ('it's probably just that her car and mobile phone have both broken down,' she rationalised without really believing it), Colleen made plans to leave the office to look for Lisa. That was before the police called.

'I knew something terrible must have happened,' she said. 'Reading between the lines, I could tell it wasn't nothing. I asked the police if I could go to the hospital but they said no. I just prayed for a miracle.'

Pat was praying too, with more purpose and passion than he'd ever done before. The wait for the police was becoming tortuous. Minutes—which so often passed for seconds in the context of two-month-long ultra marathons—dragged like hours. No God, he prayed, don't let anything happen to my precious Lisa. If she's had an accident and it's real bad, please God, help that she might just be a paraplegic.

'I really started to think the worst,' he recalled. 'All I could think about was our house and the verandah outside our bedroom—it's a beautiful verandah. I had pictures in my head that she'd been injured and thought if that's the case I could take care of her for the rest of my life. She could be outside our house and see it all finished and sit on the verandah and still watch the kids grow up. So I just kept consoling myself with those sorts of thoughts.'

Pat's mobile phone rang again. Camden police were battling traffic and had asked police from a closer station to meet him. They asked him to remain where he was, but still wouldn't provide any further explanation. After nearly 20 years of running, Pat had dealt with plenty of physical and mental torment. But this uncertainty was greater than anything he had ever experienced. Pat's brother Tony and one of his workers, James Merritt, got there before the police and tried to ease Pat's anxieties.

Finally police pulled into the carpark of Turramurra railway station. Pat awaited their news with a fear and anticipation that almost made him nauseous. The two officers quietly ushered him into the back seat of their car. 'There's been an accident and your wife has died.' The words and the moment are frozen in time in Pat's mind. A sentence that shattered a charmed life and sent him spiralling into a nightmare from which he felt he would never recover. 'We're going to take you down to Hornsby police station and look after you for a while until Camden detectives can pick you up,' one said.

A momentary numbness gave way to raw emotion. Tears rolled down a face, pale from shock and creased with anguish. For many years, Pat and Lisa had lived with the realisation that one of them might die before their time. They had spoken about it occasionally—with some sense of trepidation, but more about the practical effects it would have on children, finances, their hopes and dreams. But both assumed that because of Pat's often-perilous pursuits, it was more likely that Lisa would be the one left to face life alone.

Pat was now faced with a scenario that he had always found unthinkable. Tony was shattered for his brother; a knife had been plunged deep into his brother's heart and he could almost feel it too. Pat and Tony were more than brothers. They were best friends, comrades in arms, workmates. Lisa had played match-maker between Tony and her best friend Linda. 'You want to be careful with Tony,' Lisa had warned playfully. 'You and I might end up becoming sisters-in-law.' The prophecy was fulfilled, to everyone's delight. They had shared so many of life's joys, so many laughs and such a special bond. Now they shared a sorrow, which defied any sense of justice, or any logic in religious faith that was such a part of the Farmer family's spirituality.

'I don't understand, I just don't understand.' The words rang through Pat's head. Soon he was saying them aloud as he struggled to comprehend. 'Tony, I've got to go with the police, I'll talk to you later.' Workmate and friend James Merritt was also overcome by a mixture of emotion. While he wanted to help, he felt helpless. While he had gone there to support a mate, he almost wanted to be somewhere else. 'I felt a bit awkward, like I shouldn't be there,' he said. 'It was just so sad—knowing what Lisa and Pat meant to each other and seeing it ripped away from him like that.'

At Hornsby police station, Pat was struggling to deal with his suddenly lonely and tumultuous existence. He had lost his soulmate. Lisa was his reason for running, his reason for living. Pat's grief was for now boundless; his mind was cluttered with chaotic thoughts of sorrow and regret. The one mercy was that Lisa had dropped Brooke and Dillon off at childcare only minutes before her death. His mind couldn't cope with images of his wife and children all dying. He thanked God for sparing his son and daughter and giving him at least some reason to carry on living.

But that blessing would never change the irreplaceable loss of Lisa. A now cruel and uncertain world left Pat unsure of what to say, where to look, who to turn to. He attempted to hide his identity and his tears from visitors and station staff, who tried to comfort him.

'At the time and even now, I was touched by the kindness of the officers,' he recalled. 'They kept asking me if there was anything they could do for me or anything they could get me. All the time, the thought going through the back of my head was: "They're so considerate and so kind." It was funny to be thinking that way, but it was because I couldn't believe they were being so kind to me, when they must have been so busy and had so many other things to do. I kept thinking to myself: "This must be a common thing for them—they're treating me as if I'm the only person in the world."'

Camden police, who had attended the accident scene, arrived to interview Pat and take him to identify Lisa's body. Another dimension of the tragedy was emerging. They asked if there was anybody else, other family members, who should be contacted. Lisa's parents Barry and June Bullivant were at work at their dry-cleaning business at Granville and must be told, said Pat solemnly. Police queried whether Lisa had any health problems. 'Because while she had an accident, it appears it wasn't bad enough to cause her death,' they revealed.

Police had been puzzled from the outset. An eyewitness following Lisa saw her apparently lose control of the Mitsubishi sedan at 8.40 a.m. on the Camden Valley Way, Catherine Field, and cross on to the wrong side of the road. Lisa's car narrowly avoided oncoming traffic and halted after it collided with a steel fence. Witnesses hailed an ambulance that was passing by just minutes later. Officers treated her at the scene, but unfortunately were not equipped with a potentially life-saving defibrillator and were unable to get her heart started again before she was taken to Camden Hospital. Lisa went into cardiac arrest and was pronounced dead at 10.00 a.m.

Pat was also confused. 'The only thing I know that was wrong with her was she had a heart murmur. But thousands of people have them. A doctor checked her just a few weeks ago and he said there was nothing wrong. They said the only time it would be a problem was if she was carrying a child. She had both our children without any trouble so we didn't think anything of it.'

One of the officers confessed: 'I've got a heart murmur myself.' 'That's what I mean,' said Pat. 'I don't think that could be the problem.' Around lunchtime, police drove with Pat to Pressmatic Dry Cleaners in Granville. Lisa's step-mother June Bullivant was there managing the business. Pat stuttered as he tried to speak the words that he himself still scarcely believed to be true. 'June, I have to tell you something. Lisa's dead. She was in an accident. I need you to come and identify the body with me.' Pat was overcome again and appeared lost for any further explanation. He excused himself and headed for the toilet.

Mindful of her staff, June Bullivant walked outside with police. They asked more detailed questions about Lisa's heart condition. She organised for someone to take care of business in her absence and, against the wishes of police, drove herself to the family home at Greystanes, fifteen minutes away. 'As it was for so many of us, it was just a dreadfully traumatic event,' June recalled. 'Barry's baby was dead, his little girl was gone. Telling him was just so, so hard.'

Long after the event, Pat still has to fight back the tears as he recounts the agony of breaking the news to Lisa's father. The anguish was magnified for June and Pat as this was a truly tragic case of history repeating itself. Barry Bullivant had been 29 when his young wife Iris was diagnosed with breast cancer in 1963. It was the beginning of a long, hard fight against the silent killer. Iris had a radical mastectomy to the right breast and sickening radiotherapy. She entered a period of remission, during which she gave birth to a son, Craig, and Lisa. Just when it was thought she had conquered the illness, it reappeared. Iris Bullivant died in 1970, aged 37. She was buried on 13 February, Black Friday. Craig was aged five, Lisa was three. Twenty-eight years later, a mother was again ripped from her family. Two children were again left without a mother; the daughter was again just three years old.

This time, with old scars reopened and new ones carved out, a father and husband were bonded by their grief, united in their support for each other. 'I could understand at that very moment just how hard it must have been for Barry to have that happen to his wife and his young daughter,' said Pat. When they arrived at Camden Hospital to identify Lisa's body, Barry put his arm on Pat's shoulder. 'Son, this will be the toughest thing you will ever do.' Pat had no doubt he was right. 'I remember looking at Lisa and she looked so peaceful, like there was nothing wrong with her,' he said. 'I kissed her and felt how cold the body was. She was just lying there. It was so very, very hard. It was the worst day of my life.'

Later that day, Barry accompanied Pat to the childcare centre to collect Brooke and Dillon. Despite everyone's fears, Barry was proving to be a pillar of strength, especially for Pat. A more traumatic reaction would follow in the weeks and months ahead, but for now he was able to dig deep into his well of inner strength, to provide emotional support for others. The pair spoke to the children's teachers. By now reality was starting to hit home. Pat recalls: 'I remember looking at my daughter Brooke and thinking to myself, "Is this what awaits me in 30 years' time? Am I going to lose my daughter, just like Barry?" And that fear will never leave me.'

As police suspected, Lisa had not died as a result of the car accident. An autopsy revealed the cause of death as mitral valve prolapse—a condition that had caused a valve in her heart to fail. While no official statistics are kept, it is believed one in 250 people suffers from the disease. Most live well beyond 50 years of age.

Lisa Farmer had lived her life in the shadow of a premature death. The heart murmur was thought to be less of a health threat than breast cancer, which hung like a sword of Damocles over her head. The family appeared to be genetically predisposed to the killer disease. As well as claiming her mother and a cousin, an aunt had undergone a mastectomy and survived. Some friends believe an underlying insecurity about her health contributed to Lisa's intense love of life. The threat from breast cancer, particularly, appears to have been one of the few issues that rattled her composure. Pat and Lisa were both always wary of the warning signs of the disease. Lisa had mammograms twice a year. While she always received a clean bill of health, it didn't dispel what at times seemed to be paranoia about breast cancer. Former work colleague Ann Bowen recalls the normally unflappable Lisa getting upset once, after discovering a lump in her breast. 'She was in tears—nearly hysterical. Lisa was convinced it was breast cancer. After tests she learned it wasn't, but her fear was apparent,' she said.

A school doctor first diagnosed the problem of a faulty heart valve when Lisa was six years old. There was also a family history of this illness—her paternal grandmother suffered from the problem, as does Lisa's only brother Craig. Lisa was in the care of a cardiologist while pregnant with Brooke. During her second pregnancy, she was hospitalised for three days after suffering chest pains. After Dillon's birth, Lisa was warned the condition had deteriorated and was told to have it checked as soon as possible.

Tragically, the Farmers' hectic lifestyle meant Lisa delayed that medical appointment until seven months after the birth—just two weeks before her death. It appears Lisa was anxious about the appointment and didn't want to go alone. Her father Barry accompanied her. But due to some miscommunication between Lisa and her specialist, he was unable to give her the full range of tests. Despite Lisa's outline of her recent problems and her insistence that she needed the tests now, the medico said she seemed fine after monitoring her heart through a stethoscope. He gave her a clearance and said to come back in six months. 'Lisa was really angry when she returned home from the appointment because the right test hadn't been done. She said: "What a bloody waste of time that was,"' said Pat. It would be some time before the feeling passed that Lisa's death was preventable.

Barry and June Bullivant took on the onerous task of notifying friends of Lisa's death. Pat felt incapable of ringing anyone. His family shielded him from the unwanted intrusion of newspapers, radio and television stations. However, Pat did grant one interview, to Channel Nine News, the day after his wife's death. There was no disguising his heartbreak from the world.

Shattered and tear-wracked, he said: 'Lisa was everything I am—and so much more. We loved every day that we lived, and we lived every day that we loved. She was an ordinary person who lived an extraordinary life and affected so many people all over the world just because of the happy nature that she had, and the kindness she had in her heart for other people.'

Most friends and family can recall exactly where they were and how they received the news of Lisa Farmer's death. The day—7 May 1998—is a date they will never forget. Pat's eldest brother Bernie runs his own cleaning business in Canberra and remembers the day far better than he would like. A significant and influential figure in Pat's life, this was one of the few times when Bernie felt some inadequacy about his ability to help.

'I was doing a carpet cleaning job when my wife Deb rang up,' he recalled. 'She said she needed me to come home as soon as I could. My immediate fears were for Mum, so I whizzed through the job as best and quickly as I could. I was totally floored when she told me Lisa was dead. I couldn't believe it. Normally your first reaction would be to go straight up there, but I have to confess it took me two days to summon up the strength to go and see Pat. It affected me so much, I was worried I wouldn't have the words to say. I didn't think there was anything I could say that could help him.'

His youngest brother, Chris, was supposed to join Pat and Lisa for dinner the weekend before her death. But he and wife Sonya couldn't meet them due to Chris' work commitments as Operations Manager with ABC Sydney radio station 2BL. He recalls the day:

'I was at work the day Lisa died. Because of Pat's profile, Lisa's death apparently became a news story before I even knew about it. ABC Radio was aware of it but chose not to put the story to air because they thought I might not have known and out of respect for my privacy. I got a phone call from Mum, who I think had waited until just before I finished work to ring me. I remember standing in the corridors of 2BL just crying and people coming up to me and asking me what was wrong. I recall going home in the train thinking it couldn't be true and bawling my eyes out and people looking at me. It was a horrible feeling and a disbelief, a feeling "Maybe Mum's got it wrong, maybe there's something not quite right here and she'll be okay". There was that stupidity side of it, a denial phase, where you said to yourself: "No she hasn't really died. She's just in hospital and everything's going to be okay." It was just one of those things you never, ever think about happening.'

Ann Bowen and John Gerathy are partners in the Sydney law firm, Bowen and Gerathy, where Lisa worked for fifteen years. Lisa had been Gerathy's personal assistant; Bowen a colleague, friend and confidante. She remembers: 'Lisa had left us over twelve months prior, but she was still fondly remembered by everyone here. I was in John Gerathy's office around 5.00 p.m. when Barry Bullivant rang. John was sitting at his desk. I was talking to him when he took the call. He just put the phone down and said "Lisa Farmer's dead." I said: "She is not." Everyone in the office was as stunned as I when they heard the news and really didn't or couldn't say much. She was so full of life, so vibrant, that's why we were incredulous.'

Pat's family rallied around him—as they had done all their lives. In times of trouble, the Farmers closed ranks in support of their own. They had suffered their fair share of tragedy in this generation; just being there and helping to bear a share of the burden of grief and loss helped them all cope. There were many hours and days when they felt lost for words. They would hug Pat and hold him lovingly; occasionally relatives and friends would look at each other seeking guidance, but mindful that nothing they could say could lessen Pat's pain. 'Why you, why not me?' they thought; 'Thank God, the children weren't in the car,' they said. They all knew that even time would never completely heal this wound. Pat cancelled all engagements. Running was the furthest thing from his mind. Eldest brother Bernie arrived from Canberra, his eldest sister Catherine flew in from Tasmania. Pat's mother, Mary, embraced him with the words: 'I'm here for as long as you need me to be with you and the children.' (Two years later, she still remains.)

Some friends who rang Pat's house to offer their condolences and support were greeted by a taped message on the answering machine. The voice on the old recording was that of Lisa. The message wasn't changed for several days. It was slightly haunting for some—a sweet reminder for others.

A sea of tributes flowed forth to the Farmers and the Bullivants. The International Toastmistresses Club, of which Lisa had been the youngest member in the world at fourteen and the youngest president ever at sixteen years of age, paid homage in a special edition of its newsletter to members: 'We all loved the bright, bubbly person that she was and find it hard to believe she has gone.' Lisa dedicated inexhaustible amounts of time and energy to charity work through Rotaract and Pat's fundraising ultra marathons. The newsletter offered solace and praise in a quote from nineteenth-century American poet and essayist, Ralph Waldo Emerson: 'To know that one life has breathed easier because you have lived, this is to have succeeded.' And concluded: 'Didn't she. Vale Lisa from all your friends in ITC.'

The Granville branch of Rotaract distributed to its members a page of Lisa Farmer quotable quotes. Among them was an excerpt from one of her many motivational speeches: 'Assess and weigh up your unique talents and capacities; they constitute your potential. Develop them through determination and work and unquestionably, you will succeed.'

Mr and Mrs Bullivant made arrangements for Lisa's funeral. The notice in the *Sydney Morning Herald* paid tribute, in an understated way, to her generous, loving nature.

Her caring and sharing
will be with us always.
Forever in our hearts.
She will be sadly missed.

Appropriately, and at both families' request, mourners were asked
not to send flowers, but rather make donations to the Australian
Rotary Health Research Fund at Parramatta. Nearly $3000 was
forthcoming. The fund calls for applications for medical research
grants every year and designates a different field every year. That
year the project was family health. Appropriately, Lisa Farmer
helped others, even in death.

Around Australia, several communities were in mourning that
week—paying similar untimely tragic tributes to four other
young people who passed away, having left so much potential
still untapped. The day before Lisa died, a fuel line explosion
aboard HMAS *Westralia* killed four sailors off the coast of Perth.
Five days later, on the eve of Lisa Farmer's funeral, her local
community, Camden, also farewelled leading seaman Bradley
John Meek. His coffin was led away by a naval cortege.

On Wednesday, 13 May, under sunny western Sydney skies,
fate or God deemed it to be Granville's turn to mourn one of
its favourite children. Lisa had been raised and educated in the
local area and had been an energetic and incredibly effective
contributor to its community. At 12.30 p.m. the first of more
than 850 people from widely divergent walks of life began
arriving at the Holy Family Church. They quickly filled the pews
and aisles of the 30-year-old brown brick building. When it was
occupied beyond comfort, mourners spilled outside into court-
yards and gardens where they craned their necks to hear and see
the most moving of ceremonies. Lisa's life and achievements were
captured on two large overhead screens. Precious moments were
frozen in time of Lisa as a child, young woman, bride and
mother—every snapshot exuding vitality and vibrancy. Something of a Who's Who of Sydney attended to pay tribute to a
life of devotion to others: Olympics Minister Michael Knight,

radio commentator Alan Jones, former Balmain captain and then-coach Wayne Pearce and former federal Attorney-General Lionel Bowen were among the dignitaries.

Locals say it was the biggest event in the Granville area for decades, aside from the services for the train disaster of 1977. Police stood in the thick of traffic that congested surrounding narrow suburban streets, trying to minimise the disruption and danger. Across the road, children from the Holy Family Primary School, where Pat had been educated, peered through metal fences. Later their teachers organised them to form a guard of honour that stretched for several hundred metres.

The poignancy of the occasion was heightened for those who had sat in the same honey-stained pine pews just six years earlier witnessing the marriage of Pat Farmer and Lisa Bullivant. For many, it was the first time they had been back between these hallowed walls. Never did they envisage it would be so soon and under such wretched circumstances. Presiding over both occasions was Father James Stack. This time he told the congregation: 'From my very first meeting with Lisa and Pat it was evident that here indeed was true love. During your years together, both of you have radiated that joy in your own family circle.' Father Stack lamented the loss of a daughter, wife and mother so young. He too was crushed. The priest then wept openly—few people had ever seen a minister of religion so emotional.

Tony Farmer gave a eulogy that moved the fragile congregation even more, expressing his eternal gratitude to Lisa for the many gifts she had given everyone, including him. He made special mention of the introduction to his wife, Linda. Lisa, he said, had been Pat's greatest supporter, and had been the driving force behind his success. He was moved to recount comparisons with another tragic episode in the family's life—the loss eighteen months earlier of Tony and Linda's second son, who was born with unsustainable brain damage and died soon after birth. 'The only comfort I can find is that she will now be with our beloved son,' he said. 'Nothing, but nothing, fazed Lisa,' he said. 'You're a trooper, Lisa. We will all miss you terribly.'

Barry Bullivant told the service: 'She lived the life of a 60-year-old in just over 30 years. She would often say to friends: "We're here for a good time not a long time", and she lived her life making the most of every minute.'

Founding partner of the law firm Bowen and Gerathy, John Gerathy, paid tribute to one of the most honest and devoted workers he had ever employed. Without hesitation he said, if he had had an office full of Lisa Farmers, he would have had the most successful legal practice in the world. There was glowing praise, too, for the friendship he and his family had shared with Lisa and Pat. 'I know Lisa's father wouldn't mind me saying this, but I looked upon Lisa as a friend and daughter, not as an employee.'

All the time, Pat sat clutching his daughter Brooke and weeping. Since birth, friends and family had seen so much of Lisa's physical characteristics in her; as she had grown, Brooke had also begun to display more of her mother's personality—her unique mix of devotion, kindness and feistiness. Pat wrapped his arms around the little girl and looked like he would never let go. At one point, when mourners thought their hearts could not feel any heavier, they were shaken again by the soulful strains of Celine Dion's ode to another tragic love story, the theme song from the movie *Titanic*.

The cortege moved to Rookwood Cemetery, where Lisa was laid to rest near her mother. More than 400 mourners then gathered for a wake at the Granville RSL Club—also the venue for Pat and Lisa's wedding reception. Free of the confines of the solemn mass and burial, they shared their grief, hoping that in some small way it could begin the healing process for all of them. This, along with more projected images of Lisa smiling and laughing with friends, and dancing on tables, made them feel more at ease to swap stories of happier times and recount favourite memories. People marvelled at Pat's composure as they attempted to console him and each other. 'We have to remember how she was,' Pat told them. 'We can't forget the person she was. I can't let the kids forget her and how special she was.'

Hanging in the air was the question that no one could answer: 'Why now, why Lisa?'

2

•

Seven is enough

Survival against the odds was always part and parcel for the Farmer family. In 1927, Mary Lynn boarded a boat from Ireland with a heavy heart. She and her seven children had been apart from her husband Michael for over a year while he went in search of a better life for the family in Sydney, Australia. In his absence, her youngest child had died from pneumonia. Then followed the six-week voyage that became an ordeal no mother should have had to endure. She and four of her children developed scarlet fever and diphtheria not long after the boat left Ireland. They were quarantined from the rest of the passengers and the rest of the family, leaving her eldest child, 13-year-old John, to care for his siblings. Mary Lynn survived but tragically three of her ill children did not. They were buried at sea. More than a decade later, when John Lynn was on his way to serve as a Rat of Tobruk in the Middle East theatre during World War II, he cast flowers overboard in memory of his late sisters, as he sailed through the Dead Sea. He later had his own tragedy to deal with, losing an arm during battle when a grenade blew up in his hand. After settling into family life at Pyrmont in inner Sydney, Mary Lynn gave birth to three more children, Bridget, Mary and Peter.

When the seventh child, Mary Lynn, came to raise her own

family with Frank Farmer more than 20 years later, the battle against adversity was still ever-present. The first six Farmer children were born in a small terrace house in Ultimo, an inner Sydney suburb. In order, they were Bernard, Catherine, Annette, Michael, Patrick and Anthony. As those walls and confines were stretched with each new arrival, the family was forced to find a larger home. Their only hope of expansion was through the New South Wales Housing Commission. Frank and Mary Farmer first lodged their application in 1955 when they had just Bernard, who was then aged two.

By the time their request had been approved, ten years had passed and they had six children and a seventh, Christopher, on the way. Money was getting tighter. Frank was forced to sell the family's only luxury, a near-new Nissan Cedric car, and buy a motor scooter so they could afford to move into the rental property at Boronia Street, Granville. The low-set house provided extra space for their growing tribe, but it was a humble abode— fibro-sheeted, tiled roof, three bedrooms with a verandah that converted to a fourth bedroom. Children slept in bunk beds, two or three to a room. The Farmers were a typical Irish Catholic family of the era. Times were tough, but love, affection and kindness were handed out in large dollops.

Granville, where Pat Farmer spent all of his formative years, was always struggle town. It has several historical claims to fame. The area yielded the foundations for colonial Sydney, with vast forests of blackbutt, ironbark and stringybark being cleared to provide timber for early construction. Granville also hosted the first soccer club in Australia, established by English and Welsh migrants from the local steelworks. The first Labor member for Granville was Jack Lang, one of the most controversial figures in Australian politics. As New South Wales Premier, he was upstaged by Captain De Groot at the opening of the Sydney Harbour Bridge in 1932. He was dismissed as Premier later that year after a power struggle. Lang was later one of the greatest political influences on former Prime Minister Paul Keating. Other famous Granville products were singer Judy Stone and actor Bryan Brown. Granville pool was a mecca for champion swimmers, including legendary Olympians Dawn Fraser and John Devitt.

A champion diver also frequented the pool. Before he was a comic actor, Paul Hogan—or 'Hoges'—was a comic diver in the Parramatta City Amateur Swimming club. Hogan's juvenile sense of humour was constantly on show, riding a bicycle off the 10-metre diving board or 'bomb-diving' unsuspecting bathers. As well as being the resident practical joker, Hogan was leader of one of the gangs that hung out at Granville pool. He and his faithful followers saw it as their patch of water and generally hassled anyone who challenged their authority. The pool manager, Ted Simms, gave up trying to beat Hogan so had him join him as assistant pool attendant. The young Hogan relished the responsibility and power and became a model of good manners, even keeping his old ratbag mates in check. Granville is probably best known as the scene of Australia's worst rail disaster, which claimed 83 lives on 18 January 1977. It is a legacy and notoriety that the suburb still struggles to live down.

In Granville, people were born into a humble existence, and spent most of their lives trying to break free from the social and economic shackles that were imposed upon them. Life in the Farmer family in the 1950s and 1960s was no different. But none of the children reflect on their childhood as being one of deprivation. While there was never enough of it, money wasn't a major issue for them. Most friends and relatives were in the same boat—living a subsistence existence. Families made their own fun with whatever they could lay their hands on. Clothes were handed down from one friend and neighbour to the next, from one sibling to another. That didn't spare anyone from embarrassment when they got caught wearing a friend's hand-me-downs, but the Farmers are unanimous that they could not have asked for a happier, more secure upbringing.

One of Pat's earliest childhood memories is of his mother's generosity. It was mainly simple acts, such as bringing the postman a glass of water on hot days. 'I remember vividly Mum would greet him at the gate and they'd have a bit of a chat,' Pat recalls. 'Right from an early age I remember how my parents impressed upon me the value of being kind to people, saying hello to them and offering them help even if it was a simple thing like a drink. I remember those gestures vividly. It shaped me into being, I suppose, a generous sort of person with my time and with my life.'

Also boundless was the hospitality at the Farmers. It was always 'open house' and with seven children there was an abundance of friends happy to accept an invitation back to the Farmers. Pat remembers inviting the whole football team home after training for Vegemite sandwiches and cordial. It was expected—but not taken for granted—that Mary would always ensure there was enough food for the ever-widening circle of friends. Relatives, friends, neighbours were all welcome. A knock on the door—whether it was 10.00 a.m. or 10.00 p.m.—would be well received with the offer of food and drink.

'We never thought about where the money for food came from,' said Pat. 'We just knew if we walked in with five or even ten friends, Mum would feed every one of them. She was very resourceful; she always found enough food no matter how many kids there were. All my brothers' and sisters' friends were my friends too and vice versa. There were other houses that seemed to be that way too. People didn't have much but what they did they shared.'

Several childhood friends remember the Farmers being more generous than most families. Ray Cassally was a regular visitor at the Farmers from the time he was six years old. 'It was never too much trouble for their family,' he remembers. 'Friends who came over were made to feel like part of their clan. Admittedly, Pat's brothers used to egg each other on to mischief, especially when their parents were out—nothing too serious. His brothers were like brothers to me, especially Tony. Years later he gave me a job in his landscaping business for eighteen months.'

Colleen Chittendon, nee Young, was Pat's neighbour and grew up with his family. They were close for many years. The bond strengthened after Colleen's father died when she was ten. She remembers the Farmers displaying a true Christian sense of charity. 'They would rather struggle themselves than let someone else struggle,' she said. 'Their generosity was amazing at times. They would think nothing of giving you the shirt off their back even if they had nothing. If my Mum was too sick to cook for us, our meals would still be on the table. Mrs Farmer could make a meal out of nothing.' Pocket money was non-existent. Pat remembers being stunned when in 1968 a Year 1 classmate revealed he had $38 in a personal bank account. Pat couldn't imagine what he could spend the money on. He also seriously doubted whether his own parents had as much money lying idle.

Sport was a dominant feature of everyday life for the Farmers. While there was no great sporting pedigree in the family, Frank Farmer was a major influence, having played a variety of sports during his youth. Whenever any of the children returned home with a prize from a sports carnival, Frank would playfully remind them they had inherited their athletic ability from him. He encouraged all the children to participate in sport and urged them to strive towards achievement, but never played the role of ugly sideline parent who would yell abuse at his child for missing a goal or dropping a ball. The eldest son, Bernie, revelled in Frank's example and was a fine junior sportsman. Pat has no hesitation in nominating his eldest brother as his sporting hero. What impressed him most was Bernie's ability to place-kick a football through the goal posts from the corner of the 20-metre line during his teens.

'The rest of us thought that was incredible,' says Pat. Football games began in the 10-metre long backyard but exuberant children were soon banished to the football field at nearby Duck Creek Reserve, after inflicting damage on their father's fruit trees. While the matches continued, the younger siblings were often relegated to the role of ball boys when time came for Bernie's goal-kicking practice. 'It was rare we got a kick, we were mostly Bernie's rabbit picking up the football for him,' said Pat. 'But I remember being really impressed with my brother's dedication to a task. He'd often spend all afternoon practising his goal kicks.'

Bernie Farmer was a promising Rugby League player. When he was seventeen, he played several trials for the recently defunct Balmain Rugby League Club. They wanted a halfback but he was rejected on two counts: Bernie kept getting penalised by referees for feeding the ball into the second row of the scrum ('These days in rugby league you almost get penalised if you *don't* feed it in the second row,' he says); and he was too lean for their liking. He was told to return when he had added some bulk, but he lacked the focus and commitment to do weights training. The temptations were too great for a young man who was just starting to earn a good income—cars, girls and drinking with his mates. 'I think my brothers and sisters later learned from my mistakes,' he said.

The great Australian tradition of backyard cricket games was upheld at the Farmers'. Frank and all the children joined in. There were always too many household chores for Mary to participate. As with many things, the children had to improvise with equipment. A Slazenger 'special edition' fence paling was just the go for a bat; a metal garbage bin was preferred as stumps ('you could hear if the ball even brushed the wicket'); most times they bowled with a tennis ball. Sunday games were always memorable. The family would attend Mass in the morning. After a hot roast lunch, relatives and friends would descend on the Granville home.

It was the usual backyard rules: over the fence was six and out, if the batsman was bowled because the wicket keeper had moved the stumps a metre without his knowledge, well too bad; the third umpire could be overruled by the fourth, fifth and sixth umpires. Close games would go past dusk. These were day/night games, but only until the ambient house light was enveloped by darkness and torchlights were dimmed by weakening batteries.

When they were handing out sporting genes in the Farmer family, Pat was near the back of the queue. On his own admission, he's always been an average sportsman. His brother Bernie describes Pat as 'a gangly and uncoordinated child'. He played all the usual games—cricket, football, tennis, squash—but never shone in any of them. Pat did make a representative Rugby League team but says he spent most of the time as orange boy. 'If I was picking a team, I'd probably pick my sister Annette before I picked myself,' said Pat. 'I didn't stand out as anything. I was just one of the crowd. People say I must have had a gift and been a good runner when I was a kid, but the thing about ultra running is that I don't really see it as a sport. It's an event; it's more grit and determination than anything. It's not the sort of thing you were trained to do as a child. The most I had to run was 15 yards from one garbage bin to another in cricket. You couldn't tell from backyard games I had a talent. We were just kids being kids with boundless amounts of energy.'

Frank Farmer had a great love and appreciation for nature—a trait all his children have inherited, Pat and his brother Tony in larger doses than most. Their typically small suburban block became a hobby farm and animal refuge. Childhood playmates recall the Farmers as exuding all the qualities of country folk in suburbia. It seems the Farmers tried to live up to their surname with a menagerie that was the envy of, and magnet for, all the local children. With most of the animals adopted or donated, it was cheap entertainment. Frank built a small aviary at one point with all manner of bird life. At various stages during Pat's childhood, dozens of creatures great and small were given a home, including chickens, geese, ducks, owls, an eagle, possums, ferrets, rabbits, lizards, turtles, an echidna and even a young pig which had been given to Pat by a friend. But 'Ziggy the Piggy' didn't endear himself to Mrs Farmer, displaying an uncontrollable urge to put his head down and chase her around the yard whenever she tried to hang out the washing, much to the delight of her five boys. Mrs Farmer was ostracised from her own backyard by Ziggy, who would constantly burrow under his pen. She would have to delegate clothesline duties to one of the children who seemed less threatened by the rebel pig. Poor Ziggy must have got the hint that he'd overstayed his welcome and eventually escaped after a year. Surprisingly, common household pets like dogs and cats were banned—cats as they were a threat to the bird life and dogs because Mr Farmer thought it cruel to keep a dog in a small yard.

Tony Farmer was fascinated with snakes. During his teens he worked part time at the Flemington markets and would often find green tree snakes or diamond pythons while unpacking fruit and vegetables. While other workers would freak, Tony was unperturbed and would ride his skateboard home with the snake concealed under his jumper. Understandably, the reptiles were separated from the guinea pigs, which were among the favorite pets of the girls, Catherine and Annette.

'Catherine and I had a guinea pig each and we used to slip a home-made harness on to them,' recalls Annette. 'We used to walk them around the yard. Of course, they bred and before long we had lots and lots of guinea pigs. But the sad part was, at one stage, when they ate a poisonous plant "Deadly Nightshade", we ended up with lots and lots of graves out the back. Dad would dig the hole and put a cross in the ground.' Their deaths were mourned by all, but never for too long. There was always some other welcome distraction.

The love of nature was further stimulated during many trips to the great outdoors. The family of nine would pile into Frank's new pride and joy, a restored early-model Holden and would drive for hours to the place they called 'Paradise', Bermagui, on the south coast of New South Wales. Sandwiches, lollies and a bottle of soda water (with seven straws) kept the children occupied for most of the trip. Frank would relish the chance to occasionally light up a pipe and smoke his favourite tobacco (his only indulgence), while his wife leaned across two children in the front seat and took charge of the steering wheel on various occasions. Frank was a keen fisherman, camper and shooter and holidays were spent by the beach or in the bush—the setting for many of the children's best-learned lessons in life.

The days and the memories of simple fun are endless for all of the Farmer children—catching water dragons and racing them on the sand, being taught the finer points of fishing by a patient father, shooting rabbits and stewing them for dinner until they were eventually sick of the taste. They were wary about swimming though, especially at dawn when the presence of shark fins 50 metres from shore would put everybody off the idea for the rest of the day. The great escapes proved a genuine source of bonding for the Farmer family and have had a lingering legacy in adulthood. The venue of the back-to-nature annual camping holidays was the property of Frank's cousin and best mate, Kevin Branley, who had 290 hectares by the beach. Mr Branley later died tragically when a tree fell on him while he was clearing land for a dam. He left a widow and four young children.

With little spare money, holidays were another wonderful opportunity to create their own fun, even if it was as simple as racing iceblock sticks or thongs down the gutter on rainy days. None of the children was ever bored, especially with their father Frank's knack for making something out of nothing. He'd organise the children to make their own kites, under his supervision. Sticks would be gathered from nearby scrub and tied together with twine; plastic or butcher's paper donated by a kind shopkeeper was taped over the frame; and gathered stones wrapped in a piece of old bed-sheet were added to give weight to the tail. No better childcare ever existed than occupied children taught to make their own toy. While none of the young Farmers realised it at the time, the exercise would prove to be a valuable moral example.

'We'd spend hours and hours making the kites and all the children would make it together,' said Pat. 'We took the time to spend the time together and did it as a family. After some finicky work, we'd go down the beach or the park at the end of the day. The wind would have sprung up and we'd get to fly our kites. It was so much more enjoyable playing with something you'd helped create. It taught us all a lesson—that lesson was if you put in the effort and create something out of nothing, then you get the chance to reap the reward, and the satisfaction from that is so much greater if it's come from your own hands.

'It was a lot more enjoyable than going to the shop and buying a kite and flying it. Kids these days are sick and tired of toys after 10 minutes and want to do something else. They don't know the rewards in building a dream and not just flying the dream at the end of it all. The journey is what it's all about—that's what life's about. It's the simplest beginnings—spending time with family. There are such strong lessons to be learned and I was taught them by all of my family.'

In the Farmer family, there were no favourites and no one received special treatment. Everyone was taught to expect no more than their fair share and to show consideration for all family members. These values were promoted and underpinned by their Roman Catholic faith. Mary Farmer was the source of an endless supply of devotion and support, playing her maternal role with saintly patience. A modest, unassuming woman, she has dedicated her life to being the best mother she possibly could. Both she and Frank were very religious and would round up their growing family and begin their Sunday routine with morning Mass at the Holy Family Catholic Church, three blocks away. Later in her life, as her children grew, Mary attended Mass every day. She was the homemaker, cook, child-rearer. Mary was better educated than Frank, but they both displayed great resourcefulness, borne out of necessity.

Annette recalls: 'I always thought that she was the smartest person in the world. There was nothing she couldn't do. She was nocturnal. She'd work right through the night and she'd work right through the day as well. At night if there was the slightest whimper or cry from any of us kids, Mum was there miraculously. I don't know when she ever slept or when she ever ate because she'd always look after everyone else first.'

Michael Farmer has similar memories. 'I never remember seeing my mother sleeping. Mum would always be awake and at the ready and doing something for us or Dad—getting him off to work and waiting for us all when we came home. In between times she was out doing things for other people.'

Mary Farmer refused to be daunted or discouraged by the challenges of raising five boys and two girls. Shopping trips were done by foot and public transport and often with offspring in tow. The major logistical exercise of getting seven children out the door would sometimes mean they would miss their bus. Like circus elephants they would then make the 4-kilometre shopping expedition on foot—all holding hands in single file. If a smaller child faltered, there was always a bigger brother or sister to pick them up and carry them on their back or shoulders. Mary would carry her goods home in a string bag, leaving her fingers blue from the constant tension of the handles. None of the children can recall her ever complaining.

Frank was by all accounts one of life's real characters. He possessed a common touch and a genuine sense of fun. He thought nothing of hiding in cupboards and jumping out to scare passing children and later grandchildren, or riding a skateboard down the street while balancing with a broomstick. He was a crack shot with a .303 rifle and sometimes mused that if another war broke out, he would be drafted as a sniper. He was a regular trophy winner in one of Australia's premier shooting competitions, the Queen's Prize, and was once selected to compete in an overseas competition but dismissed thoughts of participating after cutting his finger in a band saw. Music was another of Frank Farmer's great loves. He encouraged singalongs to the accompaniment of his harmonica, especially by the campfire or on bus trips, and he could fill most song requests. His favorite tune, 'Danny Boy', would always get a run, at his own request. Frank fostered a love of music in all the children. If they decided they wanted to learn an instrument, he would make whatever sacrifices were necessary to enable it to happen. At one point he sold his beloved trombone so Bernie could buy and learn the guitar. Bernie was an outstanding soprano and alto, who won a singing bursary to the prestigious St Mary's Boys School in Sydney and sang with the Cathedral choir. He had the privilege of singing with the Vienna Boys Choir at concerts they performed on an Australian tour in the 1960s.

Frank Farmer was a nuts-and-bolts person devoid of a proper education but steeped in practical skills. Tinkering with machinery in his shed was one of Frank's great pastimes. If something was broken, he'd restore it. If it was falling down, he'd find a way to fix it. Frank had a reputation in Granville as the local handyman and would often be asked by friends and neighbours to repair washing machines, mowers and various pieces of machinery. He was always happy to oblige and rarely accepted payment. All the children remember one particular battle with a cantankerous motor mower.

'He'd been working on it for weeks,' recalls Bernie. 'He wouldn't give up on it. It was 2.00 a.m. and for some reason he was still working on this mower in the family lounge room. We were all asleep until this thing roaring to life woke us. We all walked out with our eyes like slits to see Dad in the middle of the room triumphantly boasting: "I've done it, I've done it." Mum was hysterical.'

'There was another occasion when Dad was fixing an outboard motor from a boat and he finally got it running in a bucket of water, again in the lounge room. He'd just stick at things to the end. We'd laugh about it at the time but you had to admire him. It didn't matter how long it was going to take, he'd make it happen.'

While all of the children inherited Frank's unshakeable determination to finish any job, it was a lesson that young Patrick would learn better than the others. He also acquired the greatest passion for machinery.

Frank and Mary also taught their children never to set limits on what they could achieve. Frank lacked a formal education, yet taught himself many things, mostly from reading. Armed with a coaching manual, he once trained daughter Annette's netball team.

'We were encouraged to believe in our own ability and what we could achieve,' said Pat's older brother Michael. 'Mum always told us: "You are as a big a person as you allow yourself to be." Her philosophy was you should always reach out and strive to do something better.'

But with seven children crammed into a confined area, inevitably there was someone invading your personal space and grounds for conflict. The Farmers openly admit they fought like cats and dogs. Frank had a 'strap' and, with five rowdy boys, sometimes had to venture beyond threats. There were plenty of practical jokes and much verbal jousting. Pat's eldest sister Catherine had a slight lisp. Her siblings taunted her with phrases like 'Susie sells sea shells by the sea shore'. The boys had a nickname for Annette, who had a bigger build than her slender, prettier sister. She was labelled 'Annie Oak Tree—Annie because that's her name and oak tree because she's as big as one'. While it was cruel at the time, none of the Farmers has carried any scars or grudges into adult life.

Pat gave as good as he received. He was renowned for his 'dummy spits', often sparked when things didn't go his way. No one, it seems, escaped Pat's temper. His youngest brother, Christopher, was frequently on the receiving end, although he admits he might have been somewhat precocious on occasions. One day, Pat decided enough was enough. 'Pat turned around and grabbed me by the head and shoved my head through the fibro wall and put this big hole in the wall,' Chris recalled. 'We all then panicked. It wasn't so much "oh no, my brother put my head through the wall". It was more "oh no, Dad will be home soon and he'll kill us". Lucky for Pat I was okay. He bolted down the shop to get some sort of spak filler. We all then pushed reams of newspaper into the hole and covered it over. It was just so obvious. Of course Dad spotted it the minute he got home and took it out on all of us.'

Christopher also bore much of the brunt of his siblings' taunts—especially after he displayed a phobia of the family floor polisher. To a five-year-old, the bulky piece of machinery was a fearsome sight and sound. Entrusted as baby-sitters, the older children took advantage of their responsibility and sometimes used the polisher as a blackmail tool to force their youngest brother do their bidding. Failure to obey would prompt threats to summon the beast from his cave. 'I was petrified of it,' he said. 'It had a light on the front and was an old noisy thing that shook a lot. It was very menacing. I used to climb up on the couch to escape it. I guess it was my brothers' and sisters' way of paying me back.'

Revenge was never far away for any of the Farmer children. At the age of thirteen, Pat received his at the hands of his brother Michael, who was almost two years his senior. Brothers Bernie, Tony and Chris shared one room, while Pat and Michael occupied another—all in bunk beds. After ten years, Michael, whose favourite hobby was music and having jam sessions in his room with his friends, was tiring of having a little brother cramping his teenage style. He thought it would be a good idea to get rid of Pat. Here was a challenge: Pat had to want to move out of his own accord and Michael had to persuade him. The eviction scheme was founded on Pat's fear of rodents. No one is sure when or how the phobia began, but Michael was aware of the opportunity it presented. In the Farmers' Animal House, the introduction of a few pet mice would be unlikely to raise his parent's hackles.

'I went to the local pet store where the going rate on mice was twenty cents each and bought two or three,' recalled Michael. 'When Pat came home he said: "What are they doing here?" I said: "They're my new pets." He said: "Get them out of here" and I said: "No, that's where they're staying." He said: "Well, if they're not going, I am." I said: "I can live with that." It was all too easy.'

'But I knew at that point I'd get into trouble with my parents although the damage was done for Pat. It was pointless for him to complain to Mum and Dad because I doubt he would have gone back into the room after the mice had been there. So Pat moved in with Bernie, Tony and Chris and I got my own room finally. They weren't too pleased and I was alienated for some time. I kept the mice for three weeks before releasing them into the wild. I think they were totally deaf by then because I'd been cranking up the music in my room with my friends. I seem to recall Pat eventually got his revenge on me, but it was nothing memorable.'

While the Farmers were always picking on each other, there was hell to pay if any outsider tried to inflict any verbal or physical harm on them. The children were raised to look after each other. Blood was thicker than water: if you picked on one Farmer you picked on all of them. Perhaps it was the Irish in them. This creed often resulted in blood being spilt on all sides. In spite of—or perhaps because of—his size, Pat learned how to look after himself. Fights were pretty common at school and on the bus travelling home. An ambush at the top of the street wasn't uncommon but there were always several Farmers with whom to contend.

In contrast to his home life, school days were not the happiest of Pat's life. Often, it was just somewhere to be during the day. Pat began school at the Holy Family Primary School, Granville and later moved on to secondary education at Patrician Brothers, Granville. Pat says quite bluntly that there was nothing about his school years that he liked. There was never any great love affair with learning. He lacked focus and, like many children, was easily distracted. Mind you, there were plenty of mates to do that, although Pat was frequently the one egging his friends on to mischief.

The strict, disciplinarian life at the all-boys Patrician Brothers school did not sit well with Pat. It was a threat to his independent, larrikin streak, but not an inhibitor. More than once he landed himself in hot water after he was caught pulling faces at the brothers while they were at the blackboard. He also had an irreverent side—an urge to go one step too far that he just couldn't contain. That caused trouble both at school and at home when he would write fictional essays and use characters with nicknames. But 'Pencil Head' was such a thinly disguised name for his teacher, Brother Peter, that the matter was reported to Mrs Farmer. She was distressed and embarrassed that every one else had written normal essays by comparison. Pat's cause wasn't helped with his insistence that there was nothing wrong with his work.

The cane was meted out to all students without much hesitation. Pat remembers being punished for a host of minor indiscretions—or so they appeared to him at the time. There was no such thing as children's rights; you just got hit. It was seen as character building. Hands in the pockets weren't tolerated, nor was being late for school. 'It didn't matter that I had to run to catch the bus—I was forever missing the bus and being forced to walk to school,' he said. 'It was a long 6-kilometre walk for a teenager. You got no credit from the teacher for making the effort to get to school. If you were late, you got the cane. That was the way you started the morning, which was one reason I could never get enthusiastic about school.'

Science was the only subject in which Pat showed any great interest. But those aspects that appealed to him—nature and astronomy—were topics about which his father had already planted the seeds of curiosity in Pat's favourite classroom. Pat believes he learnt more under the stars, by the water and in the bush because his family spent so much time outdoors and he found his father's lessons more interesting.

'I didn't really warm to any of my teachers or to the whole school situation,' he said. 'If someone had motivated me at school I wouldn't be running long distances, I'd be something incredible. I wouldn't just be a doctor; I'd be the best brain surgeon on the face of the earth. I wouldn't just build buildings; I'd design or construct skyscrapers bigger and better than anybody else had ever done. All it needed was somebody to relate to me and to motivate me and move me and somebody did but it was later in life. Had it been when I was at school, the path I chose might have been more academic, but no less noble a cause than what I ended up doing because I can still fundraise and I can still set the world on fire with the things I do now.' For Pat, school was a long, bumpy sidetrack in the journey of life. He laments the missed opportunities from his education and wishes he could wind the clock back and revisit his school days, armed with hindsight and a more mature attitude.

When he decided to leave school at the age of 15, Pat had helped leave a legacy for the two brothers who followed, Tony and Chris. By the time the youngest brothers were progressing through the education system, teachers had wised up to the antics of the high-spirited family and the name Farmer was greeted with arched eyebrows at the start of a new scholastic year. Last in line, Chris, didn't get half a chance to step out of line before he was jumped on from a great height. 'A Farmer hey, I don't want to hear a peep out of you,' was the refrain from the authority figure at the front of the class. However, Chris applied himself to his studies and became captain of his primary school. He progressed to Patrician Brothers, Fairfield, where again he was school captain in his final year, much to the disgust of his older brother Pat.

In 1977, Pat was a young man in search of a passion. He didn't find it in his first job as an apprentice panelbeater, where he worked for several months. But he finally had money to spend. He was earning $55 a week—a king's ransom. He was like a child in a candy store but, rather than indulge himself, his first priority was his family. He was still living at home and very much aware that they were still without many of life's little luxuries. He followed what had become something of a family tradition and tried to help rectify that, spending nearly $500 on something they had never owned—a freezer (which still works today). 'I thought Mum and Dad would love that,' he said. 'I came home and surprised the family with it. It was a good feeling to do something like that. I didn't know what to do with the money. I didn't need it, although at the time I was thinking of buying a car, but I didn't have a licence so I was in no rush.'

His newfound independence away from school also provided the opportunity to spend more time with his unruly mates, Danny Hart and Ray Cassally. Since the age of eight, fishing had featured prominently in their leisure time together. When they were younger, the boys would catch the train from Granville into Circular Quay and fish near the Sydney Opera House. They usually returned home with a good feed of leatherjacket that guaranteed them plenty of room to spread out on the 30-minute journey. There was one occasion when the trio spent the day fishing at Manly. After whiling away the hours until late afternoon, they became separated in the crowd while rushing back to the ferry terminal to beat a storm. Pat waited for them on the wharf, but his sense of duty to his mates backfired. He has a lasting image of Ray and Danny laughing and waving to him from the ferry as the boat ploughed through the green harbour wash. 'These guys were on the deck saying "See ya later Pat, sucked in",' he recalls. 'I didn't get home until after 11.00 p.m. because a couple of ferries had been cancelled due to rough seas, and then I caught the wrong train. Mum and Dad were really worried and had called the police. Even though we were as thick as thieves, I often used to curse those guys.'

In their mid-teens, they ventured further afield, heading north of Sydney to fish on weekend trips by the bountiful waters of the Hawkesbury River. There was one day when the fish proved too elusive. What else do bored teenagers do when the fish aren't biting, but light a scrub fire? Ray Cassally admits he was the culprit. It provided some brief entertainment before he and Danny Hart left the scene, believing it would burn itself out. Pat was more conscientious and thought it best to extinguish the blaze, lest it get too much out of control and do more damage. The only available fire retardant was his new woollen PT Boat Commander jacket that his father had bought for him. Pat spent ten to fifteen minutes bringing the flames under control before the cavalry arrived, in the form of the local fire brigade. Caked in soot, eyebrows singed and with a large hole in his precious jacket, he received a pat on the back from the firefighters for his troubles. 'Some fishing trip,' Pat said. 'I'll never forgive them for that one. It seemed I was always the one left behind to cop the consequences.' As punishment, Pat impounded Ray's pushbike that he'd left behind in his garage.

As idyllic as it seemed, Pat knew even in his teenage years that there had to be more to life than fishing and friends. Something tugged at his subconscious—a desire to excel at something and to rise above an ordinary existence. 'I didn't have a clue what I wanted to be. I was looking for something but I didn't know what,' he said.

3

The spark ignites

Had he been given the chance, Frank Farmer would have been a car mechanic by trade. His love affair with motor vehicles bordered on obsession. He would spend endless hours hunched over a piece of machinery, teaching his sons—and occasionally tomboy daughter Annette—about its inner workings. When Pat showed an inclination towards a career as a mechanic, Frank did everything he could to help and encourage the boy.

Pat looked long and hard for an apprenticeship. After a lifetime of doing good turns for others, family friend Doris Walsh sought to repay one. She worked at the base of Cumberland Cabs in Woodville Road, Granville. Archer's Motor Repairs was next door and serviced the cab fleet. Walsh mentioned Pat's name to the owner, Laurie Archer. He had run his own business for more than 20 years and wasn't looking for another apprentice at the time but agreed he could use an extra general junior hand around the place. There was something about the young skinny kid that impressed the white-haired, middle-aged mechanic. Mostly it was his perfect manners and his mature attitude. Pat was polite, quietly spoken, sincere and showed respect for those older and wiser than him. He didn't shirk the menial tasks— cleaning car parts, tidying the garage, running errands—and in fact tackled them with great enthusiasm. He also asked lots of questions and Laurie liked that. Within a few months, he offered Pat an apprenticeship.

Pat proved to be one of the best young mechanics Archer had ever employed. He'd given job starts to more than 200 young men over the years. After a while, he'd developed a knack for picking them and although there had been a few terrors, they never lasted long in his workshop. The self-made small business-man ruled with an iron fist and shipped out the perceived failures pretty quickly. Ninety per cent of Archer's work was on taxis, which presented their own set of challenges. Time off the road was money to owners, who always needed the repairs done yesterday. Taxi owners and drivers have a reputation the world over as whingers and they didn't breed them any differently in Sydney's western suburbs in the late 1970s and 1980s. Archer's mechanics were always under pressure to fix it fast and fix it right the first time.

Pat's strong work ethic and aptitude for mechanics—both inherited from his father—ensured he quickly became a popular and efficient worker. Frank Farmer was as proud as any parent could be as he lived out one of his own dreams through his son. Pat had always sought to please his Dad, motivated by his great love for his parents and a keen sense of duty. Within a few years, Pat was teaching his father new skills in the fast-moving world of car mechanics. At one stage, the master of Archer's garage also turned to his apprentice for a lesson. When taxis were first being converted from petrol to liquid petroleum gas (LPG), Pat's thirst for knowledge prompted Laurie to nominate him as the first mechanic in his garage to learn the new system. The course took six months, during which Pat taught the old dog a few of the basic new tricks of installation and maintenance. That was sufficient to keep Laurie going until he himself enrolled in the college course one year later.

While the good memories far outweigh the bad for both Pat and Laurie, they had their moments. Pat remembers his boss as being a 'black and white kind of guy—a real hard nut'.

'If you didn't do something right he'd literally give you a kick up the backside, because in those days bosses could get away with it, there wasn't a law against it,' said Pat. 'That was the way it was; you didn't think anything of it, you almost expected it—and in some ways it was a good way to learn. It was a hard job and you had some really bad days when things went wrong but it wasn't always your fault.'

One habit of Pat's that regularly riled Laurie was his penchant for borrowing the boss's tools.

'I'd do my block when the apprentices used my equipment,' said Laurie. 'Every apprentice was supposed to have his own private toolbox, but they'd always be missing something and they'd raid my gear. Pat was one of the worst culprits. Of course I'd only ever find out when I was looking for it.'

Laurie remembers one occasion when he went on holidays and left someone else in charge of the workshop. Pat was restoring an old Datsun at the time and was left alone to spray-paint it after work. The replacement manager was mortified when he arrived the next morning to find a fine white mist covering the workshop. 'Laurie's going to kill you,' he said. Hours were dedicated to the cleaning chore. It seems it was successful, however, because Laurie never noticed and only learned of the mishap long after the event.

Pat's interest in and love for cars quickly developed into his first obsession. This personality trait had been latent for so many years but was being unleashed now that Pat had an outlet for it. He was quick to catch the mechanics bug and once he did, there was no turning back. He envisaged transforming his LH Torana into a Porsche. It's a fixation that visits most young mechanics. The combination of youthful exuberance and peer group pressure leads young Turks to think they can rebuild their humble machines into something bigger and better than the multi-million dollar factories can produce. Pat found out the hard way that it just doesn't work like that, although he says he probably spent enough on restoration attempts to buy a Porsche.

'I was forever buying and selling cars and pulling them apart and rebuilding them; working until all hours in the workshop,' Pat said. Laurie Archer fostered an interest in Mercedes-Benz cars and Pat bought two at different stages—a 190 and a 220 S which 'looked like the Batmobile but surprisingly didn't go as fast, plus it had rusted floors'. He tried to restore both of them but was deterred by the cost of spare parts.

It didn't matter if it was his car or someone else's, Pat would become fixated with the job. It had to be finished. Nothing else mattered. The lights at Archer's garage would often glow until 2.00 a.m. as the young man focused completely on the problem at hand. By this time, he had the responsibility of opening the premises, and would return at 6.30–7.00 a.m. to start afresh. While his mates buried their faces in a schooner at pubs and clubs around Sydney, Pat, for the most part, had his head buried under a bonnet. He still socialised with friends, but it became less frequent to the point where he lost contact with some of them. Little did Pat know that the sleep deprivation, dedication and discipline of his first passion would also be the perfect tools for his next passion, ultra marathon running.

But for now, the teenage dream was revving higher. Pat's vision extended beyond a life spent as a humble garage mechanic in suburban Granville. As he soaked up the education of his technical college course, he thought beyond taxi chassis. No longer did he just want to fix cars—he wanted to build them. Not just backyard jobs but factory cars. He studied basic mechanics as a second-year apprentice during the day; by night he ventured into the same class as some of his teachers for his mechanical engineer's degree, which was going to take him six years. Pat was studying physics and chemistry on a Year 10 education, but understood them with a clarity that had been absent during his school years. Back then, so many lessons were abstract concepts that held his attention for just a few minutes. But now, with images of pumping pistons, camshafts, cylinder blocks and crankshafts in his head, he grasped perfectly all that his lecturers were saying. The spark was well and truly ignited.

But Pat's world came crashing down in 1981. The special relationship that he enjoyed with his greatest teacher, his hero and best friend ended abruptly. Pat was nineteen when his father Frank died of a massive heart attack while out shopping, just weeks after undergoing heart surgery where seven arteries were bypassed ('that's one for each of you kids,' he had joked during his recovery). His death rocked the whole Farmer family. For the first time in his life, Pat questioned his faith as he searched for reasons. A perfect family life was shattered in an instant. While the family members were united in their grief, Pat's brother Bernie stepped to the fore. He helped them fathom the tragedy by theorising that some people weren't meant to grow old, evoking images of Frank's boyish antics—like leaving chewing gum stuck on walls around the house and riding a skateboard down the street while balancing with a broom. 'If Dad didn't think it was time for us to be on our own, he wouldn't have gone. He'd prepared us for life and must have believed we were ready to carry on without him,' Bernie said.

But for Pat there were regrets. Like a longing to wind the clock back and retract the embarrassment he felt on all those occasions when his father would visit the workshop and inquire about repairs to his car. And he would lament heartfelt feelings that had never been fully expressed. Simple words like 'I love you Dad' or 'Dad, you're my hero' might have been said but not often enough and never with the emotional edge of finality. It's a painful longing that Pat has experienced more often in his life than he cares to remember.

'You just wish when you say these everyday things to loved ones that you realised that that was the final moment,' he said. 'Looking back over several times, I wish I had made those words really count. Like you say stuff and you don't think anything of it, when you wish, with hindsight, you had said it with the greatest passion you could muster. You want to say it with everything that you are. I suppose that's why I became the person that I am. The things that I do and what I say to people are with that feeling of urgency because you realise you might not get another chance. It's that passion of life—the realisation that it might be gone from me in the next second and I'm not going to be able to say it again.

'My Dad was my best friend. In some respects I've probably never really been back on an even keel since his death. Maybe the keel was lopsided in my favour with Dad around. With supporters like him, you believe you can go beyond normal human capabilities. You feel you can do anything and you do achieve great goals. When they're not around it's like being back to human again.'

Frank Farmer may have appeared an ordinary man to some. Certainly he believed he was. But his sense of charity and community earned him widespread respect. On the day of his funeral, the 1000-plus admirers who attended his service and who formed a guard of honour stretching for four streets celebrated his life as extraordinary.

For the first time, Pat also began to question his love for car mechanics and his long-time girlfriend Wendy Fraser. Some of his youthful zest for life died with his father. He abandoned his mechanical engineering studies and ended his relationship with Wendy, whom he had contemplated marrying. 'I was young and stupid in those days,' he said. 'I was more interested in cars than I was in her. I never got to the point of proposing.'

Pat continued working with Archer's and found Laurie and his wife Faye a great source of comfort and advice. Pat credits Mrs Archer with giving him one of the best pieces of advice he ever received. Pat had the opportunity to buy a cheap house block from his sister, Annette, and her husband, Ken. Mrs Archer told Pat he was crazy spending his money on cars, advised him to buy the land and even went guarantor for him. Pat purchased the land for $18 000, built a solid brick home for $42 000 and helped repay the debt by renting it out to his brother, Bernie. 'It really gave me a great financial kick-start at a young age. It was the best thing I ever did,' he said.

As momentous years go, 1984 was right up there for Pat as being both career-defining and life-changing. The year marked a blossoming of Pat's relationship with Lisa Bullivant. The pair had known each other for several months after initially being introduced through friends at a local tavern. Theirs was not the classic tale of love at first sight; in fact, it took numerous sightings before they ventured out alone. Lisa thought Pat had too many pimples and, like many young girls in search of Mr Right, felt she could do better. But Pat charmed her from the start, as he did with many women, and Lisa invited him on their first official date—the wedding of her half-brother Geoff in January 1984.

She envisaged it would be the perfect occasion, but it turned out to be much less. The 16-year-old brunette looked stunning in her pink frock with shoestring shoulder straps, matching stole and lipstick. She had been impressed with Pat's newly restored Mazda sedan and was eagerly waiting to introduce her new boyfriend to all of her relatives. Pat was oblivious to these facts and unwittingly sold the Mazda the night before the wedding. 'A guy came around to my place and offered me cash for it and I couldn't turn it down,' he said. The next day he went fishing early with his mates in a utility he'd borrowed from his boss. Later that day, and for many years on, Lisa gave Pat a not-so-subtle dig about taking her for their first date in a 'ute that stank like old fish'.

Lisa Bullivant was a remarkable young woman, possessing maturity beyond her years, so it didn't surprise 22-year-old Pat when she asked him out first. From early childhood, Lisa had been free-spirited and headstrong. While never failing any school subjects, her grades were mostly average. Teachers typecast her as a problem child and tried to restrain her. Lisa didn't aid the situation with her antics as the class jester, her healthy disrespect for authority and her desire to be the centre of attention. But it was all driven by a sense of fun, not self-centred ego. She was outgoing and easily endeared herself to a wide circle of friends. She said what she thought and never held back. 'I can't remember the number of times she was sent from the classroom,' recalls long-time friend Lisa Gayton. 'She would always be giving cheek and standing up for herself. Teachers would send her out of the class and you could still hear her telling them off from outside. They'd have to send her further down the corridor so she didn't cause any further disruption.' A born organiser, she also resented the loss of independence that accompanied teachers organising her school life.

Lisa Bullivant was also blessed with a quick wit and humour that on many occasions out-matched her elders and contributed to her attraction to trouble. Beneath the irreverent exterior lay intelligence and ambition. She also displayed an ingenuity that she applied to a wide range of situations. This came to the fore on one memorable occasion when a nun locked Lisa in a cupboard in primary school for misbehaving. Never one to miss an opportunity, Lisa occupied herself counting the jellybeans in a giant jar which was stored there as a prize for a school fund-raiser. Teachers and friends marvelled at her luck in later correctly 'guessing' the contents. Of course, she shared her spoils with her girlfriends—but not her secret. Lisa finally confessed to them on her wedding day.

Like Pat, Lisa never excelled at school, failing to find motivation in the rigid environment of the state education system. She too found her teachers were unable to adapt the lessons to suit her free spirit or find a path to her imagination. By mutual agreement, she left school in Year Nine and at the age of fourteen years and nine months acquired a job as junior administrator with prestigious Sydney law firm Bowen and Gerathy (co-founded by former Whitlam government Attorney-General Lionel Bowen). Her tender age required her to be accompanied to the job interview by her stepmother, June Bullivant.

But what Lisa lacked in formal education was compensated for by her drive and ambition to succeed in the workplace and her local community. By the time she met Pat, Lisa was a highly valued and respected staff member at Bowen and Gerathy. She was indeed a young high achiever at everything outside of school. She had been the youngest-ever member of the International Toastmistresses Club at the age of fourteen and the organisation's youngest president in the world at the age of sixteen. Lisa acquired a range of skills that served her well through her professional and personal life: speech writing, public speaking, analytical listening and interpersonal skills. She also followed the example of her parents Barry and June and joined Rotaract, the youth arm of the community club Rotary. Lisa later encouraged Pat to join and in years to come would assist him in training for public speaking engagements as his profile and demand grew.

While she was initially relaxed about their relationship, Lisa set her sights on a long-term future not long after they started dating seriously. Two years after that first date, Pat bought his second block of land at Narrawallee near Mollymook on the New South Wales south coast. The vendors were asking $20 000 for the block—more than Pat could afford. Lisa offered to go halves with him in the purchase but Pat was uncertain about whether he wanted to lock himself into a financial and emotional relationship so soon. He was also anxious about the potentially messy financial and legal repercussions if they were to break up. Pat's brother Tony agreed to provide half of the finance for the land, which they later built a house on. Pat felt pretty good about his burgeoning real estate portfolio and was boasting of his acquisition at Lisa's nineteenth birthday dinner. She produced a document from her purse and slapped it down on the table. 'Stop bragging, I've bought a block of land too,' she said. Not just any block but the land next door to Pat. 'You're not going anywhere without me, baby,' she proclaimed. Pat was gobsmacked. 'If ever you got snookered, that was it,' he said.

The other momentous event in 1984 would provide a shape and direction to Pat's life that he could never have imagined. Pat had only ever had one obsession. While ambitious, he admits that at this stage of his life, he lacked the confidence and vision to look beyond the world of car mechanics. Pat had, like the entire nation, marvelled at the deeds of the gumboot-shuffling potato farmer Cliff Young in winning the 1983 Westfield Sydney to Melbourne race. When the 1984 event, which had been reversed to run from Melbourne to Sydney for the first and only time, went past Archer's garage, the young mechanic was mildly curious to see what this apparently strange breed of athlete called ultra marathoners looked like.

'Come and have a look at this guy,' Laurie Archer called to his apprentices as the winner Geoff Molloy jogged past the garage, in what he now admits was another attempt to 'gee up the young blokes'. 'He's run from Melbourne to Sydney. He's double your age and can run twice as much. You young blokes couldn't do this.' Quick as a flash, the cocky Pat Farmer piped up: 'It's no big deal. I could do that.' Figuring his point was lost on the young upstarts, Archer ordered his mechanics back to work.

The detail of the day is indelible in Pat's mind. Lightning could not have struck at his feet and left such a lasting impression. 'Geoff Molloy was running and there was a real street parade,' he recalls. 'There were soldiers around him as a guard of honour, cheer girls and there were people lining the streets clapping him, including kids from my old school. And here was this guy—a very ordinary-looking person—running through it all. He wasn't going particularly fast. He wasn't what I expected of someone who could run those sorts of distances. He didn't have legs like a racehorse or a physique like a Greek god. He was chewing on an apple as he was running down the street near the finish and waving to the crowd.'

The triumphant finish belied a tortuous 875 kilometre struggle that had begun over six days earlier in Melbourne. Molloy, 42, a lawn-mower man and ex-champion road cyclist from Melbourne, had battled many demons on the road to Sydney. But his victory in the event they dubbed 'The Greatest Race in the World' was almost as extraordinary as Cliffy's the year before. It was Molloy's first attempt at the race and only his second ultra event (he had broken the Australian 24-hour track record only ten weeks before) in a brief four-year running career preceded by fifteen years of sedentary life. Molloy had battled knee pain, sleep deprivation, depression and exhaustion. The Victorian had taken the lead just before crossing the New South Wales border and had been running scared ever since. He kept his lead by minimising his sleep (four hours a day for the first five nights and 20 minutes on the final night) and employing a new tactic from his old bike racing days of literally eating on the run—little and often. The protracted journey through the pain barrier reduced him to tears on the final day as he fought off fast-finishing 51-year-old New Zealand policeman John Hughes.

Molloy wobbled across the line, punched the air triumphantly and was immediately greeted by glamorous cheer girls in gold tops and short shorts. He was mobbed by a horde of spectators and media, given a quick medical check and rehydrated before being presented with a large silver trophy and the winner's cheque for $20 000. An hour later, he returned to the finish line to greet runner-up Hughes with a warm embrace. The 1984 event had been extraordinary for several reasons. A field of 39 runners started, but only nine finished. It was best remembered for the controversial 'withdrawal', 17 kilometres from the finish, of Canadian runner Bob Bruner, whom race officials accused of cheating (they had spied on him from treetops in a bid to gather evidence and at one stage been stranded for hours in their elevated hiding place when Bruner's crew camped below).

Crowd favourite Cliff Young defied the orders of a medical specialist and began the race with a stress fracture of the knee. Sadly it failed to 'warm up' as he had hoped and Cliffy was never in the hunt. He battled gamely to finish seventh, 31 hours behind Molloy. The ultra veteran finished eight hours ahead of a 59-year-old novice, Bob McElwaine, who was desperate for the prize money after being bankrupted for the second time (partly due to the dwindling patronage at his Pyrmont Hotel in inner Sydney after the introduction in 1983 of random breath testing). McElwaine lost 10 kilograms during the race but finished the event despite having less than three months' training under his belt. In an extraordinary display of generosity, Cliffy gifted him the new car he had been given for the 'Best Achievement Award' for courageously completing the race despite his knee injury. McElwaine couldn't drive it for a few days because he was in hospital recovering from exhaustion. When McElwaine took his new car for a spin, he had an accident at the first intersection and wrote it off.*

The impressionable young Farmer never knew of any of these displays of camaraderie and generosity until years after the last runner passed by his door. He was too busy ringing race organisers from that first evening, trying to talk his way into the next year's event. They tried to fob him off for a week or two, but not even the most obstinate of officials could dissuade him. A new spark was ignited; his engine was idling and he wanted to hit the track for a test run. With qualifying events several months off, Pat confided to his eldest brother Bernie his desire to run in the Sydney to Melbourne race. His timing could have been better. It was the night Pat and his sister Catherine were hosting one of their famous cocktail parties at the flat they shared. Bernie wasn't just full of encouragement; his glass ran over with it. He told Pat if he was serious he would start training the next day. But that was all the stimulation Pat needed. Early the next morning, he shook off the effects of just a few cocktails, stepped through the wreckage of the party and set off for Wollongong. Fifty kilometres later, he was fatigued and dehydrated and wondering why Bernie and his sister Annette hadn't arrived with refreshments, as arranged. 'I'd been running six hours and was as dry as could be when they eventually showed up,' Pat recalls. 'Bernie didn't think I was serious and I couldn't believe they'd let me go so long without seeing how I was. With that first training run it was a case of *carpe diem*, "seize the day".'

While his family was mindful of the difficulty of the challenge, they were generally very supportive. While some friends and acquaintances thought Pat was young and foolish for tackling older, hardened athletes who had trained all their lives for an event like the Westfield run, his mother and siblings defended Pat's ambition. 'We knew he wanted to do it and we also knew that we should encourage rather than discourage him,'

---

* Phil Essam, 1999, *'I've Finally Found My Hero . . .' The story of the 1983 to 1991 Sydney to Melbourne Ultra Marathon*, self-published, South Australia.

says Tony Farmer. 'If someone wants to do something, you help them with it rather than shoot the idea down. It's the way we were brought up.'

Despite his boundless blind faith and sheer will, Pat was not well-equipped to enter the world of ultra running. He had no background or mentor in long-distance running, and bluntly admits he didn't even have a clue what he was getting himself into. He set his sights on a 24-hour qualifying event run by leading athletics club Botany Harriers at Pagewood Oval in October 1984. Training consisted of no more than afternoon jogs around a nearby park and some longer weekend runs of two to three hours' duration. It was nothing compared to what he would eventually run, but it seemed a long way to a novice and to the taxi drivers who would report having seen Pat 'on the other side of Sydney'. He also began running to work on some days but his body and mind were barely tuned for his first race. The combination of a drastically inadequate preparation and beginner's naiveté (as evidenced by the wearing of cheap, new running shoes) made it the most physically traumatic experience of his life so far.

He foolishly ran out with the leaders for the opening two hours—and quickly paid the price.

'When the gun went off I got caught up in the enthusiasm of the moment and just ran too fast,' he said. 'I was thinking this is too easy and didn't feel like I needed to have any food or drink. And then after four hours it hit me like a ton of bricks. I got blisters but they were the least of my problems. You name it, I got it—dehydration, vomiting, I was falling over. It was just a big shock to the system, especially trying to cope with sleep deprivation.'

Pat's inexperience was apparent to those witnessing the event. The race commentator, who kept calling Pat 'Mrs Farmer's little boy', pilloried him. The veterans of the ultra scene collectively shook their heads in dismay at the clueless young novice. Pat's sister Annette says it was a painful experience for the sizeable cheer squad of family and friends who were there to support him. They watched in amazement, then agony, and finally in tears.

Pat's feet swelled up considerably under the constant pounding. This put more pressure on his raw and blistered skin; with every few steps he could feel a sharp tearing at his tender flesh. At one stage, family members cut the toes out of his shoes to relieve the pain. But his feet continued to inflate to an abnormal size. 'They were so bad towards the end that we had to cut Pat's shoes off his feet and borrow a new pair from his cousin John, who took three sizes bigger,' recalls sister Annette. 'Pat would have a rest and we'd say: "We're really proud of you, but you can pull out, you don't have to do any more." But he'd still soldier on. It was physically upsetting us to see our brother go through such torment. We all got so emotional.'

But 'surrender' was a word that had been deleted from Pat's vocabulary, if in fact it was ever part of it. 'The distance wasn't so much the problem; it was the way I ran it,' he said. 'I didn't run a steady pace. I didn't drink or eat enough. I ran a miserable race but I was determined to be there at the end. I think I always knew I could finish.' This race was the harshest of introductions to the cruellest of sports. He dug deeper than ever before, spurred on by a burning desire to not let himself and his supporters down. He survived to finish fifth, running 125 kilometres in 24 hours—35 kilometres short of the qualifying distance. Thirty-five runners failed to finish—one was carried away on a stretcher. Pat had stunned his family and silenced his trackside critics. When the merry-go-round of pain stopped, Pat needed help to get off and get home. His family carried him to the car, and from the car to a hot bath when they arrived at Granville. 'We thought that was the end of his ultra career and didn't expect Pat to front up and try to kill himself again,' says Annette. 'We felt he'd done it once, he wouldn't need to put himself through such torture again.'

But amidst the agony and the ecstasy, a brilliant career had just begun under the discerning eye of one of distance running's most influential officials. Westfield race director Mike Agostini was trackside and witnessed most of Pat's race. After clarifying with his family that it was indeed his first ultra event, he told Pat he thought he maybe had what it took to be an ultra-marathoner and offered to help him in his quest to qualify for the Sydney to Melbourne event. Agostini was a timely and impressive mentor. He was a former Trinidad sprinter who once held the world records for 100 yards, 220 yards and 200 metres, was a finalist at the 1956 Melbourne Olympics and an Empire Games gold medallist. Among other things, Agostini was now Honorary Consul-General for the Republic of Trinidad and Tobago. He offered Pat help in the form of a job as a gardener at his residence in Sydney's exclusive eastern suburbs.

'It was obvious from that first day Pat had talent,' said Agostini. 'My first impression was of someone who had a dream and could dedicate themselves to it. Everyone else was older than Pat and had been training for years and yet he gutsed it out. I always have time for any person who has a dream. If you don't have a dream you're dead. There was no question here was someone with fire in his soul, which I believe is more important than physical ability. I can't tell you how many athletes I've coached or seen who looked like they had it and said they wanted it but when it got really hard, always had somewhere else to go.'

The influence of Agostini would prove to be of major significance. He offered Pat the positive reinforcement he was craving in this strange but exciting new world of ultra marathon running. While it seemed he had 'a million people' telling him how impossible it was for him to succeed, it took the belief of just one person from the ultra scene to stoke the embers of his fire. At his first test, someone outside of his biased circle of friends and family showed faith in him. But it wasn't just anyone. Agostini's credentials as an Olympian and major sports power-broker, coupled with his significant social status, gave an immeasurable boost to the self-esteem of the unknown dreamer from Sydney's west.

While he still loved his work as a mechanic, a new challenge beckoned in a bigger faster lane. Pat's life had found a new gear that could take him down roads and to destinations that he had never envisaged until six months before. He felt sad to leave Laurie and Faye Archer—they had been more like second parents than employers to Pat in the seven years he worked for them. He repaid the Archers' faith in him and repaid the debt on his Eagle Vale property before leaving. Laurie Archer admits he was somewhat devastated by Pat's decision; he'd been contemplating retirement and was grooming Pat to take over as workshop manager. 'Pat left on good terms. I never stopped anyone from furthering themselves and Pat certainly deserved to get ahead in whatever he wanted to do,' says Archer.

The casual work in the spacious gardens at Agostini's mansion was a means to an end. Firstly, it allowed Pat the extra hours for training which were necessary to develop his body and mind. More significantly, it gave him the opportunity for frequent chats with his new employer where he would soak up as many lessons as he could in this new apprenticeship. 'My picture was getting bigger all the time,' says Pat. 'I was aiming for the biggest road race in the world, which by this time had really captured Australia's imagination. I was now dealing with influential people and could really feel I was going places instead of just being a little dot on the map.'

Pat was one of the few ultra runners whom Agostini assisted and with whom he developed a friendship. His role as Westfield race director made it untenable for him to get too close to competitors. But in a more altruistic sense, Agostini was passing on an inheritance that he had received decades before. As a promising young sprinter he came under the influence of Olympic sprinters Mal Whitfield and Andy Stanfield. They had taught a wide-eyed Trinidad youth how to convert dreams into reality, aspirations into achievements. When the young Agostini had asked how to repay them, they simply replied: 'Man, you don't repay us. Someone taught us and we passed it on and we just want you to do the same.' In the circle of life, the pupils of today become the masters of tomorrow.

Pat's body was slowly adapting to the physical and mental

demands that the punishing sport of ultra marathons imposed upon him. His learning curve was steep but a new mentor entered his life—one of the very best in the business. Having failed to qualify at his first attempt for the 1985 Westfield race, Mike Agostini suggested Pat would benefit by seeing the race up close and personal as a crew member. He organised for Pat to join the team supporting the world's leading female ultra runner, Eleanor Adams from England. The 37-year-old had received her invitation to run after an outstanding performance at the Colac Six-Day race in 1984 where she broke the women's world record, becoming the first woman to run more than 800 kilometres in that period. While an experienced ultra runner, the Sydney to Melbourne event represented a new and exciting challenge for Adams. Pat and Eleanor hit it off right from the start. She was obsessed with winning every running race she entered. Pat was just obsessed with running.

Competitors in the Sydney to Melbourne races had crews of between six and eight, and two camper vans, one of which followed immediately behind the runner constantly to provide protection, food, drink and any other supplies. Pat knew from experience the horrors of night running—the unbelievable weariness that gripped the body and the fog that descended on the mind as sleep deprivation took its toll, and the fear of uncertainty as semi-trailers and speeding cars buffeted a groggy, plodding runner with their slipstreams.

Pat volunteered for the night shift, knowing this was where he could be of greatest assistance to his runner. Aspects of the job reminded Pat of his early days in his mechanic's apprenticeship where he was expected to do the menial tasks efficiently and cheerfully. He took delight in making Adams special treats to eat such as apple or banana pancakes, applying great thought to fare that would surprise, nourish and awaken the runner and her taste buds.

'Pat was a delight to have around,' said Eleanor. 'He was one of the best crew members I've ever had. The event was a real team effort. Friendships formed in these races are friendships made for life. It leaves everyone richer for the experience. Pat kept us all fed despite the heavy-handed driving by fellow crew member John Champness [a former Westfield competitor and fireman by occupation]. Pat would entertain me with stories of the mayhem behind me. In fact I think we laughed all the way to Melbourne as Pat had an endless succession of jokes or funny tales. He obviously understood the requirements, both physical and mental, of such a demanding event.'

Pat absorbed every aspect of the experience. Rather than deter him, it made him even hungrier to become a Westfield foot soldier. 'I'd never been to Melbourne and the finish was a great thrill because Eleanor was the first woman home [out of four] and seventh in a field of 28 men,' Pat said. 'She collected prizemoney of $5500 and after the race finished we stayed in Melbourne at the Parkroyal at St Kilda. I remember being in the spa on the top floor overlooking the whole of the city and I was having a beer and thinking "this is the life". I'd never experienced anything like that before in my whole life.'

Pat again failed to qualify for the 1986 Westfield run, but he was getting closer. This time he ran 145 kilometres. He again helped Adams, this time in a lead-up event, the Colac Six-Day Race in February. Pat spent much of the time playing baby-sitter to Adams' nine-year-old daughter and other local children. 'All of the youngsters made a bee line for Pat and he developed the reputation of being a Pied Piper. He certainly had a way with children,' Adams said. Keen to again savour life on the open road, Pat also crewed for the English runner in the 1986 Sydney to Melbourne race.

That event was most noted for the drama involving Adelaide runner Dr Geoff Kirkman. The 35-year-old dentist was leading the event at the end of day three when he was the innocent victim of a bizarre accident. A truck driver had stopped late at night over the crest of a hill near Kirkman's support vehicle. The driver was picking up an abandoned sack of potatoes. That action forced a following semi to swerve to avoid him. At the same time, a sedan driven by an Albury man was attempting to overtake the runner's escort vehicle. The sedan and semi collided and the out-of-control sedan careered into Kirkman, knocking him literally out of his shoes. The runner was found 12 metres away in a gully. Kirkman suffered a broken pelvis and deep lacerations and was in shock due to the loss of blood. Incredibly, he was discharged from hospital after only two days.

The motorist, Raymond Ward, 46, was killed instantly. Runners and their crews all travelled past the accident site. Farmer and Adams both remember being deeply distressed at hearing the tragic news and even more moved when they witnessed first hand the aftermath of the carnage. It provided everyone involved in the race with the most sobering and poignant reminder of the daily dangers they faced, but often overlooked.

Adams and other runners all insisted on continuing the race. Kirkman's misfortune paved the way for 33-year-old Yugoslav engineer Dusan Mravlje to win the race. This was Pat's first look at Mravlje, with whom he would be personally engaged in an epic battle across the United States nine years later. The Yugoslav's expertise in playing mind games with opponents was evident even then, when he sent a message to new race leader Brian Bloomer to expect him for dinner. Mravlje passed Bloomer several hours later and stayed in front, fuelled by his 'secret diet' of six to eight stubbies of beer every day (he increased this in the run home into Melbourne as he pub-crawled his way to the finish, buffered by a massive sixteen-hour lead).*

Adams powered home to finish fourth overall and again won the women's race—her best-ever result, as well as the fastest time and the highest placing by a female in the history of the event. But she suffered some trauma from the Kirkman accident. For weeks afterwards she would wake from nightmares of being knocked down by a runaway semi-trailer. She refused to again take part in the Westfield event until the route was changed. At Adams' suggestion, Pat contacted one of the gurus of ultra running in Australia, Tony Rafferty. He was planning an assault

---

* '*I've Finally Found My Hero . . .*'

on the road record for 1000 miles and was looking for crew members. For Pat, this was an opportunity too good to refuse, even if he had to take holidays for it.

Rafferty had escaped the ravages of Belfast's religious conflict as a 21-year-old. Along with George Perdon, he pioneered ultra marathon running in Australia, setting and smashing records at a variety of distances. He became the first person to run from Sydney to Melbourne in 1972, was the first to cross the desolate Nullarbor Plain and to run along the barren Birdsville Track.

Despite his age—over 46—Rafferty maintained a Peter Pan-like appearance in a sport where runners were like good red wines, needing time to mature. Rafferty was always keen to assist budding ultra runners in a sport that had trouble attracting young blood because of its extreme demands. Rafferty had the greatest respect for Adams—anyone with a reference from her was welcome in Rafferty's crew. Pat travelled to Queensland and filled the same role that he had with Eleanor—fuelling the record attempt with tantalising treats and assisting in the event as driver and masseur. Rafferty ran from Bundaberg to Cairns in fifteen days, six hours and 48 minutes in June 1986, creating an Australian record for 1000 miles (later that year he lowered that to fourteen days, sixteen hours and 45 minutes in Hull, England). More than anything, Rafferty opened Pat's eyes and ears to the mental and spiritual aspects of long-distance running. But at this early and formative stage of his career, Pat could not assimilate the lessons completely. In years to come, when he had experienced the extremes of physical pain, sleep deprivation and emotional exhaustion, his mind would be more receptive to Rafferty's rules.

But for now, he planned to use every piece of knowledge he had gained from working with Rafferty and Adams for another assault on a qualifying run for the 1987 Westfield event. He again ventured to Hensley Field at Botany in Sydney's east—the venue of previous failed attempts—for the 24-hour track race. But this time it was different. His body had been able to absorb enough kilometres to give him the necessary endurance. Night running was still a curse, but he had begun to gain enough control over his thoughts and emotions to extract himself from the inevitable flat patches where exhaustion gripped his body. As always, Pat had a loyal band of family and friends to pull him through. By this time, he had developed friendships with other ultra runners and there was a few athletes who also helped him survive the lows. When the clock ticked over to 24 hours, Pat had run 161 kilometres—enough to qualify. By running what was the equivalent of 100 miles, he joined a select group called 'The Centurions'. The first hurdle was finally cleared. His dream was now well and truly alive.

4

The war within

The start of his first Westfield Sydney to Melbourne on 26 March 1987 was everything Pat had envisaged. There was much fanfare with the pre-race entertainment and runners led out to centre stage of the Parramatta Shopping Centre by a pipe band. Competitors were individually introduced to the thousands of spectators, who cheered them as if they were all Olympic gold medallists. And there was the indescribable blend of excitement and fear of the unknown at the beginning of the biggest adventure of Pat's life. After three years of gruelling training and supreme sacrifice, he had finally made it in the world of sport. Pat was the youngest person ever to compete in the event, a fact that attracted a good measure of publicity prior to the race. He'd even given his first autograph. But deep down Pat was scared. He'd felt inadequate at various times of his life, but never like this. Here was the boy from Granville, part of an elite international field: aiming to match it with the best ultra marathon runners in the 'Greatest Footrace in the World'. 'I looked at all these other athletes—real athletes—and thought to myself "geez, I really fooled somebody this time". I was really wondering what was I doing there and was as nervous as could be,' he recalls.

The case of giant butterflies in his stomach was not without good reason. There had been two significant changes to the 1987 event, both prompted by safety fears arising out of the accident involving Geoff Kirkman. The race had been moved off the treacherous Hume Highway after the runners reached Goulburn, which had also extended it by 55 kilometres to 1060 kilometres. It was now the longest, toughest but richest point-to-point race in the world. As well, organisers introduced cut-off times in a bid to avoid the safety problems associated with having the field strung out over hundreds of kilometres. Runners failing to reach certain points at designated times would be disqualified. Over 218 athletes applied to start in the event; only 26 were granted entry.

For Pat, there was a great deal at stake. His struggle to compete in the Sydney to Melbourne race didn't end with the completion of his qualifying race. He still had to raise close to $10 000 to cover race entry, vehicle hire and numerous other expenses. He'd collected close to $5000 in sponsorship with the help of girlfriend Lisa and his sisters, who had approached Woolworths and ANR Elevators, the company that employed Annette's second husband, Terry. Sister Catherine, a hairdresser, had even invented the idea of a 'hair-cut-athon' to assist the fundraising. But Pat was forced to take out a personal loan for $5000, which would take him the rest of the year to repay. His crew was made up of family and friends, including three of his most loyal allies—Lisa, brother Bernie and sister Annette.

The 1987 field had the largest international field and was the strongest ever. It included three Westfield champions: Cliff Young (1983), Yiannis Kouros (1985) and Dusan Mravlje (1986). It was the first time Pat had lined up in a multi-day race against the two men who would prove to be his fiercest long-term rivals—Mravlje and fellow Sydney runner Dave Taylor. Pat ran strongly on the first day and was in equal tenth place after fourteen hours. His crew, however, took longer to get up to speed.

They'd overlooked one small detail during preparations—only two of the crew could drive a manual vehicle. Lisa, Annette and

Bernie's sister-in-law Lynn Martin were forced to learn while trailing Pat at a monotonous 6–8 kilometres per hour. They had several too-close-for-comfort encounters which had more to do with a lapse in judgment or a foot slipping than any attempt to hurry Pat along. On one occasion, Bernie was having his first rest on a top bunk inside the following vehicle, leaving learner Lynn to drive. She bumped into the back of Pat, prompting him to retort: 'What are you trying to do—kill me or something?' This immediately made her even more nervous behind the wheel. She proceeded to kangaroo-hop the vehicle, sending Bernie flying from his resting place on to the floor of the campervan. After various verbal volleys, the issue was settled with a decision to relieve Lynn of driving duties.

But the real battle for Pat was raging within. His race began to unravel on day two. He'd made the first designated cut-off at Goulburn but was in danger of being disqualified if he missed the next at Canberra, 95 kilometres down the road. Everything was an effort—brushing his teeth, shaving, just putting one foot in front of the other and keeping his eyes open. Bernie and Annette dreaded the nights as much as Pat because they knew from past runs what a desperate, depressing struggle it was for him to deal with sleep deprivation.

Along with Pat at the rear of the field was another Westfield rookie, Mark Gladwell, who was fighting his own war of attrition against the road and his body. Thirty-nine-year-old Mark had shown remarkable courage just to continue the event after being hospitalised for six hours with dehydration. He just sneaked into Goulburn ahead of the cut-off but had discarded his drip and dragged himself back on the road. Two runners failed the first test—Dave Taylor and Peter Parcell of Ipswich, Queensland had been disqualified under the new rule. Race officials had also written off Farmer and Gladwell, expecting they'd be the next to go at Canberra. But the pair had too much physical and emotional investment in the race to give up so soon. They knew what each had endured to get to the starting line, having met while crew members for different runners in previous Westfield races. This time they were reliant on their own bodies to get them to Melbourne, and struck an instant rapport. 'I feel like I've just been hit by a Mack truck,' said Pat. 'I think the same truck got me on the same road,' replied Mark.

The two began talking and sharing their painful experiences; the comfort and reassurance that flowed from the knowledge they were not alone proved something of an anaesthetic. As competitors, they shared a mutual respect. They saw themselves as the battlers of the high-profile event—putting their shows on the road on shoestring budgets. Pat was further impressed that Mark was using the run to raise $10 000 for children at the spastic centre where he worked as a contract bus driver.

Like Pat, Mark was also of working-class stock from Sydney's western suburbs. His muscular build, particularly in the upper body, was originally chiselled during three years of physical conditioning in the infantry. He was a two-tour veteran of the Vietnam War and fascinated Pat when he spoke of the ultra marathon being similar to a war zone. In both cases, battered bodies and minds were compelled to search deep within for fortitude and resilience an individual could not be sure they possessed. The Vietnam vet evoked memories of an old platoon sergeant who would tell infantrymen how they had to hit their absolute lowest point before they could think about moving forward to their highest. He told Pat: 'My old sergeant had a simple motto: "Never give up".'

As a young idealist who was trained to feel he was invincible, Mark had fought many battles against foreign enemies. It was his job to go into combat, even if it was in distant lands, and he had been very committed to the cause. On his first year-long tour, he experienced the full horrors of war during the famous Tet Offensive in 1968. His platoon was involved in a search-and-destroy mission in a village south of Saigon. 'We'd air-dropped pamphlets printed in Vietnamese telling villagers we'd be coming through,' he said. 'The village was supposed to be cleared but it wasn't. The other side had kept civilians for their own reasons. They recruited people against their will and used them for protection.' As with any war, there were innocent casualties. The worst task was burying the dead—especially the women and children. The worst battle came long after the din of gunfire and grenades had subsided—against the enemy within. The personal demons would not be exorcised and Mark volunteered for a second tour of duty. 'I thought I could undo some of the wrongs from the first time, do things better,' he said. But another eight months fighting the good fight did not assuage his guilt. He left the army, wallowed in alcoholism for years and only finally found purpose to his life when he began running.

Mark's words and deeds helped inspire Pat. For him, the war analogy bestowed prestige and honour upon a sport that was generally seen as a magnet for lunatics and misfits. 'I could see the similarities and I could see we were noble in what we were doing, just as any person was that went off to war with their own ambitions and reasons for doing it', said Pat. 'At the end of the day we were heroes because we were heroes to ourselves.' In return, Pat's youthful enthusiasm and maturity impressed the ex-soldier. The conversation proved a welcome distraction for both and they pushed each other to Canberra under the cut-off time. Mark 'came good' after Canberra but unfortunately Pat's revival was only temporary. He had stopped to sleep at a Cooma motel on the second night when officials advised his crew he was disqualified. Pat had missed the third cut-off by two hours. He awoke at daybreak thinking he had over-slept and was devastated when told of the ruling. A three-year dream dissolved in an instant. Disappointment turned to humiliation when officials insisted he take no further part in the race, stripping him of timing equipment, vehicle signage and his dignity.

'I really felt cheated,' said Pat. 'They really degraded us. They didn't say: "Oh that's a shame you didn't make it, you really did pretty well to get this far". There was nothing positive about the whole situation. It was just like I was—I don't know how you'd describe it—they didn't treat us with any respect. All the publicity I'd given them to that point didn't count. They just treated me like garbage and that was it. It was like I was wasting their time being there. They wouldn't let me have anything more to do with the event.'

But rules were rules. Westfield officials had implemented the cut-offs after discussion with police and traffic authorities. Race organiser Charlie Lynn said New South Wales police were closely scrutinising the new policy to ensure it was implemented. Lynn issued orders to on-the-road officials to give runners a few minutes' leeway, but nothing beyond that. A total of ten runners were disqualified—the most prominent casualty was the previous year's winner, the Yugoslav Mravlje, who missed the cut on day three. He continued his beer-fuelled race strategy, reportedly consuming 27 cans on the first two days, but his race went flat before he even hit halfway. Gladwell completed his fightback against ill-health, finishing eleventh—20 hours ahead of Cliff Young. Kouros was awesome, leading from start to finish and winning by more than a day.

Pat returned home bitter and disillusioned. For weeks he wanted no further involvement with the running scene. He resented being branded a failure by race officials. He stewed over the issue and finally put on his shoes to run the anger out of his system. By the time he'd achieved that, Pat was 30 kilometres from home and had made a resolution: 'That's the last time I let anything beat me.'

The Westfield runners were often called upon to put their talents to good use for charity and fund-raising events, but there was one event in April 1987 which was more unusual than most. A former accountant, Bob Squires, who was serving a sentence in Long Bay Prison for embezzlement, had been touched by the story of twelve-year-old Sydney schoolgirl Caroline Watson, who needed more than $60 000 for a life-saving heart-lung transplant in London. She was born with an illness called congenital heart syndrome. Squires asked Westfield if some of its runners could help the prisoners stage a 1000-kilometre charity run to raise the money. Pat and Mark Gladwell joined other Westfield runners, including Dave Taylor, sampling life 'on the inside' for ten hours. They arrived in time for a breakfast fit for a king, which the prisoners had conned authorities into providing for them. Transport company TNT had agreed to sponsor the 50 prisoners and Westfield runners for each of the 2702 laps they completed of the soccer oval.

Pat and Mark found it a surreal experience. At one point they were running laps with a very intelligent young man, who impressed them greatly. 'I remember a prison guard asking us later if we had enjoyed his company,' recalls Mark. 'He then told us to make sure we didn't upset him because he was a serial killer. Pat and I looked at each other. We were stunned because he looked normal. You wouldn't have picked it.'

Most of the prisoners had not trained for the event and while many were happy to assist a charitable cause, they all relished the break from the daily mundane routine. Lap counting was done by having prisoners take an ice-block stick once they had completed a circuit. However, the event degenerated into farce late in the day when prisoners began 'cheating' by grabbing handfuls of sticks after each lap. The Westfield runners thought turning a blind eye was the better part of valour. Pat and Mark were later given a guided tour of the maximum-security wing where they experienced life in a single cell. 'It was a real eye-opener—such a crappy and depressing place,' said Pat. He was moved and distressed at the notion of young lives wasting away and was particularly upset to learn that many young prisoners were given a death sentence while serving short prison terms, with AIDS rampant in prisons at that time.

But the Long Bay charity run gave life and hope to one person. The event raised more than $30 000, which helped fund Caroline Watson's heart-lung transplant. She returned to normal health for ten years and lived to the age of 22. Sadly, she died in 1997.

Pat accepted an offer by Mark Gladwell to join Mark and training partner Kevin Mansell under the tutelage of tough disciplinarian Bill Carlson. The two were new to the ultra game and while they'd run down plenty of dead ends in their lives, the world was now one long open road to be attacked with vigour.

Gladwell and Mansell had been like brothers since meeting at an Alcoholics Anonymous meeting in 1983. They were bonded by their tormented lives. Mansell, dubbed by Charlie Lynn as the greatest success story of the Westfield races, had endured the cruellest of upbringings. His mother died when he was just thirteen. With only an alcoholic father to care for them, Mansell and his five-year-old brother were placed in an orphanage for five years. Mansell was himself an alcoholic by the time he left the institution and struggled with his addiction for ten years. He was also tortured by a harelip, which forced him to endure the associated social stigma, as well as the pain from more than 30 corrective operations (he's since had more and, while he's lost count, believes they would number more than 50). Mansell had twice tried to commit suicide because he felt life was too cruel to live. He was overweight and, coupled with his 80 cigarettes a day habit, seemed to be trying to kill himself any way he could, until he discovered running. He had finished fourteenth out of 26 in the 1987 race, prompting him to declare: 'All my life I've been looking for a hero. Now I've found one . . . me.'*

Carlson set a punishing training regime that involved running 120 kilometres in the easy weeks and up to 370 kilometres in the hard ones. The most gruelling sessions were saved for weekends. The trio would leave home after work on Friday and run over 100 kilometres in thirteen hours through the darkness, sustained by supplies of bananas, chocolate and high-energy bars carried in backpacks. There was also a rain jacket, a spare pair of shoes and a change of clothes. After returning home and sleeping for six hours, they would venture out again on Saturday night and run another 120 kilometres or more through until early Sunday afternoon. While such training seemed extreme to friends and family (and occasionally to the runners themselves) it simulated some of the Westfield race conditions, building

---

*   *'I've Finally Found My Hero . . .'*

strength and endurance and toughening their minds, particularly when it came to dealing with the toughest adversary: sleep deprivation.

A few months before the 1988 Westfield, Maurice Taylor, a 38-year-old grief counsellor, joined the group. The four runners were unmistakeable and turned heads as they pounded the pavement, decked out in their red and white Westfield clothing. As their reputations grew in the local area and the running community, the group found itself a nickname. They were called the 'Awesome Foursome' and have strong claims to being the original version. Their rowing counterparts, 'The Oarsome Foursome', were created two years later and rose to sporting fame at the 1992 Barcelona Olympics where they won gold in the coxless fours. Pat organised for the ultra running quartet to have iridescent lime green t-shirts specially printed with their sobriquet. In their distinctive colours, night running around lively suburban and city streets on weekend nights proved both frustrating and hazardous. Mansell and Gladwell felt they were too old for the nightclub scene, but Pat occasionally yearned for a better social life with his friends. They often felt anything but awesome when they became regular targets for missiles launched by thrill-seeking youths in fast-moving cars. Egg raids were popular in the western suburbs and the four felt they were like ducks in a sideshow shooting gallery. Pat sported a large colourful bruise on his arm for weeks after being hit by a flying hard-boiled projectile, while Kevin was branded on the buttocks by a roll of insulation tape. The obstacles were many and varied, whether it was a group of drunks outside a hotel threatening to throw glasses at them or pistol-wielding police mistaking them for fleet-footed service station bandits. Eventually the ultra marathon men became such a regular sight in the suburbs that they became friendly with patrolling police and security guards.

As the 1988 Westfield Sydney to Melbourne race approached, Pat had developed something of a reputation among family and friends as being 'difficult' to crew for during races. Pushing body and mind to its absolute limits would produce a side to his character to which they weren't accustomed. Muscle fatigue, exhaustion and sleep deprivation would induce mood swings, the extent of which depended on Pat's condition and how well he was faring in a particular event.

Sister Annette says nighttime was the worst. 'When he was really tired, he'd go through the "horrors",' she said. 'It happens to all ultra runners. Pat would ask for Vegemite sandwiches and when we served them up he'd changed his mind and wanted peanut paste. When he looked like he couldn't run another step we'd say: "If you've had enough and want to pull out we'll back you on it." He'd get angry and say: "I've come too far, you have to support me on this, I'm counting on you guys." But when you went the other way and got tough with him and said: "Come on, you can do it" and encourage him he'd say: "You don't know what it's like. You're trying to kill me out here."'

Brother Michael remembers crewing for Pat in early races. 'When fatigue took its toll, he'd get very snappy, very quickly and we all copped a bit of that. You'd offer to do things and you'd get an earful back and you'd stand there thinking: "Now I'm trying to help this guy out, why am I doing this?" And there were times when you wanted to belt him over the head with something. I stormed off once during a race. I said: "Pat, you can have it. If that's your idea of fun you're welcome to it."'

Incredibly, nutrition was something of a dirty word for many in the ultra running scene in the 1980s who believed the psychology of complying with a runner's request for particular foods to be more important than quality calories. Bernie Farmer recalls how Pat would get crazy cravings at the oddest times in the most isolated places. 'You'd generally try to give him what he wanted, but sometimes that was impossible,' he said. 'It would be 1.00 a.m., pitch black in the middle of nowhere and he'd be asking for a chocolate milkshake. You'd say: "Where do you see a flamin' milk bar around here? Go to buggery and have a cup of tea instead."'

Pat sheepishly admits he was cantankerous in those early years. 'You're all confused and mixed up in your head and when you're first kicking off, you're all the time looking for reasons and ways to alleviate the pain and the boredom,' he said. 'You can't yell or scream at a competitor so you take it out on your crew members.' Everyone agrees that Pat gradually improved his behaviour as he mellowed and built his mental and physical strength with years of training.

His dream of finishing a Sydney to Melbourne became the shared vision of girlfriend Lisa and the entire Farmer family. Every member was involved to varying degrees, and all contributed time, money or support. Sister Annette and husband Terry drove to Brisbane with Pat to crew for him in a qualifying race held at the University of Queensland track for the 1988 Bicentennial Westfield event. They catered for his every whim and rode another 24-hour emotional roller coaster with him that stopped only after he had completed 177 kilometres—a distance that guaranteed him another start in the big event.

It seems there were few limits on the extent of sacrifice and commitment Pat's family was prepared to make. Bernie was his crew manager, occasional fitness adviser and amateur sports psychologist. The bonds that tied them were strong, but they still clashed during Pat's lowest points. 'There'd be times when he was struggling during a race and I'd say to him: "I know what you're going through," and he'd say: "No you don't bloody know, you haven't got a bloody clue." So I decided I had better find out and entered a 24-hour run myself at Wyong. I've always been of the view it's very hard for someone to tell you to do something if they've never done it. But I couldn't have been bothered doing much of the training; I probably did three or four training runs, which ended up being a gross misjudgment.'

Bernie's main claim to fame from his first ultra marathon race was that he beat the King of ultra marathons, Yiannis Kouros— on the first lap. After that it was all downhill. He suffered crippling muscle cramps and was forced to walk much of the race. It was a wonderful case of role reversal, with Pat crewing for Bernie. Having little brother become his slave for a day was one of the few satisfying aspects of the race for Bernie. He finished a physical and emotional wreck, but he finished, helped along by the Farmer iron will. 'While it was excruciating at the time, it was an experience and I'm glad I did it,' said Bernie. 'It made us both realise if you don't want to put in the effort for anything, it's going to be a bloody sight harder. I think it helped quite a bit for future events. We were on the same wavelength. I think the communication was a lot better.'

Pat insists it wasn't necessary for Bernie to walk the walk, as well as talk the talk. 'I believed he always knew anyway what I was going through,' he said. 'It was a case of Bernie felt he had to experience what it was like running an ultra marathon, more than I felt he had to. I said to him at one stage: "You're crazy, you don't have to do this." He could have still got the best out of me in future runs without doing that.' It was a true example of leading by example and brotherly love at its best.

Both Pat and his crew were better prepared for his second tilt at the Westfield event. They had reviewed every aspect of the 1987 campaign and Pat had more sponsorship money, although he still needed another bank loan. Lisa and Annette even improved their manual driving skills. The race began in controversy with talk of a runners' boycott in protest at the decision by organisers to start Kouros twelve hours behind the field, lured by a $5000 bonus if he could catch them and stay in front. The storm blew over and the race proceeded without folk hero Cliff Young, who had announced the first of many retirements from the sport. This time, Pat fixed his sights only on the finish line, visualising a triumphant run through the streets in Melbourne rather than becoming preoccupied with just making cut-off times along the way.

Pat and Mark Gladwell ran separate races for the first two days but linked up near Canberra. They welcomed the companionship—even more so this time as the pair had developed a great friendship since they last trod this long stretch of road. The fifteen-year age gap had been no barrier as Pat had always been drawn to people much older than himself. The two were also kindred spirits in their interests, attitudes and beliefs. Both men had opened their souls to each other during the thousands of hours spent training. In the absence of his father, Pat looked to Gladwell as his mentor. He provided answers to many of life's questions that Pat had asked himself a hundred times. He impressed upon the young man the value of goal setting and reassured him he wasn't being a hopeless dreamer in aiming for the highest mountains. Gladwell was astounded by Pat's maturity and honesty. In turn, Pat helped Mark rediscover his religious faith.

Ultra marathon running is probably the loneliest sport in existence. While the Westfield event was a race, runners were sometimes scattered over 400 kilometres of bitumen. They generally ran in their own little world, and might go one or two days without sighting another competitor after the start. But Pat and Mark found solace in each other and gradually realised their common goal of reaching Melbourne was best achieved by working as a team. While some of their respective crews knew each other, such was the competitive and solo nature of the event that their supporters were initially uncomfortable with the idea, fearing one would slow the other down. But they soon saw the benefits. Instead of two vehicles they had four; rather than a crew of eight they had sixteen. It was uncommon for both runners to hit a low at the same time, so this allowed one to lift the other out of a bad patch. Both remember sharing spiritual experiences on the road. One was particularly memorable and sent their morale soaring.

It was the fourth day: they had crossed the New South Wales–Victoria border and were near Cann River with more than 500 kilometres left to run. Both had struggled through another night of 'the horrors'—sleeping just four hours out of every 24 took its toll on all runners. The weariness sank deep into their muscles, compounded by each new sleep-deprived night of freezing temperatures. The few hours they had snatched this time had done little to recharge their batteries and there seemed nothing positive they could say to boost each other. The warmth from the first sunrays of a new day helped dissipate the heavy fog from the ground. They had dragged themselves over yet another hill and were descending into a valley. Dead trees stood starkly among vibrant green pastures. A large eagle stirred from its resting spot in a tree and swooped low in a long elegant arc, cutting across the runners' path. Curious cows strolled up to the fence, steam pouring from their mouths and nostrils. Dominating the scene was a huge orange fireball rising to light up the day. Pat stared in awe. The fog was sufficiently high and thick to mask the sun and allow him to look directly at it without fear of damaging his eyes.

'Look at the sunrise,' Pat said. 'Yeah,' grunted Mark through a painful grimace. 'No, have a good look, not a quick look,' he said. 'Look. How close are we to God at this moment?'

Mark also recalls the moment with some emotion. 'I was so miserable I couldn't appreciate it at first, but when I did, I saw one of the most spectacular sunrises of my life. I looked around me and it was like a flash. Pat was talking about the wonder of God and his creations all around us. When people are in pain—especially ultra marathon runners—and they've exceeded their normal coping powers, you can have a spiritual experience where it's mind over matter and the experience lifts you out of your lowest point. It wasn't a runner's high. I've found they don't happen after 300 kilometres. I'll remember that moment for as long as I live.'

Pat's deep affinity with nature made it a heightened sensory and spiritual episode. 'It was the greatest sight I've seen in my life,' he said. 'I've spoken with artists since then, asking them if they could ever paint it because I was so taken with the scene. It was like we were on another planet. I was absorbing what nature had to offer and once again I learnt another lesson from all of that. And that was to take in the surroundings: to look around you and analyse everything to the nth degree. Don't just see the leaf, but see the veins and see the shine of the leaf and every aspect of it.'

To the astonishment of their crews, the duo accelerated to a speed they hadn't run since the start, desensitised to the pain that had previously hampered them. The feeling lasted for three hours, providing the springboard for them to power through to the finish line in equal fourteenth place in seven days, 23 hours and eighteen minutes. The time was eighteen hours quicker than Gladwell's 1987 result. Pat's good friend Eleanor Adams, who had finished thirteen hours ahead of him, greeted him with a proud embrace and a bucket of tears. Kevin Mansell ran the race of his life, finishing almost eighteen hours ahead of his training partners to grab seventh place. Maurice Taylor ruptured his Achilles tendon and pulled out 250 kilometres from the finish. Kouros was again unstoppable, using his delayed start to swallow up the field one by one by the start of the fifth day. Four years after the spark was first ignited, Pat had finally fulfilled his dream of completing the world's toughest endurance event. While totally exhausted, he and his crew were brimming with pride, joy and relief. Every competitor who finished felt like a winner regardless of their position. But there was little time to smell the roses. Pat and his crew had to drive back to Sydney. They had all taken time off from their jobs and families. There were responsibilities to fulfil and bills to pay.

Some family and friends thought Pat would return to a 'normal' existence as a mechanic now that he'd achieved his goal. But Pat had a newfound belief in his own running ability and set his sights on taller peaks. He firmly believed that with a few more years of dedicated training he could win the 'World's Greatest Race'. Brother Michael, who admits he's often been the worst source of running advice to Pat through the years, was one who questioned the ongoing pursuit. 'I'd say to him: "Come off it Pat, these people come from all over the world. You're Pat Farmer from Granville, how can you be the best in the world, that's not your thing." It did take a while to click for me in terms of what drove Pat. Thankfully others in the family like Annette understood it a lot sooner and had more faith in him.'

Buoyed by their Westfield results, coach Bill Carlson encouraged Pat and Kevin Mansell to set their sights on the Australian six-day track record. The pair worked harder than ever before with training increasing from around 300 kilometres a week to over 400 kilometres. It paid dividends for Mansell, who broke the record at the Campbelltown Six-Day Race by running 902 kilometres, although the sport's governing body, the Australia Ultra Runners' Association, officially recognised it as a road not track record because it wasn't run on a standard 400 metre athletics track. Pat ventured on to the annual International Six-Day Ultra Marathon track race at Colac, Victoria, on 14 November 1988, full of hope that he could finally etch his name in sports history. Unfortunately it turned out to be one of the more disappointing yet bizarre events of Pat's career. The weather fluctuated wildly between scorching hot days and 10°C nights with thunder and hailstorms thrown in for good measure.

After a solid first day where Pat was sitting in eighth place, his race plan came unstuck. It was the same old foes—sleep deprivation, muscle cramps and blisters. Pat encountered the inevitable bad patches, but found they took longer than usual to run through them. The race degenerated on the fifth and final night when drunken louts caused major disruption. One teenager threw a dead rabbit on to the running track in front of Cliff Young, and shouted abuse as he abandoned the race. 'Mary, take me home, I've had enough,' the veteran athlete said to his wife. A second man took perverse pleasure in trying to burn the arms of passing runners with a cigarette butt. Another group of youths gang-tackled the man and stripped him of his clothes. Despite his desperate attempts to break free, they tied his hands and feet with rope and carried him in full view of spectators and dumped him in nearby Memorial Square. Pat pitied the perpetrator-turned-victim and interrupted his race to help him. He cut the rope using a knife he'd borrowed from a spectator and wrapped the man in a blanket. 'He was naked in front of all these spectators, including Lisa, and I thought it was just offensive to everybody,' said Pat. 'He was drunk as a skunk and it had all gone too far.'

In an alarming sequel, another young man stopped his drunken yelling at runners long enough to venture out on to the road into the path of a car, which struck him and dragged him

20 metres. He was taken to hospital by ambulance in a serious condition. As they sidestepped their way through beer cans and broken glass, many runners threatened to blacklist future races if security wasn't improved. Pat ran 739 kilometres and finished tenth in the race, just behind Adams and Tony Rafferty. The then world champion, 56-year-old Gilbert Mainix from France, broke the Australian record by completing 963 kilometres in six days.

Pat returned from Victoria more motivated than ever and in search of another goal. His vision was getting bigger and he desperately wanted to make his mark in the ultra scene. He and Rafferty had spoken about Pat organising an event and agreed that it should be over 1000 miles (1609 kilometres)—a distance over which Rafferty held the Australian record. Pat promptly issued a written challenge on 19 December 1988 for a race the following August. The letter oozed good-natured youthful impudence: 'I would like to prove to the public that young people have the stamina and the mental discipline to win ultra marathons and break records. Whether you accept this challenge or not will in my eyes determine if you are the "Legend" that some members of the public believe you to be, or just prove that you are passed [sic] the stage of taking on younger competitors in a one on one 1000 mile event.'

Rafferty had always loved a challenge and this one was too tempting—he had much more to gain than he had to lose. After accepting, he fired his own salvo back at Pat through the media. 'The 1000-mile race is slow torture. At times he will question his sanity,' said Rafferty. Pat was thrilled to have the opportunity to go head-to-head with one of his idols in his own event in only the world's second track race over the distance in the twentieth century. He and Lisa spent much of 1989 organising the event with the backing of the Granville Rotaract club (which was keen to use the event to promote its community work), while juggling his heavy training schedule for the Westfield Sydney to Melbourne in May.

There were two constant features about Pat Farmer's Westfield runs that surfaced again in 1989 at the lowest ebb of the run. The first was Pat's promise never to run another Sydney to Melbourne race—a pledge he would later conveniently forget after the pain and disappointment had passed. Well accustomed to this ploy, Lisa's training as a legal secretary told her she should pack a dictaphone to get it 'on the record'. She unfortunately didn't have the device handy when Pat proposed to her—again. She'd heard that before too, only to see him jokingly plead 'emotional and mental instability' upon their return.

With his mind and body toughened by five years of training, Pat recorded his best-ever result in the 1989 Sydney to Melbourne race, finishing seventh in what proved to be an extraordinary event for several reasons. He was the eighth runner across the line but was elevated one place, ahead of Graeme Woods. The Queensland runner completed the 1011 kilometre event only to be later disqualified after it was discovered he had taken a banned stimulant in a cold tablet mistakenly given to him by a crew member. Gladwell was only four hours behind Pat while training partner Maurice Taylor, who had sold a precious violin to finance his race, was fifth. Kevin Mansell showed one of the biggest improvements in race history, running a 29-hour personal best to finish third, giving the 'Awesome Foursome' four of the top ten places. Mansell had staged a fierce 130-kilometre battle through the hills near the Victorian border with Kouros, who again had a delayed start. The Greek had a custom of several years of respectfully presenting a gift of a t-shirt to a fellow competitor whom he passed on the road. Mansell did what other runners dreamed of—he passed Kouros, not just once but five times during the sixteen-hour duel. However, he resisted the temptation to return the gift each time.

The twelve-hour handicap drove Kouros to the fastest time in race history: five days, two hours, 27 minutes, but even that was not enough to overcome one of the most courageous runs in Australian ultra marathon history by South Australia's 'Colossus of Roads' [sic], David Standeven. He took line honours, defying extreme dehydration and exhaustion and literally staggered home

32 minutes ahead of Kouros. The race also saw the end of an era—the final, final retirement from Westfield events of Cliff Young. He made the announcement amid the tears and fog outside Bombala as he realised he faced certain disqualification at the next cut-off. 'I'm sad but I'm relieved in one way. No more pain. But I gave it me best,' he said.*

Pat returned home from the Westfield race and immediately channelled all his energies into the Granville Ultimate Ultra Marathon Challenge. He was hoping to use the race as a signature event: a symbol that he was the fresh new future of long-distance running. It had all the hallmarks of a classic showdown: the young bull of the ultra marathon scene versus the old bull; the 50-year-old Melbourne veteran pitted against the brash 27-year-old Sydney upstart. But what began as a good-natured rivalry ended in a feud that has lasted more than a decade and ruined a close friendship. Farmer and Rafferty have both kept their counsel on the whole event since 1989 but they welcomed the chance to set the record straight for this book.

Despite Pat and Lisa's best efforts at promotion, they couldn't raise sufficient sponsorship for the Granville Challenge and were forced to again borrow $10 000 to meet the shortfall of what was becoming an expensive exercise. Prizemoney was covered by local radio station 2KY, which agreed to pay $5000 if the world record was broken. Publicly it was a winner-take-all prize, but Rafferty says he and Pat had agreed privately that they would split the prize money regardless of the result. Pat says Rafferty proposed the deal while on a training run in Melbourne, telling him it was commonplace in top-level sport. Pat regrets the fact that he offered a muted response to the idea. 'I remember being a bit stunned when he suggested it,' he said. 'It didn't sit right with me but I didn't reject it outright at the time. I should have, but I was naive and stupid. But I idolised Tony. I had him up on the highest pedestal. He knew everything about the running game, while I was just a kid in an older man's sport. When I

* *'I've Finally Found My Hero . . .'*

went home and thought about it and spoke to Lisa, I just couldn't go along with it.'

Rafferty was livid when Pat rang several weeks before the event and informed him that the split prizemoney deal was off and the winner would take all. 'I was furious because we had made a gentleman's agreement that he broke without consulting me. I remember putting the phone down and saying to my wife Coral: "You are now looking at the winner of the 1000 Mile Challenge."' Pat says he changed his mind because the concept of 'fixing' the prize money before the race didn't sit well with him. 'Maybe I was naive in agreeing in the first place, but it played on my and Lisa's minds and I couldn't go along with it,' Pat says.

The rules of world record attempts required a third runner and Pat's local rival Dave Taylor was invited to also run. But as Rafferty lined up against the pair at Everley Park on 12 August 1989, he had 'fire in his feet' and was so motivated he would have 'run over broken glass to stay in front'. He was still seething at Pat for 'welching' on the prizemoney deal. Rafferty was also desperate to snap a two-year form slump, stung by 'know-all critics, tall poppy clippers and fence-sitters' who said the 50-year-old was over the hill after his withdrawal from the Westfield race. Added to this was the insult he felt when, six hours after the start, Pat left the track to attend the wedding of his brother Chris. He was absent for three hours, allowing Rafferty to regain the lead and establish a comfortable buffer. 'I was absolutely shocked that he did that,' said Rafferty. 'After all I had done to promote and support what was essentially his event. I rang my wife at one stage and said: "He obviously feels this is going to be a walkover."'

Pat insists he wasn't taking the result for granted. He agonised over his decision to go AWOL. It triggered a dispute with his eldest brother Bernie, who told him it was degrading to his rival and would prompt Rafferty to 'want to kick his ass'. Pat's insistence on attending the wedding at a nearby church can be explained by two of his more renowned qualities—unswerving loyalty to his family and his unique blend of single-mindedness and stubbornness. His rationale was that the 'time out' was like having an extended rest break and could be made up later. It seemed logical at the time but, years on, Pat admits he made a mistake. 'It was a stupid thing for me to do,' he said. 'I'm embarrassed about it. I deserved not to win that race. I didn't take it seriously enough. You shouldn't take on something like that if you're going to be half-hearted about it. I was young and I was silly. I've matured a lot by making major mistakes like that.'

Chris Farmer is also embarrassed in hindsight about the issue. He says there was no pressure on Pat to be at his wedding and can't recall there being much discussion about the clash of dates. He assumed at the time Pat wouldn't make the ceremony but was of course pleased when he could attend. Pat returned to the race and spent the rest of the fortnight-long event playing a losing game of catch-up. According to Rafferty, Pat adopted the unusual ultra marathon tactics of surging when his rival approached from behind, then slowing to a weary walk. 'I found his occasional flamboyant sprints incredible and thoroughly amusing. They might have delighted his cheer squad but they did little for his daily mileage total when he was forced to rest to recuperate. I doubt if these spots of showmanship were part of his plan he talked about before the race.'

Race conditions deteriorated when a thunderstorm struck on the second day. Through constant use, the grass was trampled into the dirt and the track soon became a quagmire. More rain exacerbated the problem over the ensuing days. Rafferty says they risked injury with every step and labelled it the worst circumstances he's ever raced in. Dozens of Rotaract volunteers tried to repair the surface by shovelling ash on to the track and rolling it with an industrial compactor. At one stage Pat, who felt completely responsible for the event, grabbed the compactor and assisted in the maintenance during his rest break.

There was substantial ill-feeling between Rafferty and the hundreds of volunteers from Rotaract clubs whom Lisa had organised. Loyal to Pat, they were annoyed to hear Rafferty make derogatory comments about their hero behind his back and felt he acted at times like a prima donna. Volunteer Sharon Hutchins says Rafferty 'became a really professional pig'. Rafferty was unhappy with aspects of the organisation and thought the support crew assigned to him was largely incompetent. At the same time, he criticised the adulation of Pat's crew: 'They didn't realise that to pamper a runner like Tammy Baker's poodle is not the way to win a 1000 mile race.'* However, Rafferty later sent an open thankyou letter to Rotaract in which he congratulated all volunteers and praised their 'enterprise and initiative'.

Two other issues rankle with Rafferty. He says Pat did everything to try to 'psyche him out' both before and during the race through private and public comments and the presence of a trackside sign that read: 'You can't crush the Farmer family spirit—you can win, Pat.' Rafferty says that all helped him more than Pat. If the apprentice thought he could outwit the master, he was mistaken. Rafferty had spent decades absorbing physical and spiritual lessons that Pat thought he could learn and understand in a fraction of the time. In this sport, youth was a handicap.

'He was never going to psyche me out,' Rafferty laughed. 'He had the wrong person. I'd been in the game for too long and in fact I psyched him out and worked on his mental attitude.' And with great success, breaking the old record by 33 hours in a winning time of fourteen days, eleven hours, 59 minutes and four seconds. Pat was six and a half hours behind—the second-fastest time ever and more than a day inside the old record. Dave Taylor had withdrawn 320 kilometres before the finish after apparently breaking a toe, although several witnesses reported later seeing Taylor kicking a football by day and dancing by night.

Rafferty was also annoyed to hear criticism from Pat's camp

---

*   Tony Rafferty, 1989 '1000 miles through a glue pot', *Australian Ultra Runners Association Magazine*, vol. 4, no. 4, pp. 37–9.

of his decision to leave the event and fly home as soon as he was presented with his prizes, rather than follow running protocol and wait until his rival had finished. Pat says he was upset at the time at Rafferty's early departure, but now bears no ill-will about it. Rafferty explained that after running around in circles 4000 times, he just wanted a good sleep and to get home to his wife.

'Being jacked off with everything at Granville had nothing to do with me leaving,' he said. The biggest factor was the national pilots' strike, which had divided the country and crippled the aviation industry. Rafferty feared he would be stranded in Sydney and was booked on a dawn, strikebreaking Yugoslav Airlines flight. 'It was the only guaranteed flight I could get,' he said. 'After running 1000 miles through a glue-pot there was no way I was going to stay in Sydney or go back by bus. The buses were packed anyway so that was no certainty either.'

Rafferty didn't run the 1990 Westfield but Pat fronted up for the fourth time—even more determined than ever to win it. The Awesome Foursome were now all on their own, having abandoned their coach, Bill Carlson. They finally tired of his tyrannical approach, abusive language and attempts to wield increasing control over the lives of four grown men. Pat railed against Carlson's derisive remarks that he didn't have the mental toughness to be a good ultra runner. He also failed to understand how someone like Carlson, who had not worn the shoes and run until his body screamed for it to stop, could truly understand the demands of the event. The relationship ended acrimoniously for all four. 'Bill never had friends—he took prisoners,' said Gladwell. While critical of his people skills, they all acknowledge he was a very good athletics coach. Carlson was interviewed for this book, but refused to speak on the record. In summary, he rejected the athletes' version of the reasons for the split.

All eyes were again on Kouros, with rivals unsettled by the knowledge that they'd see him sooner than last year with his handicap cut from twelve hours to eight. Pat knew his only chance of beating Kouros was to play him at his own game—

running his own race with realistic target time splits for the 1006 kilometre event. A detailed strategy that included meal and sleep breaks down to exact minutes and seconds was outlined in a pre-race briefing with his crew. Pat was within striking distance of the leaders for the first two days in his best-ever start and was in the top five when his campaign was cruelly hobbled by a knee injury. A race doctor prescribed anti-inflammatory tablets but they triggered side effects—abdominal pains and internal bleeding in the kidneys, which presented Pat with a Catch 22 situation.

'Gut ache' was pretty common for ultra runners, as was urinating blood during longer events, due to the pressure exerted on the kidneys from the constant pounding. While it was excruciating whenever he went to the toilet, Pat was more concerned about the diminishing pace and the fact that he was slipping behind his splits. 'We didn't tell him the anti-inflammatories were causing the bleeding,' says crew member Jim Chittendon. 'We approached it on a "need to know" basis. He didn't need to know the full story because it would only have played on his mind and would have been an unnecessary distraction.'

Lisa was again by Pat's side, easing his darkest moods by constantly playing the jester and helping guide him through the pain barrier. Behind the scenes, she sought constant reassurance from the doctor that Pat wasn't endangering his health by staying on the road. The anti-inflammatories were stopped and of course the knee pain worsened.

While Pat and his crew tried to maintain a positive outlook, the Holy Grail of a Westfield crown slipped further out of grasp with each passing hour. Only a change of luck would get him back in the race. It changed—but for the worse. Fate was weaving a nasty conspiracy against him. Weather conditions in 1990 were the worst in race history. Snowstorms lashed runners' faces and left hazardous, slippery black ice on the road. Freezing temperatures, hailstorms and rain further impeded their progress. All competitors struggled against the elements, but Pat's fragile state left him even more poorly equipped to deal with them.

When he revised his goals from finishing first to just finishing and accepted his lot in the race, Pat found the kilometres rolled by with less effort and he crossed the line eighteenth out of 32 starters. It was his worst result since 1987, but the reception at the finish belied his time and place. Dozens of runners and crew members cheered him home. The 'Greek God' Kouros welcomed Pat with a hug and traditional kiss. Kouros had conquered his own obstacles—a bout of the flu that left him delirious in the final stages. But he triumphed with line and handicap honours and collected the $20 000 winner's cheque. Pat's training partner, Maurice Taylor, ran his best race, finishing fourth. Mansell was ninth, Gladwell thirteenth.

The year ended with Pat and Kouros accepting an invitation to travel to the Australian Institute of Sport (AIS) in Canberra to study the elite athletes' training campus and discuss the future of ultra marathon running. It was a rich experience for Pat, spending a week eating, breathing and sleeping running with two of the finest distance runners in the country—Kouros and marathon king Robert de Castella (Deek). Both Pat and Yiannis were put to the test during training runs with Deek's squad. While the ultra marathoners could go farther, they couldn't match the AIS squad for leg speed. They had Pat and Yiannis struggling for breath during a 16-kilometre run which incorporated a lung-busting ascent up Black Mountain, which towers over Canberra. Deek astounded the pair even more as he engaged in one of his regular training run habits—delivering a passionate word-for-word rendition of Banjo Paterson's 'Man From Ironbark'. 'I couldn't believe it. Here we were running more than 15 kilometres an hour. We were struggling for breath and he was reciting poetry,' says Pat. 'I was thinking to myself: "Shut up and let me finish the run."'

While de Castella was more interested in Kouros and the secrets of his near-invincibility, he was impressed by Pat's dedication, doggedness and down-to-earth approach to his chosen sport. 'While he was a bit quiet, he seemed to have a really good attitude towards achieving his goals,' said de Castella. 'I marvel at the whole effort of ultra runners. When I think back to how difficult it was for me to do 200 kilometres a week, I think what they do is just phenomenal. To be able to back up day after day is wonderful. It was obvious then that Pat had talent and was destined for big things.' Deep down, Pat knew that too. He knew there were bigger mountains to conquer. The question was: how many and how high?

5

Wedding bells and the American dream

By 1991 the 'World's Greatest Foot Race' was on its last legs. The recession the nation had to have had bitten deep into the Australian economy and the Westfield Corporation was starting to wonder if it could get a better bang for its promotional buck. Coincidentally, many runners were riled by the way Westfield was treating them and felt the prizemoney was inadequate. Just for something different, Yiannis Kouros was in dispute with the sponsor, accusing Westfield of using the athletes to raise company profits. 'It's not in the athletic spirit,' he said. 'It's a commercial race and the people participating should be rewarded.' Kouros demanded a package deal of $80 000 just to lace up his shoes for the 1991 event. Westfield Sydney to Melbourne executive director Chris Bates said the runner had 'bitten the hand that feeds him'. 'One would hope that the sport could eventually afford such largesse, but in 1991 it is simply out of the question,' said Bates. In response to the growing howls, prizemoney was increased but that failed to appease Kouros. He put on his own show, running from Sydney to Melbourne solo under sponsorship from a Sydney fruit market. His time was never properly recorded and the finish proved an anti-climax to the main event.*

*   'I've Finally Found My Hero . . .'

Pat was also fed up with the 'freaks and fruitcakes' image that Westfield and its public relations machine had continually cultivated with a gullible media. 'It wasn't like a race any more. It had just become one big publicity stunt for the company,' he said. 'They didn't care about the sport, they just cared about the promotion of Westfield. They always depicted the race as being for misfits that were just replacing one addiction with another, which was entirely wrong. I was fairly angry about that. It didn't matter who the person was or where they'd come from, by the time they got to the start of the Westfield run they had to be athletes. I had a duty to my sponsors but it was getting harder for the real athletes to get publicity. I remember we were at the 1990 media launch and the journalists were only interested in the ex-alcoholics and former drug addicts. I said to this female journalist: "What have I got to do to get some publicity? Jump out of this window?" She said, "That would be a good start." The whole thing was just a joke.'

Westfield race organiser Charlie Lynn denies organisers tried to make the race a sideshow alley attraction. 'The Westfield race was a unique Australian event, but it was a battlers' event,' he said. 'We felt at times as if we were a mobile social welfare agency but it was the type of race that attracted people with a story to tell and something to prove. We had to maximise the publicity and to do that we had to create the stories. Admittedly sometimes we were drawing a long bow.'

While he still harboured dreams to win the Westfield race, for Pat it had lost most of its mystique. He knew there were many roads left to run and doing so could provide a path to greater glory and financial reward. Pat believed he could make ultra running a full-time job and bring a new era of professionalism to the sport. Instead of paying people so that he could run, he saw no reason why he couldn't secure longer-term sponsorship and have people pay him. Before his fallout with Tony Rafferty, the elder statesman of ultra running had taught Pat many important sport and business lessons.

Rafferty showed Pat the value of presenting himself as an

all-round package: you had to be a good athlete (but not necessarily a great one), be prepared to work hard for your sponsor, present well and speak well. 'I realised I needed to be able to offer people something more than just a runner if I was to secure enough sponsorship so I could make a comfortable living,' Pat said. 'At the end of the day, most sponsors don't give a rat's backside whether you're a good runner or not. All they care about is how well you could help sell their item and that's what the other ultra runners never saw.'

Pat also looked for examples in other sports of 'packaged sportsmen'. He had met AFL legend Ron Barassi and former test cricketer and raconteur Max Walker through Rotaract functions. They stood out as two worthy role models, and lessons gleaned from their presentation skills were valuable, especially when Pat's profile was high enough for him to make a quid on the public speaking circuit. Throughout his career, Pat had become increasingly image-conscious. That was driven partly by a level of insecurity that left him eager to please people and anxious about what they thought of him. But he also realised image was vital to his 'saleability' in the sport.

'I was aware that everything about my appearance and my performance would impact on my appeal to a company,' he said. 'Aside from Tony Rafferty, I was the only one who was thinking that way because all the other ultra guys were just in it for whatever they could get—a pair of socks, a pair of shoes, or whatever. They were never looking at the big picture of the sport, the big sponsorship deals.'

Rafferty describes their relationship before the fallout over the Granville race as a master–student one. 'I helped him where I could,' he said. 'We had an excellent rapport for the first few years. He was a real doer and was willing to learn. I guess in the early days I did see him as the next Tony Rafferty—he had what it took. But Pat's whole thing was he wanted to become famous. He was looking for a big-name signature run—a first— but unfortunately just about everything had been done in ultra and solo running in Australia by then.'

But Rafferty had also assisted Pat in a more practical way. The countless hours spent as Rafferty's crew member in 1986, and later as his house guest in Melbourne in planning for the Granville Challenge, had helped him understand and appreciate the role of the mind in running ultra marathons. Most long-distance runners will tell you the physical exertion is less important than the mental application and believe between 75 and 95 per cent of the battle is fought and won in the mind. Rafferty had seen Pat struggle in various races and thought he could help.

'Tony taught me the importance of training your mind as well as your body,' Pat said. 'He once said to me: "Pat, you have to be part of nature when you compete in these events. You need to feel the wind on your face going through you rather than against you. You need to feel the sun's rays, but let it shine through you rather than let it burn you. If you fight those elements too much they'll kill you. If you blend in with them they won't harm you, they'll go right through you." When I tried it I found it seemed to work.'

Rafferty helped Pat tap into the spiritual side of running through positive thinking, affirmations and relaxation music. Rafferty gave Pat some reading material about the power of the mind and penned a number of affirmations that he himself had used as motivation. Pat asked his brother Chris, who worked for ABC Radio, to set them to music and has since almost worn the tapes out. Some of the affirmations were:

'I must at all times think of success.'

'Pain is normal and natural in every race. I must accept it as part of the event and push on.'

'Belief is the motivating force that enables you to achieve your goal.'

Pat also credits Yiannis Kouros with helping him master the relaxed and meditative state of mind that ultra runners need to succeed. Few dispute that Kouros is the greatest ultra marathon runner in the history of the sport, the 'Bradman of long distance running'. Kouros was a unique athlete, apparently winning most of his races on limited physical training. He claims he ran no more than 150 kilometres a week and only began his preparation a few months before a race, although few of his rivals believed this because most marathon runners would run further in a week of training and have a longer build-up. But the Greek runner dominated ultra running like no athlete in the history of the sport by ensuring his mind was perfectly tuned for the event. 'I believe fitness is not enough to complete an ultra marathon race even if you are training every day,' says Kouros. 'Your body will be exhausted once you go past 100 kilometres no matter how much you've trained. Your mind is the main part.'

Pat was astute and bold enough to ask the questions that many other ultra runners didn't—he was ever the inquisitor, seeking to glean as many success secrets as his mentors were willing to offer. 'I thought he could do great things if he could put more emphasis on the mental aspect,' said Kouros. 'You have to be a unique person to go beyond your physical limits. I thought Pat could do that but it depends on your mind. We all have faults and it depends on where you get your inspiration from.'

Kouros also taught Pat about the need for discipline—not just with issues like crew management during races, but the discipline of mind over body.

'Yiannis told me the toughest race was within and that you should never get too concerned about the other competitors in the race,' Pat said. 'And what makes you slow down or get held up is not the other runners—it's you, within yourself. And so if your mind can beat your body you can win that internal battle every time.'

The ninth and last Westfield race started on 15 May 1991 without Pat Farmer and past winners Kouros, Cliff Young and Dusan Mravlje. But among the current crop of novices was a young man whom Pat had inspired. Twenty-three-year-old Craig Rowe had emerged from a troubled youth far from unscathed and unscarred. His body was battered by drug, alcohol and nicotine abuse and he was heavily tattooed. Orphaned at birth, he squandered an inheritance from his adopted grandfather to pay for his teenage indulgences. Pat's trail-blazing success as a young man in a mature person's sport appealed to Craig. Just like Pat seven years before, he had been searching for some meaning and direction to his life. Just as Mike Agostini had done at the start of his career, Pat passed the baton of faith to Craig Rowe. Later, Pat's rival Dave Taylor weighed in with coaching advice. Rowe gained special entry to the final Westfield event, which had prizemoney increased to $60 000. It was a handi-capped race—the first and only one. Craig and the other 22 runners were started in stages with Julie Anthony singing 'Advance Australia Fair'.

Rowe, who still smoked, survived past the two-day cut-off, defying the predictions of race organiser Charlie Lynn. Over the next four days, the margins by which he scraped through each checkpoint became narrower. By day six he was last in a field that had been reduced to fourteen. Rowe showed enormous courage to battle through the pain of near-hypothermia and exhaustion that reduced him to tears and induced hallucinations. Believing his entire future hung on the race, he dragged himself a further 100 kilometres to just 90 kilometres before the Mel-bourne finish. Fellow competitor Helen Stangar, who was with Rowe at the end, said it was one of the finest displays of bravery one could ever wish to see. 'He pushed himself beyond the accepted limits of endurance,' she said.*

Wet shoes and socks from constant rain had rubbed numerous layers of skin from his soft feet, acting like sandpaper on soft and ageing paint. The race doctor advised Rowe that he was in danger of causing permanent damage to his feet and should withdraw. Still he refused. It was only when told he would be disqualified that Craig Rowe bowed to the inevitable. His sister Sharon Knight lived through every minute of the torment. 'His feet were virtually raw with no skin left on them, but it meant the world to him to finish that race,' she said. 'This was going to be the start of a new life by meeting such an incredible

---

* *'I've Finally Found My Hero . . .'*

challenge. When he was forced out of the race we just lay together on the side of the road in tears. Despite an iron will, there was a physical limit to what his body would let him do. If I could have finished the race for him I would have.'

Victorian runner Bryan Smith overcame his 24-hour handicap to win the 1991 event in what was his fourth Westfield attempt. Pat's training partners Maurice Taylor and Kevin Mansell finally cracked the placings, finishing second and third respectively. Mansell joined eighth-placed Mark Gladwell in the record books as the only runners to finish five consecutive Westfields.

Pat becomes visibly moved when he reflects on Rowe's story. 'I was fortunate enough to have the chance to motivate him a bit and cheer him up and help him. We had a few heart-to-hearts. I didn't realise I'd made such a great impression on him, but I was glad to assist him to achieve at least some of his dreams at later stages.'

Craig Rowe used the shattering disappointment of the West-field withdrawal to further fuel his running ambitions. His tattoos were a curse, restricting his job opportunities to work as a cleaner and forcing him to run under the cover of darkness to avoid harassment. But he was possessed and obsessed by ultra marathons and in August 1993 finally made his mark when he broke the world 1000-hour record for endurance running, held by Queensland's Ron Grant. He also raised several thousand dollars for sick children in his local area of Manly, Sydney. But just when his career was about to blossom, Rowe died aged 27 in November 1994 in a Kings Cross hotel of a drug overdose. His family firmly believe he was not a regular drug user when he died and suspect he was the victim of misadventure. His fiancée Jenny and 20-month-old son Ashley survived him.

Meanwhile Pat was looking for a new challenge. He was also determined to create his own 'ultra marathon first'. It was while staring at the map of Australia that he realised one still remained—running the entire length of the east coast of the country, from Cape York in Queensland to Cockle Creek, the most southerly tip of Tasmania.

He learned Diabetes Australia needed someone to spearhead an awareness campaign. Pat had several diabetic friends and family members who were among half a million Australian sufferers, so the cause was close to his heart. Using running to raise money for charity made perfect sense to him, while also fulfilling his generous, giving nature and the social conscience the Farmer children had inherited from their parents. Frank Farmer had told his children the gesture of giving a gift only counted if what you were giving was of value to you. Pat's sisters remember him following his father's advice on two notable occasions. Catherine says once Pat returned from a training run just before midnight and grabbed his prized leopard-print doona from his bed, tucked it under his arm and ran out the door. He later explained he had seen a homeless man sleeping under the Granville railway station steps who looked cold. Annette remembers another time when Pat spontaneously signed his Holden car over to her after inspecting her ageing vehicle and finding it was unroadworthy. 'It's too dangerous for you to drive with the kids,' he told her. 'Besides I'm young and single and I've got legs.' 'Pat didn't make a big deal of it,' says Annette. 'He just did it because he cared for us. It was a wonderful gesture and I really appreciated it. But all of my siblings are like that to each other. We would do anything to help each other.'

And it seems all of the Farmers learned the personal rewards of extending a helping hand well. Older sister Annette shared an enriching friendship with 82-year-old Polish-born Ted Mcawski. She met him while driving into Bowral from her home in nearby Mittagong. He was making his regular daily pilgrimage to visit his wife, in a nursing home 20 kilometres from their home. Mrs Mcawski suffered from Alzheimer's disease and, while she often didn't remember him, he knew she would have shown the same loyalty had the roles been reversed. Annette sympathised with his plight when he told her he walked 40 kilometres on weekend days due to the unavailability of public transport.

Every Saturday and Sunday for two years, Annette planned her family's weekend activities around chauffeuring Mr Mcawski to the nursing home, despite her own very hectic lifestyle. 'It wasn't a chore at all,' she says. 'He was truly a gift to me. He was an incredible man, so grateful. He used to amaze me and the kids with his stories and vast knowledge. He spoke five languages.' The tale that captivated her most was of Mr Mcawski's life as a prisoner of war in a German concentration camp in Siberia in World War II. A hairdresser for a theatre company before the war, he had survived by making himself useful to the Germans. He would make elaborate and beautiful wigs from rope and string and dye them, for use by prisoners who entertained their captors with stage shows. It was here that Mr Mcawski met his wife, a Red Cross worker. They married after the war and emigrated to Australia. For them, love had triumphed over so much adversity. Annette relished the chance to help keep it alive.

Pat's run for diabetes was a logical extension of the same Christian principles that had guided the Farmers through life. The valued items in this case were his time and effort and the loss of three months' income. The solo run was pieced together with the Aboriginal and Torres Strait Islander Commission (ATSIC) as one of the event sponsors and Pat and his crew flew north to spend several days on Cape York islands before the run began on 8 August 1991.

The significance of his mission hit home when they visited Indigenous communities on Thursday Island. Pat met many men and women who had lost limbs because of nerve damage resulting from poorly controlled diabetes. He walked around the island and visited the three schools, where he spoke about his challenge and what he would to do to help. Later he was official starter at a school athletics carnival, releasing free-spirited children to run and jump their way through an afternoon of joyful play. 'Overall the visit was a very moving experience and I was so glad we did it,' Pat said. 'When we left it was like a scene from a movie. Dozens of islanders were standing on the wharf singing to us in these beautiful harmonious voices. I felt like we'd made some lifelong friends.'

The most vivid memories of the run itself are also bound in far north Queensland where the thermometer often nudged 40°C and fine red bulldust from the unsealed roads caked every piece of equipment and clothing. Pat often ran alone, sending his support vehicle 5 kilometres ahead to avoid choking on the car dust. He regularly encountered wild animals. In scenes that would have sat comfortably in *Crocodile Dundee* Pat occasionally had to stare down feral pigs and buffalo to negotiate a safe passage. Crossing crocodile-infested waterways was also a challenge with the red-blooded runner opting to run through anything that was no more than waist-deep. The man-eaters sounded like barking dogs on the riverbanks but Pat reasoned if he closely followed his vehicle he'd be safe. He was thankful the reptiles didn't challenge such a flawed theory.

Pat found the entire run taxing yet exhilarating. He had often felt that ultra running was one of the few modern pursuits that allowed athletes to feel like pioneers. In remote areas especially, he felt truly in touch with his spirit of adventure. He found another source of inspiration when he ran through Cooktown in North Queensland, stopping at the statue of explorer Captain James Cook which bore the epitaph: 'He left nothing un-endeavoured'. 'I've often thought about that when I've been running over the years when I've been faced with every difficult challenge in my life and I've spoken about it to people quite regularly. It really struck a chord with me,' says Pat.

Pat's run had three main aims: to raise $100 000, to have 20 000 people tested at the mobile unit and to generally raise community awareness of diabetes. He spread the diabetes pre-vention message through cities, towns and on lonely country roads, running an average of 55 kilometres a day without a day off. Various friends and family members volunteered their time and services as support crew. Accompanying them much of the way was a mobile screening unit that tested for diabetes with a simple finger-prick blood test.

Pat's mother Mary was the stayer who remained with the crew from beginning to end, playing the role of cook, homemaker for their travelling caravan and occasionally, when tempers got frayed, peacemaker. Lisa joined Pat on the road on several occasions and later proudly headed the reception party when he stopped in Sydney after 75 days of running. Thirty insulin-dependent diabetic children joined Pat in a 2-kilometre fun run through the city. Pat was welcomed in Martin Place by a large lunchtime crowd and another leading sports identity, former test cricket captain and broadcaster Richie Benaud.

After an epic 110-day journey, Pat arrived in the hamlet of Cockle Creek, the last place on the map of Australia. He ran his final steps down a dirt track until he was confronted by a sheer cliff face. He climbed down a steel ladder and clambered across a beach of black rocky pebbles, reaching his finish line at Lion Rock. After running 5963 kilometres, Pat Farmer could finally etch his name in the record books as the first person to run from north to south. He had completed the longest run of his life and raised more than $50 000, half of the original target, but no one was disappointed. Diabetes Australia public relations manager Carol Webster said the funds provided an enormous boost to education programs around the country. Before he left Cape York, Pat had dipped a bottle into the warm Torres Strait. It was carefully transported in the support vehicle for the entire 110 days. After reaching Cockle Creek, he did the same, collecting another sample from the cooler South Pacific Ocean. When he returned to Parramatta, he joined the two bodies of water together to symbolise the completion of the run and the unity of north and south.

Pat then set his sights on a much shorter distance—the 30 metres to the altar to wed long-time partner Lisa Bullivant. Mutual respect had long since blossomed into mutual love. Like any young couple, they'd had their moments and had come close to separating at one stage. Pat had come to dislike festive occasions such as Christmas, Valentine's Day and Lisa's birthday because they heralded a certain expectation—by Lisa as well as family and friends—that he would use the event to announce their engagement. Pat had refused to give her a friendship ring for fear that even that would signal a future he couldn't guarantee.

Some friends and family thought Lisa had no future with Pat because of his reluctance to make a commitment—indeed, at various times she'd been advised to forget him. They had their own pursuits: running dominated Pat's life while Lisa was heavily involved in Rotaract and the International Toastmistresses Club, as well as her job as a legal secretary. Lisa had held numerous office-bearing positions in Rotaract and as western district representative, and was constantly a driving force, especially when it came to playing peacemaker among fractured Rotaract clubs. Even though Lisa got Pat involved in the club he was initially viewed with some suspicion among her Rotaract friends.

'I guess we all loved Lisa so much we were a bit possessive of her,' said Brad Hutchins, a close and long-time Rotaract friend. 'A lot of us initially thought she was too good for Pat. We saw him as an outsider and he didn't mix much with us. Lisa was on her own all the time at our social gatherings. Pat always seemed to have something else to do. Lisa had plenty of other admirers and there was a view that "if this bloke's not going to do the right thing there are plenty of others who will".'

Pat would not be rushed into marriage. He was unsure whether he could juggle the commitment of marriage with his unwavering dedication to his running, which by its very nature was all-consuming and selfish. Lisa had gradually dispelled those concerns with her constant devotion and by investing much time and energy to help him realise his dreams. Pat also got a case of the 'wobbly boot' after the marriage break-ups of his sister Annette and younger brother Tony. His friend Mark Gladwell spent many hours on training runs reassuring Pat about the positive side of marriage and his belief in Pat's readiness.

Pat says he knew after a few years that Lisa was his soulmate, but rebelled when he felt she and others were subtly pressuring him into marriage. It appears a bit of reverse psychology did the trick in the end. Lisa looked like she was giving up hope and friends stopped asking questions about the Big M. Given some clear air, Pat contemplated marriage in his own time and for his own reasons. The first hint Lisa had was when she discovered a receipt for an engagement ring in Pat's pocket.

Her friends were surprised when Pat finally popped the question in a quiet moment on Christmas Day, 1990. Among those who celebrated was the man who was considered Lisa's second father, John Gerathy, her boss at the Sydney law firm Bowen and Gerathy, where she had worked for ten years. He was a senior partner in the firm and had seen Lisa evolve into a poised, confident and elegant young woman. But she hadn't always been like that. Gerathy and Lisa shared an uncommon boss–employee friendship. She called him Barney Rubble, thinking he looked like the character from the *Flintstones* cartoon show. Gerathy says there was a touch of *My Fair Lady* about their relationship, with the well-educated lawyer engaged in a well-meaning attempt to help Lisa refine her ways. 'I called her Eliza Doolittle because for a long time she would constantly drop the letter 'h' in words,' he recalls. 'Even after a while she'd slip and I'd correct her and say: "Come on Eliza, don't forget your aitch." I used to jokingly say: "The rain in Spain stays mainly on the plain." She didn't seem to mind the correction. I think it benefited her, especially when she rose through the ranks of Rotaract and the Toast-mistresses Club. She had a friendly, infectious personality. I wanted to see her get ahead and prove herself. I was also always at her to do something about her nails. She constantly bit her nails when something was worrying her.'

Pat and Lisa were married on 14 March 1992—Pat's thirtieth birthday and just three days before Lisa's twenty-fifth. Pat spent most of the day kicking a football and having a few beers with his groomsmen and dropping in on old friends. He blissfully followed a fine family tradition—being late for his wedding, a habit begun by his father and continued by his eldest brother Bernie. While some believe Pat was stalling, he insists he just lost track of time. In contrast to the normal celluloid scene, the bride was consoling her father on their third circuit of the church block. Barry Bullivant feared the runner was 'doing a runner'. Lisa, however, was confident Pat was just late—again. 'When we looked at our watches the wedding was starting in five minutes and we still had to get dressed and drive about 10 kilometres from my mate's place,' remembers Pat. 'Five of us piled into this one little white Corolla. We were on two wheels most of the way and ran every red light. Finally we pulled up out the front. We were still buttoning up our shirts and suits. We were late as hell and all 200 guests stood and applauded as we ran down the aisle.'

Hell hath no fury like a woman delayed on her wedding day. Pat felt the full force of Lisa's anger after the ceremony when they realised they were being charged overtime on the limousines because of his tardiness. The reception at the Granville RSL club was one long and late party. The bride and groom lingered to the point where some guests wondered if they would ever make their big farewell. Their honeymoon retreat was on Lord Howe Island. They climbed mountains but running was off the agenda for at least that week.

In December of 1992, Pat and Lisa ventured overseas together for the first time to New Zealand, on what became a second honeymoon. More importantly, Pat had been selected to run for his country for the first time at the inaugural 100 kilometres Australasian Championships at Campbell Park in the Waitaki Valley on the South Island. Pat has always proudly worn his patriotism on his sleeve and he regarded this as one of the highlights of his running career. As usual with the ultra marathon game, Pat had to pay for the privilege. The race was held on a bitumen road that ran through a sprawling farm owned by a wealthy American. The Australian team stayed in a replica Scottish castle and spent a relaxing two days before the race, trout fishing and hunting for rabbits, wild pigs and wild goats. 'We didn't catch or shoot anything but we had a fantastic time. I hit it off with everybody,' said Pat. Lisa and Pat's mother accompanied him. Their host's son wheeled his favourite toy, a Harley-Davidson, out of the garage and took Lisa for a joyride.

The Australians upset the fancied New Zealand team and won both the men's and women's individual and team races. Don

Wallace and Lavinia Petrie were comfortable winners of their events. It was 5°C when the race started and 27°C when they finished. After running close to the leading pace for the first 50 kilometres, the 'wheels fell off' for Pat and he faded badly to finish eighteenth out of a field of 35, three and a half hours behind Wallace.

Pat said he was still recovering from a dose of flu and had ignored the advice of Dick Telford, the head of Sports Science at the Australian Institute of Sport, who had been coaching him for a few months. Telford has coached many of Australia's best long-distance and marathon runners, including Lisa Ondieki and Andrew Lloyd. But it didn't work out for Pat. As with other coaches who had not been ultra runners themselves, Pat just couldn't gel with advisers who hadn't experienced the slow torture of body and mind.

A pattern started to emerge as he looked for his next challenge. Pat needed to find something bigger and better that would keep him focused on training, and that would appeal to sponsors and gain them the necessary public exposure. He turned his thoughts overseas and found an event that finally fired his imagination—the Trans America footrace. It had a fascinating history, having begun in 1928 as a promotional vehicle for Route 66—the first coast-to-coast road in the United States—by vision-ary promoter C.C. Pyle. With unemployment spiralling upwards and the divide between rich and poor widening with the Great Depression imminent, the race and the US$25 000 first prize lured 231 men (women weren't allowed to enter until the fol-lowing year) to the Great Bunion Derby, as it was called. The winner, Andy Payne from Oklahoma, took 84 days to run 5370 kilometres from Los Angeles to New York. Fifty-five runners finished.

A smaller field of 168 headed west in 1929 on a reverse route from New York to Los Angeles. After 78 days of running, Johnny Salo, an immigrant policeman from New Jersey, beat Great Britain's Peter Gavuzzi by less than three minutes. But both were the victims of daylight robbery. The promoter Pyle went bankrupt and none of the runners was paid.*

Aside from a two-man duel in 1985, the race looked consigned to the history books. But in 1992, two American running enthusiasts, Jesse Dale Riley and Michael Kenney, revived the event, backed by a $45 000 loan from Riley's rich businessman uncle. California's Dave Warady, 35, won the first modern Trans America footrace by almost seven hours.

The race barely made headlines in America, let alone on the other side of the world, which made Pat's endeavours to attract sponsorship even more difficult. He finally made a pitch to health insurer Manchester Unity, which had given partial backing to Pat's Diabetes Australia run. David Fookes, who as sales and marketing manager controlled the purse strings on such matters, had been very impressed with the exposure they'd received from that event. 'When Pat came back to me I didn't have a lot of hesitation because I knew he'd work his arse off to promote us—he had that fierce determination in his persona,' said Fookes. 'I got dozens of applications from athletes seeking sponsorship, but Pat fitted our image because he was a young married man thinking of starting a family and he and Lisa needed health insurance.'

Manchester Unity put up $10 000 which covered most of his air fares, accommodation and race entry of $1400, but Pat still ended up out of pocket. The 1993 Trans Am was lucky to proceed, after looking financially shaky a month before the start on 19 June. Matters weren't helped when the 1992 eighth-placed finisher Ed Kelley paid his entry fee on the eve of the 1993 race with a bounced cheque, knowing it would be weeks before Riley and Kenney would tumble to his ploy. However, things began to look up when a Japanese businessman came to the rescue. Toshihiko Okada was the chairman of Moonbat, a wholesaler of fine fashion items to Japanese department stores. He was drawn

---

*   Blaikie, D. 'History of Trans America Footraces', *Ultramodern World News*, Ultramarathon World Home Page.

to the race because of his background as a competitor in long-distance races up to 100 kilometres. He heard about the Trans America race through a Japanese runner who had entered. Moonbat sponsored the race for $110 000.

The 1993 race had thirteen starters from America, Europe, Australia and Asia. Having never raced competitively over such a distance, Pat admits his goal was to survive and finish. It was a tough assignment for any athlete: 4719 kilometres from Huntington Beach, California to New York, New York—an average of 80 kilometres a day, or two marathons each day for 64 days with no days off.

Pat ran conservatively for the first few days, finishing in the middle of the pack while he assessed the capabilities of his competitors, particularly early race leader Ray Bell from Florida. Unbeknown to Pat, Bell was even more circumspect about his own prospects, initially treating the event as a one-week race. He'd run his first multi-day event just the previous year (the 525 kilometre Trans Colorado race) and Bell confesses he never thought he would finish the 1993 Trans Am. The 46-year-old had been flat out winning a raffle lately, let alone a competitive road race. His last victory had been in 1989.

'I was getting weaker and my times were getting slower,' he says. 'And the only reason I entered Trans Am was that I was trying to make it to Las Vegas just to go there and have a vacation and I was planning to head home after that. I only took enough shoes and clothing and money for that. I actually didn't think I'd make it to Las Vegas. I didn't think there was any way I'd ever, ever make it across the United States.'

But Bell's attitude belies an experienced race-hardened runner who quickly proved he was a formidable rival. Neither runner had heard of the other before the race, but they soon developed a healthy mutual respect. Pat dubbed Bell 'The Rocket'; the American recognised Pat was super-competitive and knew that would drive him to perform day in, day out. Pat decided to test out his rival's boosters on the fourth day. Pat got some hint that Bell had the 'right stuff' when he out-sprinted the Australian in the last 100 metres. By the end of the first week of the world's toughest footrace, competitors had begun to drop like flies. The searing 51°C heat of 'The Devil's Playground' in the Nevada Desert claimed three men and one of only two female competitors, Diane Dakan, reducing the field to nine.

On the first stage out of the desert, Pat took advantage of his redoubtable strength on the hills to break Bell's hot streak of ten consecutive daily stage wins. Pat out-kicked Bell at the end of a lung-busting 85-kilometre climb through the high country of Utah to record a one-second victory. But the next day Bell put two hours on Pat to increase his overall race margin to twelve hours after two weeks. Now it was getting serious. The pair had developed an intense rivalry that saw them barely speak to each other through the entire 64-day event. Ray says Pat was more the source of it, although admits his regular derogatory jibes at Australia's lack of sophistication probably didn't help.

While Bell's lead might have appeared invincible, Pat was getting stronger and fitter by the week and hadn't given up hope. He lost further time to his rival on the backroads through the endless wasteland of Utah but the arrival of day 20 and a camera crew from Channel Nine's Los Angeles bureau triggered for Pat a new burst of faith in himself. It was typical of his positive attitude that he began to believe he had a chance to win the race. But he had to gamble now before Bell's lead became totally unassailable. Pat beat Bell into Fruita, Colorado, which began an awesome string of 37 wins in the final 45 stages.

Ray Bell's friend and compatriot Mike Sandlin pulled out on day 22 and Pat gave a moving farewell speech. There was a camaraderie among the runners—even between Pat and Ray, although to a lesser extent—and having covered 1500 kilometres, they were all saddened to see another of their number drop off. With just seven left in the field they were now willing each other to the finish.

Pat used the famous Rocky Mountains of Colorado to make inroads into Bell's lead. The climb into altitude of 4000 metres ripped at his lungs and left him feeling like he was struggling for breath to live, let alone breath to keep running competitively. He pushed his body until his legs felt like jelly. Pat tried desperately to break Bell's spirit—he even hoped his rival, who many regarded as a hypochondriac, would succumb to one of the many illnesses or injuries he often talked about. Despite Pat's supreme effort, Bell had shown enormous courage in ensuring Pat cut no more than two hours from his lead which still stood at sixteen hours by the time they left the Rockies. 'I didn't have any expectations about how much time I should have been pegging back,' said Pat. 'I would have loved to be making bigger inroads, but I was happy to get any time off him.'

As well as confronting every physical challenge, the runners also had to contend with the mighty extremes of Nature. One night in Maryville, Kansas, the home of the Pony Express, a state trooper delivered a grim tornado warning to the runners. The advice about seeking ground-level shelter was ringing in their ears when a vicious storm struck the next day. There were no twisters, but a deluge sent most of the field scuttling off to seek refuge in vehicles. Torrents spilled over from the elevated corn-fields, leaving the road covered in knee-deep water. Pat thought it a chance to gain a break on Bell, but his rival matched his determination and the pair ploughed on through the floodwaters.

The storm signalled the start of once-in-a-century rains in Oklahoma and Kansas that made for truly miserable running conditions. The only consolation was the additional rest compet-itors received from their unrelenting schedule when the swollen waterways converged. The mighty Missouri and Mississippi Rivers burst their banks and swallowed up vast tracts of lowlands. The inland seas were 40 kilometres wide at some points, forcing organisers to make 300-kilometre detours.

Through all of the natural adversity, Pat and Ray continued to hammer each other mercilessly, neither preparing to concede any seconds unnecessarily. It was no longer a matter of just surviving—every day was a serious match-race. The tension was palpable. Still they refused to talk, despite spending much of their nine-hour day on the road within whispering distance of each other. 'The duel was just incredible,' said organiser Jesse Riley, who watched it at close quarters on his mountain bike, marking the turns and checking runners' progress. 'Most times it was a battle to see how close they could stay without saying anything. It was their way of torturing each other.'

It was an enormous psychological battle, with both runners using whatever tactics or tricks they could to gain a slight advantage. Pat began using the cover of darkness with the 5.00 a.m. daily start to get an early break. He slipped out of Bell's sight on two mornings before his rival got wise and began carrying a torch so he could keep track of the Australian. Pat would also throw in numerous surges, or sprints, to test him out.

Drink stations were also used as a tactical weapon when the race was close, with both runners often using the strategy of faking a stop to take refreshments, then sprinting away. A gap of seconds could sometimes be converted to soul-destroying minutes. Pat was so desperate to gain any sort of a break on his rival that he turned inventor. He smashed a mirror and made a makeshift rear vision mirror by taping it to a stick and attaching it to his cap. It worked a treat for a week, allowing him to see when Bell was stopping for a drink or a toilet break behind him. The invention mysteriously disappeared one night while Pat was sleeping.

Most of the time the pair ran at 11–13 kilometres an hour, but there were plenty of stages when they'd step on the gas and run up to 16 kilometres an hour in an attempt to psyche each other out. The effort seemed even more incredible after weeks of pressure-filled running in the heat, rain and mountains. Bell's strength was the Saturday time trials, where runners ran individually against the clock, as opposed to each other. Bell enjoyed this form of racing and would push himself even harder. Pat found it incredibly frustrating—he would whittle minutes from Bell's massive lead mid-week only to see his opponent beat him by more than half an hour in the weekly time trials.

The runners in the Trans America often felt like they were fleet-footed backpackers. Very few of them had support crews and accommodation was often primitive. It was America on $20 a day—the pain was complimentary. Most of the athletes had brought little spending money with them—although it was rare they were in places that had extravagances for sale. On the admission of Riley, 'it was an unimaginably difficult event to compete in', given the conditions. Most nights were spent crashed out in a sleeping bag on the floor of a high school gymnasium or church hall. The luxury of a real bed in a motel was thrown in once every three nights, on average. Nutrition was poor.

'I had no access to decent food,' said Pat. 'Most nights we'd just pay the organisers to go buy us food and we were eating garbage just about every night. Usually it was pizzas or donuts or some other rubbish takeaway. There was never enough to go around. I'd have only a few pieces of pizza and this was after running flat out all day. Just about every night I went to bed hungry. During the day it was snacks on the run—fruit, sandwiches and a few cookies. Drinks were a problem, especially in the desert stages. Organisers would leave water out for you but it was 30 degrees by 10.00 a.m. so you hardly felt like drinking hot water.'

After more than a month of relentless racing, Pat and Ray were finding the daily routine was the most harrowing and mind-numbing experience of their entire lives. The discordant sound of various alarm clocks stirred runners from a restless slumber between 3.30 and 4.00 a.m. Internally the mind and body waged a war about how to face another day. Sleep was invariably difficult. Pat would go to bed with his head pounding from the heat and exertion and wake up feeling like he had a king-sized hangover. His legs constantly ached—never more so than the morning—with the buildup of muscle-numbing lactic acid ensuring his first movements looked very robotic.

Ray also dreaded the mornings. His joint and muscle stiffness was so bad from the daily toil, it would take him five full minutes before he could struggle from his sleeping bag into a chair and then half an hour of slow warm-up running before he was ready for each new day of torture.

By day 54, the front-running pair was so exhausted other runners in the field began to finally challenge for stage wins. The only woman who had survived the race rigours was 34-year-old Lorna Michael from Wisconsin. Michael was relatively fresh after running very cautiously for the first half of the Trans Am. Runners began each new daily stage together and Michael put herself into a position to become the first runner since day one to beat Pat and Ray. They insist they let her win to encourage the other runners to 'have a go' out front and revive everyone's interest in what had become a two-man race.

Despite trailing by more than 80 hours overall, Michael was now confident she could serve it up to the big boys. She was fourth and closing fast on third-placed Ed Kelley, who was just an hour ahead, with two weeks left to run. She finally passed a shattered Kelley on day 52 and never looked back, employing the clever tactic of using Pat and Ray to drag her along to increase her buffer over Kelley. Pat and Ray resented her presence and worked hard to avoid being shown up by her. Pat thought Lorna was trying to 'nark' him by running ridiculously close to him, to the point where she clipped his heels numerous times. 'She was suddenly transformed into this aggressive new runner, it was like Jekyll and Hyde,' said Pat. 'I said to Ray after we let her win that stage: "We've created a monster here."'

In Pennsylvania, just five days from the finish, Michael's spirits were further boosted by the arrival of a long-time friend, Dave Obelkevich. For $130, he was allowed to enter as a stage runner on day 60, a fundraising and promotional ploy used regularly by the organisers. A top-class sub-two hours 20 marathon runner, he paced and coached Lorna, helping her to open up a twelve-minute lead on the field by 70 kilometres. 'It's a set-up,' said Pat, referring to the assistance of Lorna's friend Dave, 'but that's okay. That just means I'll kick 'em *both* in the arse.' Michael was too strong for her partner and found herself running alone with Pat and Ray closing in. 'I'm going to have to earn it,' she repeatedly told herself. When a train threatened to cut her off at a level crossing, she sprinted to beat it. A signalman switched the gate and she crossed safely. Close behind was organiser Jesse Riley following on his mountain bike, who narrowly avoided the locomotive—by just a metre.

With his protests to race organisers falling on deaf ears, Pat dug deep into his reserves, running down Obelkevich and leaving him in an exhausted, sweaty heap by the side of the road. Bell joined Pat as they set their sights on Michael. Pat cranked up the pace once he got Michael in his sights, leaving both her and Bell in his wake. She was unable to fight off either challenge and finished almost seven minutes behind a triumphant Pat. Despite Michael presenting no threat to Pat's overall race position, his super-competitive streak wouldn't allow him to concede time or a victory.

Pain had been a constant companion throughout the race but Pat had long since learned to accept it as a companion, not an intruder into his comfort zone. Mentor Tony Rafferty had once warned him that pain was an integral part of endurance sport, but Pat extends the theory. 'I also realise that pain in various forms is an inescapable part of life. Sure you can spend your time trying to avoid the hurt or shielding loved ones from it, but you may end up leading a very unhappy and less fulfilling life. We have to accept that pain goes hand in hand with us. What you have to do is to draw strength from it.'

The 64-day race had been a dramatic roller coaster for competitors and supporters and the final 50-kilometre leg was no different. With a sixteen-hour lead, Bell merely needed to finish the leg to win. But halfway through the stage, he was in trouble after tripping and badly lacerating both knees. While his safety margin was enormous, there was a danger of disqualification had he not finished before the nominated cut-off time. Bell's injury slowed him down, but when his family joined him from Florida, they encouraged him to push through to the finish in Central Park.

Pat was oblivious to Bell's problems as he made his own triumphant final run through the Big Apple. His emotions were mixed—relief and pride at his stunning second place in the world's toughest footrace; a hint of regret about what more could have been done to go one place better; and sadness that his wife Lisa couldn't share in the excitement. For Pat, the pain of separation had often exceeded the physical pain from running. It was reflected in the $1600 phone bill that faced him when he returned home.

These things almost overwhelmed his feeling of utter exhaustion. No run had ever taxed and tested him so much—he had lost 10 kilograms during the event. Pat carried the Australian flag as he ran the final kilometres through Central Park. New Yorkers barely flinched from their activity—they'd seen stranger things in the Big Apple. Ten metres from the finish, Pat's eye caught a familiar figure. This was the face that had carried him along thousands of gruelling, lonely kilometress. The feeling of Lisa's embrace was even more comforting than he had ever remembered.

'What are you doing here?'

'David Fookes and Manchester Unity flew me over here. They thought you'd like a surprise. I got my hair done. What do you think?' said Lisa. Pat confessed that after three months apart he had forgotten how it used to look. 'It's fantastic,' he replied. 'It cost me $100,' said Lisa. 'What! We can't afford that,' said Pat.

He had run 4685 kilometres knowing there was not one cent of prize money. For now it didn't matter. 'I had the best prize of all. I couldn't ask for anything more,' said Pat.

6

The quest

Since 1907, Sydney's Camperdown Children's Hospital has had a reputation for expert medical care. Rotary District Governor Denis Green certainly owed the staff a debt of gratitude for saving his eyesight after he was left temporarily blinded by an infection when he was twelve years old. He had little hesitation in agreeing on Rotary's behalf in taking up the challenge of helping to fundraise $2 million over three years when approached by the Chief Executive Officer of the proposed new Children's Hospital, Dr John Yu, in 1993. Dr Yu, the 1996 Australian of the Year, was committed to maintaining the relocated Children's Hospital's standard of medical excellence. While the New South Wales government was funding its construction and equipment, the hospital board needed another $30 million to build an outstanding facility. Denis Green knew Pat Farmer and approached him to do a charity run to help raise funds.

Initially they wanted Pat to run 40 kilometres from the old Children's Hospital at Camperdown to the new one at Westmead, in Sydney's west. That was barely a training run for Pat, who was always searching for more imaginative challenges. Mindful that the Children's Hospital was the main metropolitan medical centre for country kids, Pat and Rotary thought it appropriate to take the message to the bush. 'From Sydney to the Black Stump and Back' was conceived as a 42-day fundraising journey around country New South Wales that began on 21 March 1994. Pat originally planned to run a marathon a day, but as the event unfolded, he found himself sometimes running up to 85 kilometres (two marathons a day) as he visited schools, hospitals and functions the length and breadth of the state. The response and donations were initially slightly disappointing, perhaps fuelled by rural cynicism about a bloke many country folk had never heard of asking for donations for a city hospital.

But word quickly began to spread on the bush telegraph about Pat's mission and his inspirational message. No sooner had he left a town than the money began rolling in behind him. He would be on the road to the next stopover when they would start lining up for another function. In pubs and halls from Cootamundra to Coonabarabran and Gunnedah to Gundagai, Pat regaled avid audiences with stories from his Trans America race and other adventures on the road. Many times Pat concealed the day's exhaustion from exertion. It was just over six months since he had finished the epic race across the United States and his body was still ailing, with a lingering kidney complaint and soft tissue injuries. His listeners were amazed and moved. Functions went for hours, with many of his newly acquired fans loitering after his speech to 'have a yak'.

When he returned after running 2500 kilometres they had raised $70 000. But Pat had touched a chord in most country towns and Rotary's fundraising drive slowly gathered momentum with receipts swelling to $300 000 by the end of the year.

'Pat worked his guts out to help raise the money,' said organiser Denis Green. 'It was hard motivating local Rotary clubs initially because they had their own local priorities to worry about. Pat created the desire among clubs to stage functions and activities for months after he'd passed through their towns. It gave us a great kick-start to our $2 million target.'

'It was very worthwhile,' said Pat. 'Like all of my runs there's not a gold medal or the prestige like football players receive, but there is the fulfilment in knowing you were able to do something special and help other people along the way which a lot of the other sportspeople don't do.'

While Pat never seemed to tire of telling Trans Am anecdotes and jokes, his crew grew weary of hearing them. Friend and training partner Mark Gladwell and Pat's cousin, Gerard Lynn, spent night after night at functions passively listening to the same stories. To relieve the boredom, they found themselves reciting the stories almost word for word in hushed tones to each other, ahead of Pat's delivery. 'Pat always spoke well and was highly motivating but I'm afraid it lost its appeal for us after a dozen sessions,' said Gerard. 'We would challenge Pat to let us tell the story because we reckoned we knew it as well as him.'

But there was something different about Pat's rhetoric now. His second place in the Trans America race had stoked the fires of ambition like no other event. Previously he never knew how far he could go in ultra running or how good he could be. Pat just knew he wanted to be the best he could be. He now realised that his best was maybe good enough to take him to the top, to make him the best ultra marathon runner in the world. Before Trans Am, he dared not aspire to such lofty heights. But now it was a burning desire and, as family and friends knew, once Pat had an idea in his head, he wouldn't rest until he saw it through. The landscape gardener from Sydney's west had gone from pretender to contender and knew he had to return to America for another shot at the title.

'I ran out of my skin in the Trans Am and I realised the overseas competition wasn't as tough as I thought it would be,' he said. 'I thought a lot about the 1993 Trans Am and at times was hell to live with for poor Lisa because I realised that I needed to go back there and have another shot at the race just to prove to myself that I could be number one. I thought if I learnt from that experience and took my own crew and did things better I could win the event.'

While the 1993 Trans America had carried no prizemoney, Pat and Ray Bell did not go unrewarded. Mr Okada, chairman of Moonbat which had sponsored the run, was so impressed with the commitment of the pair and the spirit of competition between them, he felt compelled to acknowledge it. He offered all-expenses paid trips for Pat, Ray and their partners to represent his company at the 100-kilometre World Challenge at Lake Saroma on the Japanese island of Hokkaido on 26 June 1994.

'I appreciated the fact that even after 3000 kilometres of the Trans America they were still challenging each other,' said Mr Okada. 'I liked Pat Farmer very much. I remember one night he was crying out of frustration at the mental ordeal and the fact he could not reduce Ray Bell's lead. He promised himself he would try his best effort even if he couldn't get first prize. The runners, when they run like this, they challenge life itself.'

The 100-kilometre World Challenge had both quantity and quality, with over 2000 of the world's best ultra runners competing. Pat and Ray always knew this would be too short and too fast for them (it was a bit like a marathon runner lining up to run a 200 metre sprint), but they welcomed the chance to run in such a world-class event. The early pace was frantic for an ultra race. Pat and Ray picked up their rivalry where they left off in New York one year earlier. It was as if time had stood still in between. Bell went out hard and was amongst the top 50 athletes, cruising through the first 50 kilometres in three and a half hours, before losing momentum. He heard commotion behind him and was passed by the leading two female runners who were accompanied by a television crew in an open-back vehicle. Ever the opportunist, Pat flashed by him at that exact moment on the other side.

'He went by pretty fast and I thought: "That's it. I'm never going to see him again."' Bell said. But Pat was soon beset by stomach cramps and a bout of vomiting between 70 and 75 kilometres, perhaps induced by some local food that disagreed with him. He was reduced to a walk. Bell couldn't believe his luck when he spotted Pat in the distance. Instead of surging past him, Ray slowed and asked Pat how he was feeling. He accompanied his friend and rival for a short distance and offered words of encouragement, then the American ran ahead. Bell's actions helped lift Pat's competitive spirit. Within a few kilometres, Pat's pain had passed. Before too long he began feeling better and picked up the pace. He gradually caught Bell and kicked past him—the next he saw of Pat was at the finish line. The proud Australian ran a huge personal best to finish in eight hours, five minutes. Bell was 25 minutes behind. Russian Alexey Volgin led the field home in six hours, 22 minutes and 43 seconds.

Despite arriving in Japan one week before the race, Mr Okada invited Pat and Ray to stay on for another week. It was one of the best trips of their lives.

'We had a fantastic time and Mr Okada paid for everything which was incredibly generous,' said Pat. 'Lisa was pregnant with Brooke, so she wasn't too keen on the raw fish. We made a lot of really great friends over there. Most of them were on Mr Okada's staff. They were pretty stiff-collared but by the time Lisa finished with them—especially on the karaoke nights—they were as loose as could be. They really chilled out.'

Ray Bell's daughter Audra accompanied him on the trip. Audra and Lisa spent plenty of time together. At one stage, the ladies went exploring their hotel in search of a bathtub, after surprisingly learning their rooms were lacking in this facility. They found two doors that they thought led to the communal hot tubs. Unfortunately the signs were in Japanese so they had no way of telling which was the women's bathroom and which was the men's. They took a guess and of course got it wrong, walking into a room of smiling naked Japanese men. They made the most dignified exit they could. When their momentary embarrassment subsided, they laughed until tears rolled down their aching cheeks.

Pat was now race-toughened and in peak physical shape, ready to again match it with the best on home soil. He had been invited to compete in a star-studded ultra marathon in Tasmania, dubbed 'Hell in Paradise'. It was a seven-day 650 kilometre race that began on 6 August 1994 and brought together the best male and female multi-day long-distance runners in the world in what amounted to a Tour de France on two legs. Among the field of 27 was current and former world 100 kilometre champions Janos Bogar from Hungary, Konstantin Santalov from Russia and Roland Vuillemenot from France, Westfield Sydney to Melbourne winners Bryan Smith (Australia) and Dusan Mravlje (Slovenia) and women's world champion Eleanor Adams. Yiannis Kouros was enticed out of semi-retirement for the event. For three years, Kouros had done little competitive running, but didn't consider he would be handicapped by the lack of training.

Australia's Don Wallace was the surprise packet, leading Kouros by almost three minutes after the first two days which featured stages of 90 kilometres and 92 kilometres. Competitors ran straight into an Antarctic blizzard that made a difficult race a survival test when confronted by 90 kilometre per hour winds, blinding snow, sleet and slippery roads. Pat had never seen conditions like it. 'It was incredible. The snow was blowing sideways because of the icy wind,' said Pat. Eleanor Adams cheated death when she was hospitalised after suffering from dangerously low body temperature and blood pressure induced by the cold. She discharged herself and continued to race. Pat never ran well in cold conditions and struggled into fourteenth place after two days. As one local scribe wrote: 'It was hell all right—forget the paradise.'

Wallace again led the field on the third day until the 25 kilometre mark, when he was crippled by a torn stomach muscle that severely hampered his running. He surrendered his two-minute lead to Kouros, Bogar and emerging Russian Anatoly Kruglikov, and then watched half of the field swallow him up. Runners marched on by, none of them offering assistance or words of consolation, as Wallace lay helpless by the side of the road. By the time Pat had caught Wallace, the injured runner had received some massage from his crew and was able to at least get his legs moving. In a gesture of true sportsmanship, Pat slowed down and ran with Wallace for 3 kilometres, conceding valuable time to his rivals—in a scene reminiscent of John

Landy's famous 'helping hand' to a fallen Ron Clarke at the 1956 Australian mile championships in Melbourne.

Wallace's legs again refused to function properly and he was forced to stop. Pat paused and tried to motivate his wounded colleague. 'Us Aussies don't give up,' Pat said, before pushing on alone at Wallace's insistence. 'That really struck a chord with me,' said Wallace. 'He didn't have to sacrifice his race to help me—no one else did. I really appreciated the gesture.' Wallace battled bravely to the finish in eighteenth place but retired from the race the next morning.

At the start of day six, Pat had fought his way back through the field to be in ninth place. While he was no threat to overall race leader Kruglikov, trailing five and a half hours behind, Pat's strength and confidence had been building with each stage. The Russian had buried Kouros's hopes in the snow and freezing conditions of the 85 kilometre run to Cradle Mountain in northwest Tasmania on the fifth day. The Greek King of ultra running feared for his life as he finished half an hour behind Kruglikov. 'There is nothing more important than your life, your family, your friends,' Kouros said. 'That's what I thought about in those hills. I didn't want to leave my bones in those hills.'*

The attrition rate was high. The field had been reduced from 27 to 18 and Pat decided the time was right to have a crack at the leaders. He employed 'catch me if you can' tactics from the start at Strahan on the west coast, using his strength on the early hills. The ease with which he opened up a three-minute break surprised everyone, above all himself. 'People were cheering me and saying I had a good lead, but I didn't want to get carried away,' Pat said. 'I knew I was flying. I was running out of my skin and when my lead was almost one kilometre, I started to feel tired and I began to have doubts and wondered: "What am I doing so far in front?"'

Halfway through the 78-kilometre section, Pat heard Greek music. Kouros's support crew had driven ahead of their runner

* Rogers, M., 1994 'Russian leads by 31 mins', *Hobart Mercury*, p. 1.

The beginning of an incredible journey, Sydney to Melbourne, 1987. Pat was bitterly disappointed not to finish his first Westfield ultra marathon.

1988. The war within was at its worst during the night as sleep deprivation exacerbated the pain of weary muscles. Night running tested Pat to the limit.

1989. A triumphant finish in the 'world's greatest foot race'. Pat manages a smile as he realises his dream of finishing the Sydney to Melbourne ultra. As always, Lisa was by his side through the good and the bad.

Promoting the Granville Ultimate Ultra Marathon Challenge in 1989 with mentor Tony Rafferty and Dave Taylor. Pat and Tony both broke the world 1000-mile record, but the race shattered their friendship.

Pat and Dave Taylor at the Campbelltown 24-hour Ultra, 1989. This pair shared a rivalry that lasted more than a decade.

Collecting water at the southern-most point in Tasmania, at the completion of the Diabetes Australia event in 1990. Pat's 5963-km solo run consolidated his place in the record books.

Pat is reunited with wife Lisa, a perennial source of inspiration, at the finish of the 1993 Trans-America race in Central Park, New York.

The American Dream, Trans-America Race, 1993. Patriotic runner-up Pat Farmer with race winner Ray Bell, at the end of their exhausting 64-day duel.

A race to the bitter end—Pat and his deadliest rival, Dusan Mravlje go stride for stride through the desert in the 1995 Trans-America race.

Pat crossing the finish line in Cisco, Utah, after another day of toil in the 1995 Trans Am. Three days later, a crippling stress fracture ended Pat's dream of winning the gruelling event.

Support crew help Pat to take a life-saving swim at Eyre Creek in the Simpson Desert in 1996. Pat came closer to death during this event than at any other stage in his career but, remarkably, broke Ron Grant's record for a desert crossing.

International success in the 1997 Trailwalker team run in Hong Kong. The 'dream team' of (l to r) Mike Sandlin, Bryan Hacker, Pat Farmer and Ray Bell finished strongest out of the 720-team strong field of runners.

Pat and Lisa Bullivant's first date in 1984, at the wedding of her half-brother Geoff, was a memorable event, as much for Pat's arrival to pick Lisa up in a 'ute that stank like old fish'.

Pat and Lisa's wedding day, 14 March, 1992. Pat followed the family tradition of arriving late for his own wedding, raising fears in the bride's father that the 'runner was doing a runner'.

The perfect family. Pat and Lisa with son Dillon and daughter Brooke, just months before Lisa's tragic death at the age of 31.

The start of the longest journey. Pat's epic Centenary of Federation Run around Australia. Pat at Parliament House with Brooke, Dillon, mother Mary and Prime Minister John Howard. (Photo: Auspic)

Putting one foot in front of the other was the simple philosophy that drove Pat to success and inspired a nation in his record-breaking 14 986-km Centenary of Federation Run to promote awareness of Australia's impending 100th birthday celebrations.

Prime Minister John Howard and the Federal Parliament bestowed rare honours on Pat and his family upon his return, on 8 December 1999, having completed his greatest achievement.

and stopped alongside Pat in what he thought was a deliberate attempt to strike fear into him. 'Good on you Patrick Farmer. Yiannis looks forward to joining you soon,' they teased. Their prophesy was fulfilled sooner than Pat would have liked. He could hear the footsteps, but was powerless to repel them.

'When Kouros and Kruglikov passed me, my legs felt like a ton of bricks,' said Pat. 'I stopped and vomited by the side of the road because I'd really hammered the pace. I just looked at them moving off into the distance. My sister Catherine who was in my crew said: "Never mind Pat, you did really well to get where you are." I looked ahead and something clicked. I said: "It's not over yet."'

When a runner is 'dropped' or passed in distance races like this, their spirit or motivation is usually crushed and they rarely come back. Kouros and Kruglikov had opened up a substantial 400-metre lead and could reasonably have expected that Pat would be easy pickings for the rest of the field. No one had predicted Pat would serve it up to the big guns of the race, viewing him as one of the battlers who were there to make up the numbers. But serve it up he did, recovering the lost ground over the next 5 kilometres. Kouros and Kruglikov were stunned when Pat caught them and regained the lead. As the trio passed the other runners after the final turnaround, Pat was boosted by their enthusiastic support. The lead changed hands until the final downhill run into Queenstown. Pat remembered from his long discussions with Kouros that the Greek didn't enjoy downhill running and the challenger let gravity and his leg speed do the rest.

Kouros faded but the Russian Kruglikov stayed with Pat until they reached the final flat run home. Excited compatriot Don Wallace appeared on the footpath telling Pat: 'You've got him now. You've just got to hang in there.' Pat lifted the tempo and 'hammered it like I've never done before over the final 3 kilometres'. He spent every ounce of energy to finish 45 seconds clear of the Russian, with Kouros a further second behind in third. It was the first time Pat had beaten the King of ultra running. The Greek embraced an exhausted Pat and gave him the 'Kouros Kiss'—a prize reserved only for competitors who beat him or for whom he holds the highest respect. 'That's the greatest kiss I've ever had,' Pat said later. 'It meant more to me than any trophy. It's not often you beat the best in the world.' Kouros says he shared in the joy of Pat's victory.

'I was surprised but pleased Pat changed his mind that day and stopped running conservatively and decided to run hard from the start,' he said. 'He ran very smart in that race because he knew we were exhausted from the previous days of running hard. He had the physical ability to challenge us. I knew that if he was doing enough in the mind he could do that almost every day.'

Pat still regards that as the finest individual race victory of his career. The stage win helped him to finish seventh overall in the 'Hell in Paradise' event, which was won by the Russian Kruglikov by 44 minutes, with Kouros second—his first defeat in a multi-day race in Australia. Kruglikov won $8000 and, in a rare show of equality, women's winner Eleanor Adams also pocketed $8000, then announced her retirement from international competition. She did a Cliff Young, however, and returned to racing several months later. Pat had one of his rare pay-days from ultra running, receiving $1000.

• • •

The rosy lips pursed and broadened as a contented look spread across an innocent face. Pat drew his cracked and weather-beaten lips closer to the soft skin. This too was a sweet kiss. The birth of Pat and Lisa's first child, Brooke, on 24 January 1995 was a memorable occasion. 'I was present for the birth and I was just awe-struck by the miracle of life. It's like nothing else. I was so proud of Lisa that she'd produced this beautiful child,' he said. Although he enjoyed every aspect of first-time parenthood, Pat admits he was a real novice. 'Like all babies, Brooke was only interested in feeding and sleeping for the first three months and it was hard for me to get too involved, especially with all the running I was doing,' he said. 'I admit I didn't have a clue, but Lisa handled it like a pro.'

Pat added baby bathing and nappy-changing to his daily routine as he began the most intensive training for the 1995 Trans Am. He increased his weekly workload from 200 kilometres to 350 kilometres a week. In a highly unusual move for an ultra runner, Pat even began doing some sprint sessions on a track. He reasoned that he needed the leg-speed so he could produce important mid-race surges and decisive sprint finishes. Pat linked up with a new coach, Phil Austen, but the association was short-lived. The speed sessions led to more soft-tissue injuries and Pat felt Austen tried to exert too much control over him. As always, Pat was his own man and found it hard to bend to the will of others.

Daily life was a major juggling act. Pat would rise between 4.00 and 5.00 a.m., run 20–30 kilometres and then be on site to labour for a day as a landscape gardener with his brother. Tony Farmer says he never went easy on his brother. Nor would Pat have expected or accepted it. Fellow workers vouch for Pat's willing labour ethic. He would then spend another two to three hours training after work, often running home from the worksite. The heavy manual work was not conducive to good training but bills had to be paid and money had to be put aside to pay the mortgage during his three-month absence. Lisa was forced to return to her job as a legal secretary. Pat had secured the biggest sponsorship of his life with Manchester Unity, but it was only enough to pay for the Trans America race expenses.

Despite the lure of the dream, there was much heartache attached to his decision to run in America. Mindful of his responsibility as a husband and father, Pat agonised over his decision to leave his wife and newborn baby for more than two months. Some people, including Lisa's step-mother, were angry with Pat over his decision to go to the other side of the world for what they saw as a selfish pursuit.

'Everybody that cared for Lisa didn't care for what I was doing and I don't blame them,' said Pat. 'Lisa's mother, June, is a practical person and she couldn't understand why I would take off to America and not have an income to provide as a result of it, and not have any prize money to chase or anything. She thought it was just crazy to leave them with no means to look after themselves. But I had the ability to be the best ultra runner on the planet and at the time I thought I'd be crazy if I didn't take up the chance and give it a go. Thankfully Lisa saw it my way and she loved me so much that she supported everything I did.'

This time he could afford to take his own crew. Pat invited his 24-year-old cousin, Gerard Lynn, to be his one-man support team. Lynn wasted little time in grabbing the unique opportunity, although he confesses he had only a vague idea what he was volunteering for. He was forced to take almost three months' unpaid leave from his teaching job, but categorised it as one of those 'not-to-be-missed' life experiences.

Pat was in the best physical shape of his life going into his second Trans Am race. But any feelings of strength or invincibility were offset by two events in the lead-up to his departure. Like all competitors, Pat was asked by race organisers to sign a death and responsibility waiver. It read, in part:

'I realise this event entails many risks including, but not limited to, death, severe and permanent injury, exposure to the extremes of weather, severe weight-loss, overuse injuries, interference by local officials, collisions with vehicles, primitive living conditions, and damage, loss or theft of personal belongings.'

As if that wasn't sobering enough, Pat got a further reality check while soaking his weary muscles in a hot bath one night after a training run, just weeks before his departure.

'Pat, there's a couple of things we have to get sorted out,' said Lisa, grabbing a moment when he was stationary long enough for her to address pressing matters.

'What are they?' Pat said.

'First of all I need you to sign Brooke's passport application.'

'I thought we agreed Brooke wasn't coming over.'

'Well I just think you better sign it in case something happens and we need to come over there in a hurry. I also need you to sign this.'

'What's that one?' he asked.

'It's your will,' said Lisa.

Being young, it was the last issue on Pat's mind but he accepted that Lisa, with her legal background, was not being alarmist, merely practical. She was trained to think like that.

Pat's final preparation was also disrupted by dental work just a fortnight before he left. An upcoming wisdom tooth was causing him grief. He visited one dentist who performed an extraction, but left part of the tooth and an exposed nerve, which exacerbated the pain. Pat sought out another dentist, fellow ultra runner Tony Collins, who was forced to do root canal surgery. 'It's just as well you saw me because this would have caused you all sorts of pain and problems. I wouldn't like to have been running across America with it,' he said.

When Pat and Gerard arrived in Los Angeles on 24 July 1995, things started looking up. A local Rotary Club member greeted them at the airport and showed them some good old-fashioned American hospitality. They had a week to overcome jet lag, acclimatise and finalise preparations and needed a vehicle, so he loaned them his spare car—a Mercedes Benz. At the pre-race media conference, Pat eyed off one man who he knew would be the greatest barrier to achieving his greatest dream, Slovenian runner Dusan Mravlje. While 1993 winner Ray Bell was seeking to become the first two-time winner, Pat knew Mravlje, with whom he had duelled in several Westfield Sydney to Melbourne races, was a world-class runner. He had the perfect attributes for ultra running—tall, well muscled all over, with an ungainly, yet economical running style. But was he mentally hardened to cope with the incredible pain and suffering they would all be forced to endure over 64 days and 4719 kilometres? Pat asked the same question of himself. The real war—the decisive one—would be fought not between each other, but within. Pat hoped and believed he could win that battle.

Despite two years of planning and preparation, the quest to be the best ultra runner in the world had a less than perfect start. He was as determined as hell that no one, especially Mravlje and Bell, was going to get a big lead in the first few weeks. Pat had to stay within striking distance, no matter how much it hurt. He struggled to find his rhythm on the first day, 17 June, although he ran with the leaders for the first 40 kilometres. But the summer heat and his failure to consume enough fluids knocked him around. Complicating matters was the misfortune that befell Gerard halfway into the 80-kilometre opening leg. The crew member was almost as anxious as Pat to get off to a good, smooth start, but he misjudged the softness of a dirt shoulder when he stopped on the side of the road, bogging the support van up to its hubcaps. 'Hey, that's the way we drive in Australia,' was Gerard's feeble explanation to Pat's American friend Will Campbell, who had joined the team for the first few days. It was several hours before the local Automobile Association could extricate the vehicle from the mud, leaving Pat to run the final 40 kilometres—just shy of a marathon—with no support team to provide snacks and fluids. 'Don't worry about it, those things happen,' was Pat's understanding response to Gerard's apology. But such sympathy had shallow limits, as Gerard would soon discover.

By day three, with legs of 80 kilometres, 75 kilometres and 60 kilometres, Pat had surrendered a three-and-a-half hour lead to Mravlje—more than he would have liked, but not enough to trigger panic. He was in fifth place overall. Contrary to logical belief, the first few days were among the toughest in this form of racing. The freshness of body and mind actually worked against most runners as they came to grips with the shock and ardour of the intense race pace.

But it was now time for Pat to dig in a bit and serve it up to the Slovenian. They went head to head through California's Mojave Desert in oppressive heat that reached 42°C. They passed the famous Baghdad Café *en route*, but had no time to admire the setting of the 1987 art film starring Jack Palance. Both runners tested each other out with some fast running, inter-spersed with occasional faster surges, but neither was prepared to push himself to the limit just yet. Pat and Dusan tied for first on day four, running back-to-back marathons in an incredible average time of three hours, 38 minutes for each 42.2 kilometre split.

It was the first of seven consecutive ties between the pair. It took little time for the mind games to begin and bag of tricks to be opened. Mravlje would try to fake a shadowing Pat at the aid stations, pretending to stop for food or drink, but then sprinting away in a bid to grab a decisive break. Pat covered every move, matching the Slovenian's tactic of cutting his rival off at corners. The pace was much faster than any previous Trans Am and had developed into a four-horse race between Pat, Dusan and Americans David Horton and Ray Bell. Aside from the inevitable blisters from the scorching hot roads and sunburn, Pat was in good shape, sitting in third place after ten days.

His resolve faced its first test, as he knew it inevitably would, on day eleven when he began urinating a substantial amount of blood—a sign of abrasions in the bladder caused by dehydration. The pain was at times debilitating, forcing Pat to slow down. His stomach felt tight all day. At its worst, it felt as if he had been punched in the gut. He was concerned, but knew it was almost inevitable with ultra runs in the heat. The health risks from such an ailment were not serious—yet. All he could do was drink more water which flushed his kidneys and eased the pain. As the Trans Am runners crossed into their third state, Utah, Pat charged into second place, overtaking Horton, with a series of second placings behind Mravlje.

The 1000-kilometre milestone was reached on day fourteen, as the runners climbed through the mountains of Utah, with snow-capped peaks providing an eye-catching backdrop. But Pat was soon in no mood to appreciate the scenery, as he was inexplicably beset with sharp stomach pains and vomiting. He dropped off Mravlje's pace, two-thirds of the way through the 80-kilometre day.

His crew member, Gerard Lynn, felt completely helpless, only able to serve up food, drink and reassuring words. 'It scared the hell out of me,' says Gerard, 'because he went from being so good to so bad in the space of 3 kilometres. He looked like death warmed up. It was the lowest I'd ever seen him to that point. The race rules stipulated I could only give aid every 3 kilometres and not stop in between. I wasn't sure of the consequences, but I was seriously tempted to break the rules.'

After half an hour, Pat's nausea and vomiting passed just as quickly as it arrived. 'We're back in business,' he said, breaking back into strong stride. Pat finished the day in reasonable shape and felt a crisis had been averted after losing just 36 minutes to Mravlje, while holding second place.

The presence of camera crews from Australia's Seven and Nine Networks the next day lifted Pat's spirits and provided him with plenty of incentive for a comeback. Mindful that Pat wanted to perform well for the cameras, Mravlje laid out his cards early into the race.

'You want a war today?' he said.

'Yes,' was Pat's blunt reply.

'You don't want to finish together? I'm feeling good and can run very fast today.'

'No, I want to win.'

'Well, it will be war then.'

Today was one of the shortest days of the entire event—just 45 kilometres—but there was nothing easy about it. The pair duelled through the canyons where Butch Cassidy and the Sundance Kid once roamed lawless, going stride for stride, running faster than at any other stage of the race in the cool, overcast conditions. There was no way that Dusan was going to let Pat look good for Australian television. In fact, race observers thought the Slovenian wanted to humiliate him. But Pat was like a terrier at his loping rival's heels, refusing to concede any advantage.

With 3 kilometres to go, they started to increase the pace until they were engaged in a headlong gallop to the finish line.

Dusan out-sprinted Pat by just one second. Race organisers thought they were both foolish, but Pat claimed a psychological victory.

'I thought it was stupid of Dusan,' said Pat. 'He led me by over four hours but he was prepared to run the risk of injury in a big sprint with me, just for the sake of a few seconds. He just got the shits with being challenged. He was cranky about having to run so hard just to win the stages but the battle line was drawn and that was all there was to it.'

Running, it appears, was Dusan Mravlje's life. The 44-year-old was able to train for a living, explaining he was a 'no-fighting, just running' soldier in the sports division of the Slovenian Army. He was a superb athlete and a shrewd competitor. But he was also the most unpopular runner in the history of the event. 'Everyone resented his arrogant, superstar attitude,' said Trans Am organiser Jesse Riley. 'He had no respect and would taunt his rivals in his macho way, saying things like: "I am soldier. Don't challenge soldier. You will not beat me."'

In one of the few interviews he gave to Australian television, Mravlje told the Nine Network's Nick McCallum, in broken English: 'I think all the field in this race is physically very, very strong but the winner in this race is the man who is strongest in head. I think at this stage I am maybe very, very strong. Maybe I can win this race.'

His considerable ego was dealt a blow the next day when Pat scored a breakthrough victory of twelve seconds, pouring cold water on the Slovenian's hot streak of fifteen consecutive stage wins. Pat's confidence was riding high despite a substantial overall deficit. He knew Mravlje had had several DNFs (Did Not Finish) in longer ultra races, with minor injuries forcing his withdrawal. The Slovenian was also untested in races over ten days. Pat's strategy was simple. 'While he was very fiery, I thought he was mentally fragile and I just thought if I could keep the pressure on him and force him into these stupid blitzes he might get injured and crack,' said Pat. But having challenged the soldier, Pat had to contend with the counter-attack and the daily war of body and mind that followed. His relationship with Mravlje continued to deteriorate out on the road. He seemed concerned by Pat's renewed presence. As his threat to the race leader grew over the coming days, what little conversation there had been almost evaporated into a stony silence.

Any attempts at discourse rapidly degenerated into argument as the crafty Slovenian tried to cut a deal with Pat. They were the best two runners in the field and if they both cooperated, they could sew up the top two places, he told Pat. Mravlje of course wanted first prize. Pat was insulted by the offer. 'That was a sign of weakness by him. I just wasn't going to lie down and hand it to him and let him have a picnic and enjoy it,' said Pat. 'As far as I was concerned, I had the Australian flag on my back. I was representing my country and I had to give it my best, win lose or draw.'

After winning another tense sprint finish by one second, Mravlje couldn't resist a shot at Pat. 'No injuries. I'm sorry.' Pat was seething and returned fire. 'I'll be in New York. Will you?' Their relationship went completely sour a few days later as the pair went 'hammer and tongs' running into the town of Fruita (Spanish for 'fruit'), Colorado. Race organisers had impressed local community groups with their tales of kindness and cama- raderie among runners. That illusion was quickly shattered as Pat and Mravlje elbowed and jostled each other through the finishing chute in the main street. Townsfolk were shocked to see Pat career uncontrollably into the finish line, sending the structure crashing to the ground. Organisers ignored Pat's plea to disqualify his rival, ruling it a tie.

'Pat was still angry that night,' said Gerard. 'He thought it was dirty pool and that Dusan was completely to blame. I didn't see it happen, but Pat is as competitive as anyone else out on the road and I wouldn't put it past either of them to be doing something as silly as each other at that stage.'

'It was deadly serious and we put each other through deep pain after the first week,' said Pat. 'It was like being in a war. It wasn't an enjoyable place to be. It wasn't a fun race and in fact wasn't even like a footrace. It was a matter of doing whatever you had to do to win that day. If Dusan and I could have shot each other we would have. I hated that figure in front or behind me and I'm sure he felt the same way. If we'd been allowed to don boxing gloves and punch it out at the end of every day I'm sure we'd have done it.'

Pat had forgotten how depressingly painful this race could be. He'd also forgotten how uncivilised living conditions could be. Steamy nights sleeping on hard gymnasium floors under siege from insect plagues of seemingly biblical proportions; in community centres which were sometimes infested with maggots or located next to rail shunting yards with only a bush shower to clean himself. On some nights, runners found they were better off in sleeping bags under the stars. They spent one night in a veritable ghost town, Cisco, Utah, where the local contact was listed as 'Casper the Ghost'. The only sign of life was snakes, and plenty of them. Reports of snake pits under building floorboards and the earlier sighting of a 'rattler' curled around a roadside drink bottle were enough to force Pat and other runners into their vans for the night. Even when a gift horse came his way, in the form of a four-star room with a spa and fridge full of beer no longer required by a *Sixty Minutes* camera crew, it was Gerard not Pat who benefited. Race rules required all runners to sleep in the same standard of accommodation. Pat's one-star motel room was decrepit and looked like it had been trashed by a maniac with a lousy golf swing. The infrequent 'luxury' of motel rooms saw runners forced to share rooms, but never Pat and Dusan. In halls and gyms, the pair bedded down at opposite corners.

Disrupted nights were broken by the cacophony of alarm clocks around 3.30 a.m. and occasionally a collective groan among runners at the prospect of another day of torture. 'Quite often I'd wish they'd switch off the lights so I could go back to sleep and forget about the whole thing,' said Pat. It felt like they were living the worst day of their life over and over. 'Groundhog Day' they called it, after the Bill Murray movie of the same name.

Substandard living conditions were the source of great angst between runners and the race organisers Jesse Riley and Michael Kenney—or 'Tom and Jerry' as they had been dubbed after the cartoon characters. Nightly team meetings became a hotbed of complaints. Runners felt the organisers didn't treat them with enough respect but Riley says it cut both ways.

'I could see it from their perspective because I'd run other ultra races myself,' he says. 'Everyone was always tired and in a crabby mood but I thought their attacks were unfair because we were on a really tight budget and were always trying to stem the financial bleeding. We mortgaged our future to put the event on, and as I told them, Michael and I had been putting up with shitty conditions for four years.'

With the benefit of hindsight, the onset of Pat's stress fracture, 22 days into the 64-day event, was foreseeable. Pat had felt good the previous day after leading the field through the foothills of the Rocky Mountains. Another stage record ended in another tie with Mravlje. Pat's leg problems struck out of the blue early the next day. The pain built steadily through the 67-kilometre stage, reducing him to a limp for most of the day. 'It was just shocking,' he said. 'It really gave me hell. I knew I was in trouble after the first few kilometres and after that, for want of a better word, it was just shit,' said Pat. 'Everybody started to overtake me and I found myself floundering at the back of the field.' When Pat arrived at the finish line, a curious Mravlje and Ray Bell were waiting for him but Gerard was on hand with their van so they could make a hasty getaway to the privacy of their motel room. That was typical Trans Am '95 tactics among rivals—tell 'em nothin', take 'em nowhere.

Despite constant ice therapy, the injury didn't improve in the ensuing days. There was no readily available medical treatment, but that was almost inconsequential. Stress fractures only heal through rest and that simply wasn't an option, as missing one day would result in automatic disqualification. The next three days were totally demoralising as Pat endured hour after hour of debilitating pain, dragging his leg through the Rocky Mountains in temperatures exceeding 30°C. He climbed the steepest section of the race, to an altitude of 3600 metres. But the crisis deepened when he reached the zenith. Pat's pace slowed to half his normal speed and he came within half an hour of being disqualified after nearly failing to finish one day in the stipulated time period. 'I was pretty worried about him that day because at one point it was looking touch and go as to whether he'd make the cut-off,' said Gerard. 'He put on a brave face for the *Sixty Minutes* cameras but he wore a grimace every other minute of the day.'

It was thoughts of Lisa that helped Pat fight through each hour, each day of gnawing pain. His reward was a phone call home at the end of the day and the prospect of loving, comforting words. 'Lisa's voice meant everything to me and I constantly thought about hearing her voice and Brooke's voice at my lowest moments during the day,' he said. 'I'd replay our conversation in my head the next day a million times. It was a lifeline to reality because I was living in this surreal world on the road that didn't count for anything in the real world.

'It was so, so hard to get through the days but I just had to break it down into each 2-kilometre aid station and take them one at a time. But I'd started the race just so determined to win. I was prepared to die out there rather than give in.'

Having hobbled over the Colorado Rockies, Pat suffered even more while negotiating the steep downhill on the other side.

'That was the longest day of my life,' said Pat. 'I didn't think the pain could get worse but it did with the extra jarring of running downhill. It felt like somebody had shoved an ice pick into my leg and with every step it felt like they were hitting it with a hammer. Every time my left foot hit the ground it was a painful reminder that I might not even finish this day. That constant reminder of possible failure really gets your spirit down and you're so aware that there is a long, long way to go.'

His morale was wounded even further with the withdrawal of two brothers-in-arms—Mike Sandlin and Ed Kelley. 'That was really depressing because it brought back to me the reality that you can be this far into the race and just not make it,' he said.

They were exhausted from fighting their own battles with injury. Sandlin surrendered to pain, Kelley was disqualified after missing the cut-off time by just four minutes. 'But I think Pat's injury was also a factor in their withdrawal,' said Gerard. 'To see someone as spirited as Pat so down with his problems, I think it just took the edge off them.' After four days of incapacitation, Pat had fallen more than 24 hours behind Mravlje and slipped from second to fourth. While Pat clung to the hope that he would recover and a similar fate might befall the Slovenian, Jesse Riley said he knew the Australian could not win. For Pat, it laced the event with a bitter irony. He had told Gerard only days before injury struck that he would finish the race, even if he had to do it on one leg. The Rocky Mountains were also where Pat had thought he could make a comeback and gain a winning break on Mravlje. Instead it was where the race and the dream slipped from his grasp.

By way of small compensation, fortune and favour finally smiled upon him. Melting snow from upper elevations flooded certain roads, leaving them impassable. Riley took a unilateral decision to cut 28 kilometres from the race course one day and 16 kilometres on another day. Pat was not the only competitor struggling with ailments, but certainly he was the worst. While many organisational decisions during the Trans Am were un-popular, this was indeed welcome news to all the field, affording runners a few extra hours to rest niggling injuries. It wasn't much, but small mercies were magnified in the context of the world's toughest footrace.

The shorter days certainly had the desired effect for Pat. Days of intensive acupuncture—courtesy of a therapist with one of the Japanese runners—reduced the swelling in his leg, allowing him to resume his joust at the front after a week with the back markers. While everyone else had written off Pat's chances, his optimistic side believed the coveted first prize was not yet out of his reach. He had been pushed to the edge, but had not toppled over it. His bravery had not gone unnoticed back home. Pat was being bestowed with a level of hero worship in Australia that was without precedent for him. Somehow an avalanche of mail made it through to the nomadic runner. Strangers offered advice on how to heal his injury while mothers and school-children thanked Pat for 'doing Australia proud'. The support of family, friends and compatriots imbued him with a new lease of energy. He felt mentally stronger than ever. He would fight on, feeling he was destined to finish.

When Mravlje was struck with a mystery injury just days after Pat's recovery, the Australian thought his big break had arrived. While he reclaimed more than an hour over four days, the Slovenian bounced back quicker than what Pat would have liked. Mravlje learned the hard way that a more conservative approach to the second half of the race would make him unbeatable. Under this risk-free strategy, Pat could only ever peg back minutes rather than hours on Mravlje and his dream slowly disappeared into the endless cornfields of Kansas.

Having run the previous Trans Am without organised support, Pat found it a major bonus having his cousin Gerard as his backup. He also had the assistance of a 21-year-old Japanese physiology student, Yuki, who made Pat the focus of a study. While Pat was civil towards Yuki, Pat admits he and Gerard 'fought like cats and dogs'. Jesse Riley was more blunt. 'Pat treated Gerard like dirt,' he said. Gerard knew from past experience that Pat could be moody and demanding during ultras, but the intensity of the daily racing, coupled with the emotional roller coaster they found themselves on, made for a rocky relationship.

'We had probably one or two moments a day when we lost it with each other,' said Lynn. 'Often I wanted to chuck it in but then I'd call home, talk to my family and get things off my chest. It was an experience but I wouldn't do it a second time. It was absolute frustration at times. Pat had two golden rules about food while he was running: no meat and no dairy products. But one day, in the middle of nowhere, he insisted he wanted a cheeseburger. When I couldn't deliver, he made me feel like I was the worst person in the world. That was just one example. There was a lot of other stuff and I couldn't help but take some of it to heart.'

Years on, Pat is apologetic. 'I know I was short with Gerard sometimes because I had nobody else to take it out on,' said Pat. 'I feel bad about it now. But the race got to the stage where it took all my strength and energy just to survive each day. It was so bitter and difficult. There was nothing enjoyable about the 64-day event.'

For 2000 kilometres and throughout the last month of the race, Pat grappled with the incessant dull throbbing from his stress fracture which had not healed. Pain was a constant travelling companion. Unless Mravlje succumbed to another serious injury, first place was now out of reach. He frequently struggled for motivation, questioning the logic of his endeavours. No matter how hard he ran each day, he was no closer to beating Mravlje. Pat did some serious soul-searching and even began to question his proudest trait, his refusal to never quit on anything. Sometimes, like now, that vow was a curse. As well, there were regular bouts of vomiting and nausea. But all the physical pain paled in comparison to the ache in his heart. Pat became desperately homesick for Lisa and Brooke.

'I missed Lisa more than I had ever done in my whole life and while I'd ring up most nights and it was great to talk to Lisa and hear Brooke's baby noises, the heartache would grow sharper soon after I put the phone down,' he said. 'I wore two watches most of the time so I knew the time back home and my mind drifted to thoughts of what they were doing. Lisa had an American map to chart my progress and several times a day she'd tell Brooke where I was and play videotapes of me. Lisa would send me pictures of Brooke and I used to gloat over them and show everybody. You can't imagine how much I missed them.'

Pat finally found a new reason to run in the last few weeks and rediscovered an old one. Japanese runner Nobuyaki Koyago was finishing like a steam train, taking advantage of the power vacuum at the front caused by the absence of Pat's fierce duels with Mravlje. Pat found himself in a dogfight for his new trophy, fourth place. A string of seven consecutive stage wins saw Koyago move ahead of Pat overall. 'Fourth, fifth, what's the difference if you can't win?' he thought.

'It was very hard to find motivation in the last four weeks,' he said. 'But I remember taking my shirt off one night and looking at the Australian flag on my back. I really looked at it hard and that meant a hell of a lot to me and it reminded me of all that I stood for and all that I believed this country represented. Our flag stands for the battler, for the never-say-die attitude. I thought about Gallipoli and thought about how Australians have really shone through the difficult times in life. That gave me new purpose to dig deep.'

Pat reclaimed fourth as Koyago paid the price for his gallantry and lost ground with an injury similar to Pat's. But in the final week, the Japanese made one last lion-hearted assault on the now-coveted fourth place. After another series of brutal races with Mravlje, the Australian and Slovenian declared a cease-fire in the hills of Pennsylvania, just a week before the finish. Fittingly, an old foe turned friend as they passed through Gettysburg, the scene of one of the bloodiest battlefields in American history. Mravlje helped Pat over the final days to minimise Koyago's inroads into the Australian's lead. Crewman Lynn's training as a mathematics teacher was also invaluable, as he was called upon to do regular sums to ensure the buffer was not completely eroded.

As Pat proudly carried the Australian flag through the streets of New York towards the finish line with fourth place secured, patriotism and personal pride blended with feelings of relief and disappointment. While his fellow runners revelled, Pat was deep in thought. He was at peace with himself, having conquered the demon of pain. Ultimately success was a state of mind, he thought. While the result was not what he'd envisaged, in some ways the race had been more successful than he could have dreamed. He wanted to be the best ultra runner in the world. That prize would have to wait for another day. His reward this time was more intimate—the knowledge that, in the true Anzac tradition, he was a proud Australian who would never, ever quit.

That night after the finish, all of the Trans Am runners and crew gathered for a 'celebration dinner'. They went to a restaurant named after American baseball legend Mickey Mantle. After the longest two months of their lives, the Trans Am survivors were ready to relax and reflect. The Slovenian Ambassador to the United States accompanied the winner, Dusan Mravlje, who was now a national hero back in his country. All of the finishers were presented not with prizemoney, but simply with a plaque noting their achievement. The trophies all contained numerous spelling mistakes. The most glaring was 'New Yory', instead of New York.

Years later, the disgust still lingers with Pat. 'I thought: "How poor is that?" We were prepared to lay down our lives and they couldn't even get the plaques right. We were all disappointed. Dusan and the Ambassador walked out in a rage. I've got my so-called trophy buried in a corner of my office. It isn't worth spitting on.'

7

Piece of cake, Bern!

Pat's homecoming was sweeter than any previous one. Months of pain and heartache dissolved the instant he touched Lisa and hugged his daughter Brooke at Sydney airport. He was always a winner to his family, but here was adulation on a grander scale than he could ever have imagined. As well as more than a hundred friends and acquaintances, hordes of children from Little Athletics clubs waved banners bearing inscriptions such as 'Welcome Home Pat' and 'Well done Pat, our Aussie hero'. He had to run the gamut of one of the biggest media scrums he'd ever seen and completed the circuit of national television current affairs and sport shows which began the day he finished in New York.

Pat took a complete rest from running for several weeks—his longest break in eight years. For weeks he limped around like an ageing cripple, especially after lying down for any period of time. But duty and commitment again called. He returned to labouring after just a week off and, three months later, hit the road again to fulfil a long-standing commitment to help Rotary reach its $2 million fundraising target for the Sydney Children's Hospital. Pat ran almost 100 kilometres a day every day for a week through country New South Wales. The days were long and tough. He still suffered leg pain from the healing stress fracture, a reminder of his American ordeal.

'I asked him if his leg was hurting on the second day,' said former Rotary District Governor and event organiser Alan Grady, 'and he said: "The leg's fine. I don't want you to ask me about it again." It wasn't fine, but he just wanted to block out the pain. Another day, I was standing at the top of a tough hill with refreshments. Pat said: "I wish I would have joined Lions and not Rotary." He was dead-pan, but I knew he was joking.'

As usual, the more he ran, the better he felt. Pat backed up from a hard day's running with nightly motivational speeches. The run gave renewed momentum to Rotary's fundraising and it achieved the target of $2 million in three years. The Rotary wing at the Children's Hospital was opened on 17 July 1998.

Pat's continual overt displays of patriotism also saw him chosen to be an Australia Day ambassador in 1996. The Australia Day Council was thrilled when Pat offered to do more than a fly-drive hand-shaking chest-thumping series of speeches. Again he wanted to let his feet do most of the talking. He proposed a ten-day 1100-kilometre goodwill mission from Sydney to Tweed Heads on the Queensland–New South Wales border. He left on 14 January and stopped at more than a dozen regional communities where he spoke about the Trans America runs, his other achievements and how privileged he had been to carry the Australian flag with him. 'It was his idea to talk to people all along the way,' said Australia Day Committee chairman John Trevillian. 'He had such a natural enthusiasm about life, but especially about his running and Australia. He wanted to combine national spirit with the message of achievement. I was impressed with the energy he showed in all the talks he gave at country towns along the coast. He speaks in common language and people really related to that.'

But charity runs were never far from Pat's agenda. He agreed to tackle the world vertical mile record to raise funds for the Autism Association of New South Wales. The stairwell of the tallest building in the Southern Hemisphere, Sydney's Centrepoint Tower—a steep, steamy and claustrophobic location—was not every runner's idea of a challenge. But on 28 May 1996, Pat spent five hours entombed in the concrete cavern. He made 26 lung-busting, muscle-burning trips up the 1350-step structure—a total of 33 382 stairs. While he was a strong hill-runner, the difficulty and intensity of this endeavour surprised him. 'My legs began to burn after a while, especially my hamstrings and calves,' he said. 'It was hard work because the stairs in the tower zig-zag, so I became a bit dizzy and disoriented towards the end.'

Pat missed his goal of the world vertical mile record by 22 minutes, but his time of two hours, two minutes and 55 seconds was the best attempt ever made by an Australian stair climber. He also failed to reach his monetary target. Instead of $100 000, he only raised $10 000. But he was still a mile-high hero to all who witnessed the event, battling heat and humidity that was so intense Pat was forced to change his sweat-drenched t-shirt six times. Despite regular snacks of bananas and sports drinks, he lost more than two litres in body fluid and 2 kilograms in weight. Friends say he looked as exhausted at the end of the event as they'd ever seen him. He spent almost half an hour soaking in a spa bath, which had been set up by the event sponsor Sundance Spas. He recovered quickly after the run but, not surprisingly, had difficulty walking up and down any stairs for a week afterwards.

While the Trans America race had once again been consigned to the history books, Pat linked up with some of his former rivals for the 100 kilometre Trailwalker Run in Hong Kong in November 1996—the toughest team race in the world over that distance. The event began as a training exercise for the local Gurkha army regiment but had expanded to become a massive fundraising venture for the Hong Kong branch of the charity Oxfam. Teams paid a race entry fee and were expected to seek corporate backing. It had proved a major fundraiser with millions of dollars donated to the world's needy: projects included the construction or refurbishment of nearly 300 schools in Nepal; the resettlement of 300 000 people in Sudan; teaching women literacy skills in Bangladesh. Pat formed part of a four-man team with Ray Bell, Mike Sandlin and Nobuyaki Koyago. The team ran under the banner of the company of Trans Am sponsor Moonbat. Mr Okada had invited the athletes to run and, as usual, had paid all their expenses. Despite taking an early lead, the team's superior speed and fitness were no match for the guile, experience and mountain-climbing ability over rugged terrain of the Gurkhas. Their teams finished first and second with Pat's Moonbat team 20 minutes behind.

But all of his 1996 events paled into insignificance compared with the final test for the year. Like a mother after childbirth, his body quickly forgot the pain from the previous encounter and steeled itself for the next event. Never had Pat challenged nature and one of her most hostile environments as he was about to. Ron Grant's 1986 record for crossing the harshest piece of country in Australia, the Simpson Desert, had been like a magnet on the record books for Pat.

The bread vendor from Caboolture in Queensland had been the first man ever to run across the Simpson. His maiden crossing was completed in the autumn of 1981 in four days, eleven hours and 44 minutes. Always keen to notch up firsts, and never one to shirk a challenge, Grant went back in January 1985. In temperatures that averaged 25°C higher than in 1981, he slashed an astonishing fourteen hours off his own record to set a new benchmark of three days, seventeen hours and 52 minutes.

In the first-ever race across the desert against Tony Rafferty—a nationally publicised event, Grant set a new record, defying ground temperatures of 65°C to win the race in a time of three days, seventeen hours, 52 minutes and eighteen seconds—two hours and 43 minutes inside his old record. Upon completion, an exhausted Grant said anyone who tried to break his record was 'stupid'.

When Pat decided to have a shot at Grant's record, he rang him at his Caboolture home. They had raced several times when Grant was in the twilight of his career and Pat in the dawn of his, but there was no deep-seated rivalry. They were kindred souls with a respect and understanding for each other's feats. Pat asked Grant for any advice on tackling the Simpson. Grant warned him about the totally unforgiving nature of the heat and suggested he be well-prepared. But Pat admits this 'went in one ear and out the other'. Grant also cautioned him: 'I will only acknowledge my record as being beaten if you run the Simpson at the same time of the year that I did.'

• • •

Pat stared into the redness. The flames danced and jumped erratically. He could feel the heat on his face. It was comforting amidst the cold, dusty winds that had greeted their arrival at base camp. From this distance, it was a pleasant companion. Yet, strangely, he yearned for greater discomfort from the fire, to experience more of its intensity.

'Penny for your thoughts,' came a voice.

Pat's eyes remained transfixed by the glow. 'I'm wondering how close I can get to it before it burns me.' His voice drifted off. His thoughts wandered to the desert and the challenge it would present.

Simpson Desert sunrises take the breath away. The rich colours spread across and above the horizon with the passing minutes, as the earth strokes life into a new day's canvas. Pat had slept fitfully. By the time they had flown in and completed the five-hour drive to Alka Seltzer bore near the South Australian–Northern Territory border, established their primitive camp and unwound from the journey, it was almost 1.00 a.m. before Pat and his entourage of twelve crawled into their bedding, such as it was—plastic ground sheets, thin foam mattresses and light sleeping bags. As Pat ambled around the camp collecting his thoughts and his running gear, he became aware of his final conscious thoughts as he'd lapsed into slumber last night: 'Is this the last run I'll ever do? Is this where it all ends?' He'd stared at the stars, more mindful than at any stage in his life of his mortality. He'd prayed and drifted off to sleep.

It was 27°C and Pat was shivering. It was after 6.00 a.m. and he was wearing a tracksuit in the middle of summer in the hottest place in Australia and still couldn't get warm. He had risen early for a breakfast of potatoes and bananas—good energy food. The starting line was crude—paper towel laid across the sand. '10, 9, 8, 7, 6, 5, 4, 3, 2, 1, Go.' The first steps. Relief. Pat knew exactly what lay ahead—at least geographically. The arid land-scape was interspersed with 1162 sand hills, spread over 379 kilometres. Pat was to run the seismic survey track known as the French Line, plotted by a group of seismologists in the 1960s. It was the shortest reliable route east across the Simpson to Poeppel Corner, but had been poorly maintained over the years since Reginald Sprigg first surveyed it in 1963 for a French petroleum company. However, the original survey pegs still stood and would be Pat's guideposts. After a 35-kilometre trek around Lake Poeppel, it was then just a matter of following the QAA Line for another 162 kilometres through to the finish line at the famous Birdsville Hotel.

Starting also helped Pat to at last clear his head and allow him to focus on the brutal job ahead. He was satisfied with his training and preparation for the Simpson Desert Challenge. After running for the last 43 days in the 1995 Trans America race with a stress fracture in his lower leg, he had heightened confidence in his tolerance to that constant companion, pain, as well as newfound respect for his body's capabilities. In the preceding months he'd trained on the sand hills at Botany, in Sydney, and ventured out for some weekend runs in the middle of the day, with temperatures in the low thirties—not as many as he would have liked, but surely sufficient to assist in a quick adjustment to the climate and terrain and improve the odds of breaking the record. But elder brother Bernie wasn't so sure. 'I knew he hadn't prepared well for it, I just knew it deep down,' he says. 'But Pat convinced me otherwise.' Those arguments, so persuasively pro-nounced to a concerned older brother included the following: it had been a decade since Ron Grant set the record and there had been numerous advances in science since then; Pat was using some of the crew who had guided Tony Rafferty across the desert and had the benefit of their experience; and Pat was younger than Grant (not always an advantage in ultra running, although in ten years in the game Pat had proved otherwise).

Bernie was a reluctant crew manager. He hated the heat, any heat—suffered acutely in it—but knew this was one run where Pat would need all his emotional support and experience. He grasped the enormity of the challenge and had his usual sage advice. 'Forget about your Trans America runs and everything else you have done. This will be the toughest endurance feat that you've ever embarked upon.' He received a typically cheeky response from his little brother. 'Piece of cake, Bern!'

As he embarked on another remarkable journey on 12 December 1996, Pat pondered over the unnecessary self-imposed pressure in the weeks counting down to the Simpson run. There was pressure too on wife Lisa. He reflected on how he had sacrificed time with his 22-month-old daughter Brooke. Endless hours spent away from his family on lonely trails, toughening his body and mind for this event. He thought of Lisa's endless supply of patience, support and love. But Pat knew this was another mountain that had to be conquered in his attempt to prove himself the best long-distance runner in the world.

'I was so determined to achieve what I'd set out to do and break the record by seventeen hours. I felt it was a make or break race for me, but then I think they're all like that,' he said. 'A different person might think, "I'll give this a shot and see what happens." Not me. I believe in the saying that you're only as good as your last achievement. That's how I think people will judge me—they'll think I'm no good if I don't succeed. I can't allow myself to fail, not once.'

Heat, not distance, was always going to be the major factor for Pat, and it came into play sooner than anyone expected. By 10.00 a.m.—less than four hours into a four-day event—the mercury had climbed to nearly 50°C. The ground temperature was a sizzling 65°C and Pat's campaign was in trouble. He had misjudged his early pace in the stifling conditions. Experience had told him to hold back. Despite his apparent restraint, he still went out too hard, burning through too much of his body fuel—glycogen—for the conditions. He simply underestimated the effect of such extreme heat on the human body while exercising.

Pat was well prepared in other respects. As well as being layered with SPF 15 sunscreen, he wore desert garb—a cap with a flap at the back to protect his neck from ultra-violet rays, a long-sleeved top and boxer-style shorts to prevent sunstroke. The fabric was supposed to be Pat's secret weapon. It was a special cloth called 'Sportwool' which had been developed by the CSIRO in conjunction with the Australian Wool Secretariat, designed to assist in the convective cooling of an athlete involved in endurance sport. It allowed his skin to breathe and body heat to escape—essential for running in hot climates. Pat was the first to trial the fabric outside a laboratory.

Every member of the crew had been aware of the importance of maintaining Pat's fluid levels. But the heat was an insidious enemy. While its presence was apparent to all, its life-threatening consequences came, like a Stealth bomber, silently under the human radar. Bernie noticed after the first two hours that Pat was taking no more than a few sips from his water bottle and then disposing of the rest into the red sand. 'I thought I was drinking enough, but obviously I wasn't,' he said. 'I didn't have the discipline to just keep pouring the drinks down my throat until I felt sick.'

Also problematic was the issue of chilling drinks. Ice was a rare and precious commodity in outback Australia in summer. The support vehicles had been unable to purchase enough for the journey. As well, their portable fridges proved inefficient due to constant opening—drinks were barely cooled when they were produced and quickly got warmer once exposed to the sun. All fluid lost its appeal for Pat once invaded by the heat.

Just 30 kilometres into the 379-kilometre event, Pat was suffering the early effects of dehydration. His pace had slowed noticeably—instead of running like a champion athlete he looked like a weekend jogger. He found it difficult to swallow and even breathing became a chore.

'Every inch of my body progressively began to feel uncomfortable and then slowly more painful,' he said. 'I went from feeling fit and strong to feeling terrible in a fairly short space of time. It felt like the rest of my body was being deprived of blood and oxygen just to supply my legs. My heart began to ache, so did my head and brain. My tongue and throat swelled up and it became hard to digest anything. I was getting headaches from my brain more or less drying out.'

The other, even more paralysing, problem was the cramps in Pat's muscles. The major muscle groups in his legs—calves, quadriceps and hamstrings—were in uncontrollable spasms. Their erratic pulsation would have been a comical sight had the situation not been so dire. Every muscle, it seemed, was screaming in protest at Pat's exertion. It looked to him as if they were trying to burst through his flesh. The pain—or so it seemed at the time—was worse than running with the stress fracture across America. In a scene reminiscent of the Sigourney Weaver science fiction movie thriller *Alien*, Pat felt like 'other forces were controlling my body'.

'Something was going on that was like nothing I'd ever experienced before and it was pretty freaky,' he said. 'It was a shock to the system. I felt helpless. I had no control over what was happening to my body. There was a moment when I thought I was really going to die. I realised why so many others had died out there.'

The cramps were triggered by Pat's inability to correct the fluid loss and imbalance in electrolyte (body salt) levels in his body. That imbalance arises when severe demands are placed on the body, especially in the heat. (The onset of cramps in climates of extreme heat is also known as 'Stokers' Cramps', so-called by nineteenth century physicians because it was first noticed that men who stoked the fires that kept factory machinery alive suffered debilitating muscle spasms.)

A similar feeling of helplessness descended upon Pat's crew.

As well intentioned and qualified as they were in their own fields of endeavour, there was very little medical expertise among the group. Some members held first aid certificates from years long past, but no one was able to provide an adequate explanation or solution to Pat's predicament. He tried several times to walk the cramps out, but any exertion drew resistance from his shattered body. When the pain seemed unbearable, he reassured himself with positive statements and used a mantra that had helped him through other tough times: 'I've never quit, I've never quit.'

Rest and massage were the only answers, but the relief they provided was negligible—certainly insufficient to embolden most of the crew with confidence in his ability to finish, let alone break the record. As Pat lay writhing on the ground, no one could recall seeing a human being in such agony. The raw emotion was graphically captured by a Channel Nine camera crew and later shown on *A Current Affair*. They had been invited to document the triumph, but suddenly their presence was an unwanted intrusion.

While it may have started as just another story to the camera crew, and just another outback job to the support crew, that had changed. Gradually, as they witnessed Pat endure such physical and mental torture, their involvement and emotional stake began to increase. 'This is ridiculous. Call it off, he can't take any more,' demanded cameraman Drew Benjamin, confronting tour leader John Deckert. Deckert was a farmer from Nhill, Victoria, who'd had a long-time love affair with the outback. He and wife Bev specialised in Simpson Desert four-wheel-drive tours. They were contracted to provide vehicles, drivers and supplies.

'I refused to call it off,' said Deckert, ' because I was hired by Pat to get him to Birdsville. I wasn't there to tell him he couldn't run. I knew from crewing for Tony Rafferty that men of this incredible will and spirit couldn't be dissuaded from the task, no matter how gruelling it seemed. Don't get me wrong; I would have done anything in my power to make sure he finished. Everyone there would have. Pat inspired and commanded that much respect from everyone for all sorts of reasons. More than anything, it was the effort he was putting in. You could tell he was giving it absolutely everything he had to give. But it was also his attitude—his mental attitude, his personal attitude and his moral standards—which made Pat Farmer even more admirable.'

'I've really done it this time haven't I?' Pat looked and sounded like a man who had been to war. Bernie and Annette had seen their brother endure pain previously, but this was a side of the pain barrier they'd never been to. As always, Bernie tried to keep his composure and his sense of humour. 'You bastard, I know you have,' says Bernie. As a brother, friend, minder and occasional fitness adviser, he had a duty to see Pat through the ordeal.

'I've seen him beaten up on runs but never as bad as this,' said Bernie. It was a given that when you're running in the heat of the desert, you'll encounter pain, but I was honestly scared. We were out of our league and we were so far from help it wasn't funny. We were making it up as we went along, but while I was fast running out of ideas, I wasn't going to panic and pull him out prematurely. I would have known at what point it got dangerous and I somehow felt we hadn't quite reached that point.'

With the original day one target revised downwards from 140 kilometres to 100 kilometres, Pat was still a long way behind schedule. He had run just 60 kilometres in sixteen hours and needed to cover another 40 kilometres before the end of the first day to give himself even a remote shot at his three-day goal. Despite Pat's dilapidated state, Bernie realised they must take advantage of the night. While the crew slept, they quietly decamped, armed with just a flashlight and two water bottles. At first Pat staggered through the sand. His muscles were still shell-shocked from dehydration despite three hours of rest and copious amounts of fluid, some fruit and other small snacks. It was just as important, thought Bernie, to get Pat's mind moving as well as his muscles. Distract it, take the focus away from the physical pain, and concentrate the athlete's thoughts on more pleasant memories. It was a technique they'd used with good success in many ultra marathons and one commonly used by long-distance athletes. For Pat there was one place in his consciousness that offered constant comfort—his childhood.

As Pat and Bernie struggled down that dark, sandy desert track in the most inhospitable of environments, they looked to the stars—the same stars that a patient and devoted Frank Farmer had used as the subject of astronomy lessons to his attentive tribe years before. It was elementary for the younger children but became more detailed as they grew older and wiser. They were the same stars that provided solace for the Farmer children whenever they escaped from their city environs into the country to go fishing and shooting. The deep, cold waters surrounding the old whaling village of Bermagui, south of Sydney, were fertile grounds for all manner of marine life. Frank had several rules for fishing. No unnecessary talking and one lure per trip. If you surrendered it to the ocean or its inhabitants, that was your bad luck. And there were plenty of chances to do that, with sharks and stingrays hunting for a free feed.

They made their own fun. There was always a game of ten-pin bowling to be had. With no bowling alley for miles and miles, the entire family would forage for honeydew melons that grew wild near the coast. The less ripe they were, the better they rolled. More durable too. Sticks and tree limbs for pins. Low tide was the perfect time to play—the sand, massaged into a smooth crease-free surface by the gentle withdrawal of the ocean, was as reliable to a child as any polished wooden floor. Shame about the slope, but they soon learned to compensate for it. They would cheer each strike with youthful exuberance—willing each other's melons to miss the thin, crooked targets. They barracked, too, for shapes out to sea—just below the horizon they could distinguish the spinnakers of the Sydney to Hobart fleet as it whipped down the coast. Gleaming craft with wind and hope filling their sails. Men with stories to tell on the way and more to tell upon their return. Pat would gaze at the boats: the adventure of tackling the elements appealed to him. Through the eyes of a child, these things are bliss. In the mind of an exhausted runner, these memories are a powerful mental tool.

Bernie paused the grainy reminiscences rolling through his head to take stock of the present. A chilling thought interrupted the indulgence. 'I hope we're going the right way!' he thought. He wondered if they had missed a turn or fork in the desert track. Its definition was less pronounced under the ambient light of the half-moon and the narrow band of torchlight. With sudden acuteness, his mind began to focus on the possible outcomes of that mistake. With just one litre of water between two men and no food, the relentless heat of another day would show them no mercy and would grind them to a limp, fluid-starved state within hours. Bernie was thankful for their slow progress, deducing that if they were separated from the crew, they might not be too far apart and rescue would come sooner rather than later. Hopefully. He kept his fears private, not wishing to burden Pat with any more concerns. But the same scenario had occurred to Pat.

Separately, reluctantly, their minds were cast back to pre-race warnings. Fifteen people had died trying to cross the Simpson Desert. Authorities had told them of two recent deaths, in a bid to either dissuade or disturb them sufficiently to reconsider. One was a trekker who tried to walk across the desert. He went missing after a week and was never seen or heard from after that. The park ranger found some of his gear and notepad weeks later. Four years on they found a set of keys, but that was all.

The other was a motorbike rider traversing the desert with two mates. They took some precautions with water bottles and tubes fed through their helmets. But one rider failed to listen to his body. His fluid consumption couldn't keep pace with his soaring body temperature. He literally cooked in his suit and collapsed off his bike after his brain shut down. One friend stayed with him as he lay unconscious, while another rode for help to a station 50 kilometres away. The Royal Flying Doctor Service was called. Help arrived too late. Aborigines called the Simpson Desert 'land of death, home of evil spirits'. Neither Pat nor Bernie could escape all these chilling thoughts as they struggled from one sandy peak to another.

There were many nervous glances over their shoulders in the small hours of 13 December. When finally the tiny lights of the four-wheel drive vehicles pierced the distant darkness, they relaxed. Their spirits and tempo were lifted as the three vehicles came past them. The grind of the engines in low gear, usually the only accompanying background noise, was imperceptible below the horn tooting and cheering from the crews. As the sun rose to renew its assault on the desert challenger, Pat was filled with new hope, not old dread. The walk became a slow jog. 'It was a brand new day and a brand new challenge,' he said.

As the clock ticked over the 24-hour mark, Bernie's eyes shot to the speedometer. The revised first-day target was 100 kilometres. Pat's achievement was 100.2 kilometres. He had 200 metres in the bank—about two minutes. 'Despite the fact it was so fine, I honestly knew at that point we were back in with a chance at breaking the record,' says Bernie. 'If it was going to go off the rails—and it very nearly did—it was going to go off the first day. I just felt it was never going to get any worse than it had.'

But Pat's nemesis, the heat, was just as hostile on day two. By midday it hovered around 52°C. By now his body was slowly acclimatising. The crippling muscle cramps had eased and the sharp, stabbing pain that permeated his muscles had passed. It was substituted by a dull muscular ache. But Pat felt as if he was in a daze. He thought maybe he was desensitised to the pain. Mentally he had adjusted to the threshold and he was now coping better. Curiously, without the pain on which to focus, his awareness of other extraneous factors was heightened. Other things were 'making life hell'—like the flies. Every time he opened his mouth, they were hovering. The great Australian salute was in vain; the exodus of one squadron of insects merely cleared a runway for a new wave. In the end, he covered his hat with netting and accepted them as nature's inevitable passengers.

The sand, too, was becoming more of a factor. Baked dry by the extreme heat, it was soft and fine with none of the density and texture of beach sand—more like talcum powder. It made some tracks almost impassable to traffic, bogging Pat's support vehicles on several occasions. Pat noticed how little it supported his feet upon contact, especially when he tackled the dunes which, while decreasing in frequency, were increasing in height and steepness. As he leaned into the red slope, it felt like his shoes were slipping backwards with each step. The sand seemed like a treadmill beneath him, stopping his progress. He feared his crew would think he was not trying, but Pat was sure he was giving out more effort than at any previous stage. At times, he pushed his hands down on to his knees in an attempt to acquire greater traction. The sand was irritating. It seemed to hang in the air, filling his mouth and his lungs with each gasping breath. Protective covers stopped it from filling his shoes, but it still gathered in a fine layer on his clothes, exposed skin, the openings of his drink bottles and his food—on his pillow when he rested. The basic pleasures of life, such as eating, drinking and sleeping—the only things that could make him feel human—were less pleasurable.

Despite the existence of, and its tolerance to, extreme climatic conditions, the Simpson Desert is a fragile eco-system that demands respect. By now the crews had developed a system where one vehicle leapfrogged the other two support crews to establish the next rest stop. When Annette felt a call of nature, she discreetly excused herself from the crew armed with toilet paper and a box of matches. They were under instructions from the park ranger to burn their toilet paper after use (it can take decades to decompose). Having completed the task next to a small dry shrub, she promptly proceeded to put the matches to use. Just as the paper ignited, an ill-timed gust of wind caught the flammable material and began to disperse it. With little time to react Annette aimed her foot at a piece of evasive glowing tissue. It moved mid-strike and instinctively her foot followed, landing in what could only be delicately described as 'unfinished business'. Her embarrassment was heightened when she realised she was wearing her only pair of joggers. Annette slunk back to the four-wheel-drive having been only moderately successful at scraping her shoe clean. She managed to secrete the offensive shoes in a plastic bag and confided to Bernie brief details of the episode. At the first opportunity, he betrayed that confidence. While the levity was timely for the rest of the crew, Annette wished it were at someone else's expense.

Back on the track, Pat was making few inroads into the schedule. Since his early morning comeback, he had held his own with the clock, but failed to get in front of it. Crew members again began to have doubts about Pat's ability to beat the record. Bernie and Annette remained as faithful as ever. Among the doubters was Deckert. In a private moment, he seriously began questioning Pat's prospects to wife Bev. 'He'll never do it,' he said. But Bev's respect for and belief in a young man chasing a dream that seemed ludicrous and far-fetched to others had quickly grown to unshakeable limits. Their acquaintance could be measured more accurately in hours rather than days, but it didn't matter. Her solidarity with Pat was linked in part to the loss of her son Glen, at the age of 16, in a traffic accident five years earlier and an unfulfilled longing that he might have lived longer so she could help him achieve his dreams. She refused to tolerate such negative talk. 'He can do it and he will do it. It's not up to us to say he can't,' she told Deckert.

'I could just see Pat was a super man,' she later revealed. 'By that I mean a super, super athlete, the type that you rarely see. I just felt that, despite his condition, he was so fit and had such a great mental attitude that he would prevail. He had that much faith in himself, even at the lowest point, that I couldn't help but believe in him.'

Bernie and Annette tried to shield Pat from any negativity. Inevitably, some of it filtered through and in his fragile state that upset him. 'I began to worry what members of my crew were saying about me, as I always do,' he said. 'I didn't need people quitting on me. If anyone was going to quit it was up to me, not them. I needed all of my crew to believe in me. I needed them to believe I could pull a rabbit out of a hat.'

Pat became more conscious of the need to refresh his mask of self-control and self-belief. He worked more deliberately and purposely towards putting on a 'brave front'. By fooling them, he believed he was also helping to deceive his own mind and body. This was another exercise in distraction—something else to focus on rather than internalise his pain. At least it helped his mind escape from the moment.

While Pat is a religious man, he never expected to see an angel in the desert. Much less a moustached one in a khaki uniform in a four-wheel-drive. Don Rowlands, the Ranger-in-Charge of the Queensland section of the Simpson Desert, has an affinity with the desert that matches his respect for its wild frontier qualities. When Pat's crew radioed through a wish list, Rowlands appreciated the psychological value of little luxuries in such harsh conditions. When he swung open the door to his portable fridge, Pat and his crew thought Ranger Rowlands must truly have been heaven-sent. It was filled with chilled soda water, lemon squash, beer and ice-blocks. Pat felt that surely his luck had changed. He grabbed a handful of ice-cubes, crunched them and allowed the icy granules to melt in his mouth. Cold beer never, ever tasted so good. It was a welcome change from the fruit, yoghurt, rice custard and sports drinks that had replenished him to this point.

'In fact I seriously pinched myself for fear that it was a mirage,' he said. 'I could not believe it. There was this fridge stocked with all sorts of goodies. It was like a corner shop in the middle of nowhere. That did several things for me. Physically it helped rehydrate me. Mentally it lifted my spirits enormously and I started thinking: "If he's driven out from Birdsville to meet us here, the finish can't be too far away." From then on things clicked. I got my head together.'

Mercy dashes were not uncommon for Rowlands. While Pat's was one of the most dramatic situations, more than three years later Rowlands answered another important SOS. He drove six hours into the Northern Territory desert to deliver 24 rolls of toilet paper to stricken camel trekkers. They were still over

100 kilometres from Birdsville and suffering from diarrhoea. Rowlands' mission was equally appreciated then.

After resting to allow the worst heat to pass, Pat found fresh legs and even acquired some additional running company, with Rowlands jogging alongside him for short distances, until his heavy work boots slowed him down. The next stage, the run around Poeppel Corner, was of great strategic importance. It had taken Grant more than fourteen hours to travel around the lake. The magnification of the sun on the flat white saltpans made this one of the hottest places in Australia and Bernie realised if they could time the run around the lake and avoid tackling it in the middle of the day, they could steal back valuable time. It meant slowing Pat's progress, but the timing was perfect, as they approached it late in the day.

The break allowed the crew a longer than usual break for dinner. Meals were always basic and there was nothing *cordon bleu* about this one—cold soup straight from the can. But surprisingly, it was a winner. 'The soup tasted fantastic, it was just what we wanted, funnily enough,' said Bernie. 'I guess we wouldn't have wanted hot soup in the desert. We felt it was like Christmas. We all raved about how good it was. If your wife served it up to you at home, you'd throw it back at her, but it's funny how you adjust your standards when dealing with adversity.'

Pat ran through most of the night, covering the flat 38-kilometre flat section around Lake Poeppel in good time. He made up four hours and was running 'like a steam train'. But by this time there was another drama unfolding. Bernie had begun showing signs of advanced dehydration. For the past two days, his focus had, inevitably and unselfishly, been directly on Pat. Unfortunately he had done little to accommodate his own needs. His level of exertion had been modest compared to his brother's but he had spent many hours absorbing the full impact of the sun alongside Pat, with limited fluid intake—all this while wearing fleecy-lined track suit pants. 'I figured it was already hot so what's a few extra degrees,' Bernie said. 'I was worried about sunburn on my legs and didn't want the hassle of constantly applying sunscreen and having it quickly layered and gritted with sand.'

After two days of gradually depriving himself of vital fluid, he began hallucinating. Others thought he was joking at first when he began talking about naked women off in the distance—another mind game for the men, thought Annette. But as his insistence grew—'I'm telling you, they're not trees up ahead. They're naked women, must be 30 or 40 of them'—so, appropriately, did his sister's concerns. When his motor functions began to disintegrate to the point where he was staggering, Annette adopted her most authoritative manner and ordered him to rest in the vehicle. Even in a state of delirium, Bernie was not an easy man to persuade. When they finally lured him out of the sun, they had to lock the vehicle's doors.

Annette suddenly felt more vulnerable and frightened than she had at any other stage of the journey. She had sensed danger before leaving the comfort of her Mittagong home, perhaps more than her brothers. She had updated her will, ensured her affairs were in order and said slightly more emotional goodbyes than usual to her family. With her heroes and protectors both hovering near physical shutdown, she had a heightened awareness of the perils of their exploit. But surrender—be it physical, mental or emotional—was totally foreign to the Farmer family. While her best sporting days were behind her and she was not in great physical condition, Pat was now in almost constant need of company. She walked with him, handing him snacks and drinks. She also nourished his spirit with words of strength and support. They talked—of the elation of finishing, of home life, of missing their families, of past runs and, of course, of childhood—endless hours watching their father tinker in his shed, passing tools and passing the time with the man they also called their best friend. Slowly, the sandy red kilometres ticked by.

When morning broke, Bernie was again coherent and had made a good recovery. Despite Pat's supreme overnight effort, the record was still a line-ball call. Ranger Rowlands returned with two more angelic supporters—wife Lynnette and son Ashley. The timely injection of their energy, enthusiasm and company on the final day, with Birdsville still 80 kilometres away, boosted everyone's flagging spirits. Finishing now was attainable but there was much less certainty about the Grant record. Pat's muscles were in an advanced state of fatigue, exacerbated by sleep deprivation. They had been working on autopilot for many kilometres and would continue to do so. The ability to continue running and override the exhaustion was driven by a small section of the brain that communicated to Pat's lethargic muscles hidden reserves of 'mind power'. The supply and value of this fuel had in the past been inexhaustible, its limits indeterminate. Pat knew he had come close in the past to tapping the bottom of the well. He was about to find out how deep that pool really was.

By Birdsville standards—where hardly anyone exerted themselves for the heck of it, especially in summer—Lynette and Ashley were keen athletes. Forty-three-year-old Lynette was a compact 56 kilograms; Ashley was 17 and lean-framed. While neither had ever covered more than 5 kilometres in a single training session, limits of endurance had to be cast aside in deference to the extent of Pat's already extraordinary achievement. There was no room for their own self-doubts. One final day of supreme effort was required from all; it was a chance to participate in an historic achievement and mother and son were willing to step up and be counted. Pat abandoned his walking pace and again managed a respectable jog.

'With fresh legs to push me along, it took my mind off the sheer exhaustion I was feeling at this point,' says Pat. 'Lynette was very encouraging and a strong runner. We kept the pace moving along. I'm sure she ran way beyond herself just to keep me going. And here was this schoolkid looking up to me like I was something special and that gave me a huge lift. You see, with the physical and emotional depths I had encountered, and with the record looking doubtful, I had felt at various times over the past two days like I was an embarrassment to everyone. But with Ashley there, I thought: "This kid doesn't know me but what

I'm doing really means something to him, I've got to impress him." He told me he wanted to be a runner and I began offering him advice about the rewards of hard work and achievement and how to stay motivated about a passion such as running. With such a positive thing to focus on and talk about, it was another helpful diversion.'

Despite another merciless 52°C day descending upon them, the trio made good progress. But each dune seemed to require extreme exertion and Pat wondered after each one whether he could summon another similar effort. There was now more distance between the peaks—up to a kilometre at times—but each ridge seemed to be steeper and higher than the last. Up to 40 metres in height and a gradient of more than 50 degrees. Pat could sense them building to a crescendo. Somewhere ahead, 30 kilometres from Birdsville, lay Big Red, a dune notorious among desert trekkers. He became anxious about it and concerned about the effort it would take to conquer it and how much it would take out of him. The margin for error and the line between success and failure were ever diminishing. A record that had throughout the entire preparation been measured in days and hours was now an equation of far finer parts. For the first time, Pat demanded to know the exact detail of the Grant record—in minutes and seconds. He didn't want to contemplate that it could come to that, but quietly feared it might.

Bernie resumed his role of tactician, constantly seeking ideas to keep Pat moving and motivated. There was a nearby water hole, not too far off the track, which Deckert suggested might provide some relief and refreshment. Eyre Creek sat in a flood-plain that often filled to the brim in the annual wet season. At the end of typically arid winters and springs, the creek dried out, leaving mere remnants of the last big April rains. This time, just a few waist-deep puddles had survived months of evaporation, protected only by large coolabah trees that fringed the creek. Bernie had reservations about the value of the detour, but did a reconnaissance.

He was initially repulsed by its grey muddy waters—this was no Surfers Paradise, he thought to himself—but agreed it was worth a risk. Pat took more convincing, fearful that an unscheduled fifteen-minute break could be the cruel difference between success and failure. He was also worried that the indulgence might weaken his concentration for the final homeward drive and diminish his barrier of fortitude. But the temptation was too great. He plunged into the cool waters fully clothed. A broad smile creased his face as he emerged from the water. Its soothing properties seemed to penetrate through his leathery sun-parched skin to his aching muscles. It was a true oasis in the most hostile of deserts. Bernie joined him. They felt yabbies biting their toes, but barely flinched.

Those muddy waters proved to be a fountain of youth for Pat. As he trotted back towards the main track with some of the old bounce back in his stride, Pat hesitated, unsure of his bearings and shouted for directions. Leigh Goldsmith, who had been recruited from the Northern Territory by Deckert to pilot the third vehicle, ambled after him and steered him back on course.

'Thanks very much, see you down the track,' enthused Pat. His energy and spirit amazed the hard-bitten Territorian. There was excitement in Pat's voice. He seemed thrilled to be running again—after two and a half days of torturous exertion. To Goldsmith it seemed incomprehensible. As Pat jogged away, Goldsmith couldn't control himself. The emotional roller coaster had taken its toll on all of Pat's support crew and the Territorian was no exception. He cried. Just a few tears at the boundless courage and grit of one man in pursuit of a dream. It was a vulnerability he didn't expect to encounter. He later shared the event with the Deckerts. The outburst of emotion had surprised him. It astounded them.

In the darkness, Big Red was nothing more than an ominous outline—four storeys high and one of nature's proudest creations in this showpiece desert. The conquest of Big Red was significant because it was the most taxing of the 1162 sand hills Pat had encountered; it was the Mount Everest of the event due to its height and angle (somewhere between 60 and 65 degrees). It also marked the end of the desert—the last great dune. Lynette could sense Pat's anxiety as they approached it. He went quiet and stopped talking, as it loomed larger. She understood and was happy to conserve her breath and energy.

Pat's pace was livelier as they neared the base, and he moved several metres in front of her. He surged at the base, arms and legs pumping furiously. He put his head down and leaned into the slope until he looked to be doubled over. Pat quickly went into oxygen debt. His breathing became exaggerated as his lungs screamed for more air. The thin line signifying the summit was out of Pat's vision . . . he simply buried himself into the mountain of red sand. He focused on one foot strike, then another, then another. The motion was frantic compared to the last few hours. Only one minute of complete exertion was required. Pat dug deep—deeper than he had for a long time. His shoes sank into the red sand that seemed to swallow each step before it was able to take grip and provide the drive for the next one. Just a few metres more, he told himself, then you can rest. The seconds dragged. He sneaked a desperate look for the peak. Finally it was there within his narrowed vision. His running form had been abandoned as he reached for the top. The final few strides felt like they had been taken in slow motion. He doubled over in pain as he reached the summit. 'I can't describe how good it felt to reach the top. I was so relieved that I had gone through another barrier of pain. I really felt that the record was now that much closer,' he said.

The handful of lights in Birdsville combined to form one glowing beacon. He tried to picture the finish and imagine the feeling of lying down and not having to get up. It was after midnight and he doubted whether too many townsfolk would disturb their precious sleep to greet some crazy runner. As he rounded a bend, he could see that the gloomy track ahead was punctuated by light. Finally the desert was behind him, giving way to a gently undulating gibber plain.

Pat had to negotiate 30 kilometres through Sturt's Stony Desert (named after explorer Charles Sturt) on the final run home. It is a bumpy surface covered with a dense pavement of shimmering stones, the remains of weathered rock that have been slowly eroded by wind, water and time. The stones—varying in size from marbles to eggs—have a polished surface and are coated with a 'desert varnish' of silica, iron and manganese.

Pat's scrambled brain took several minutes to deduce that the lights were car lights. As he neared, he could distinguish small, silhouetted figures and hear children's voices. A home-grown fan club of Birdsville residents had been rounded up to cheer this strange but welcome conqueror. After more than three days of desolation, their appearance lifted him. He felt their energy and appreciation for his heroics and increased his tempo in further defiance of the logic of physiology.

It seemed to Pat that his adopted supporters multiplied with each passing kilometre. He had seen some leapfrog ahead of him, but there was no doubt the numbers were multiplying. There were now 30 or 40 crowded into utes, tray-backs, dual cabins and four-wheel-drives. In a town where the stable population was measured by the dozens, this was big numbers. They lined the final kilometres, at least one cheering, waving well-wisher every hundred metres or so until the Birdsville Hotel loomed in the distance. Its verandah lights were blazing—although just an hour ago the pub had been shrouded in darkness until one of Pat's crew woke publican Kim Fort by throwing a rock on to the roof.

Pat could see the spotlight of a television camera glaring at him. As he charged to the finish line in a final desperate surge more reminiscent of a 1500-metre runner than an ultra marathoner, Pat broke the tissue-thin finishing tape with his hands—despite his momentum, the paper almost clung to his drenched clothing. Bernie stopped his watch, but needed to see the numbers to confirm that what he suspected was in fact true. The record was broken by 20 minutes and 35 seconds. A local drinker gave Pat an admiring slap on the back as he staggered past without spilling a drop of the precious amber fluid from his glass. 'Well mate, you look better than Ron Grant did,' he said. Pat slumped into the arms of Annette and wobbled his way to a spa bath that had been specially flown in by sponsor Sundance Spas.

As Pat blinked the sweat from his eyes, he focused on two beaming figures sitting in the spa. His face, creased with pain, quickly changed expression. In a surprise gesture, *A Current Affair* had flown Lisa and Brooke to Birdsville. Pat leant across the fibreglass structure into the arms of both. There were whispered words—just a few. 'I love you and I'm so proud of you,' said Lisa. Pat slowly and painfully clambered up the few steps into the swirling bubbling waters. He closed his eyes and was enveloped by the warm and familiar embrace of a loving wife and child. He felt safe, relieved, contented. Mind and body were numbed by exhaustion. There was nothing else to feel.

8

•

Enemies—Simpson 2

Pat came closer to dying in the desert than he would admit. The newspaper headlines around the country told the story. 'Ultra Runner near Death', 'On the Road to Hell', 'How Pat Survived Run of His Life', they screamed. It was only one year later when he had a full debriefing with scientific experts that he fully grasped the severity of his plight. 'He was in grave danger,' said Dr Martin Thompson, head of the University of Sydney's Exercise and Sports Science Department and a former international ultra marathon runner. 'He hadn't acclimatised and his early pace was unrealistic for the hot conditions. His body temperature was obviously elevated and his advanced state of dehydration meant he wasn't getting a proper blood flow to vital internal organs. The flow of blood sugar to the brain could have also been compromised. It could also have affected the function of the kidney and liver. In fact, he could have suffered kidney failure and liver damage.'

Thompson's colleague, Dr Helen O'Connor, a dietician-nutritionist, was equally alarmed. 'Pat ate and drank so many wrong things it's amazing he not only survived and finished, but that he also broke the record,' she said. 'We don't know how dehydrated he was but if you suffer 5 per cent dehydration that's enough to kill you and from what Pat told me I'd say he was pretty close to that.'

Pat's physical condition after his Simpson Desert crossing was testament to his statement that it was the toughest run he had ever undertaken. For weeks, he suffered severe fatigue, finding simple daily tasks tiring. At stages, he felt like he could never run again. Despite his weary state, he could not sleep. He would toss and turn and wake lathered in so much sweat it looked as if he'd been doused with a bucket of water. But incredibly, within days of finishing the Simpson Desert run, he was telling journalists he was still keen to accept a long-standing invitation to tackle another desert run in just four months—the annual race across Africa's Sahara Desert, which attracted some of the world's leading ultra runners. He later declined the invitation after being unable to raise the necessary $20 000 in sponsorship.

When he finally began to feel normal again after a month, rather than being more aware of his mortality, Pat felt more invincible than ever. The Simpson Desert conquest had been a breakthrough, signifying the first time Pat had broken and held an existing long-distance record in his own right. It also engendered a newfound belief in his abilities—not just the physical, but also the mental—and proved to him his ability to apply and rely on the lessons of mind power, in the face of what appeared to others to be a hopeless situation.

'After doing something like that I believe there is absolutely nothing that I cannot do,' he said. 'I believe you can do anything if you really want to do it. You just have to believe in yourself. I'm able to blend with nature and be out there in impossible conditions. Most people would die just by being out there, let alone trying to run, but I can blend in with the conditions to the degree that I can live there and compete there. The sun—sure it burns me, but it doesn't kill me.'

After his near-death experience, Pat gladly returned to more mundane domestic issues. Top of the list of priorities for him and Lisa was building their 'dream home'. Like all of Pat's successes, it had been a long and hard struggle. The couple had bought a 2-hectare block of land in 1995 in the semi-rural suburb of Catherine Field, one hour west of Sydney. Given their love of nature and the outdoors, it was inevitable they would move to acreage. They sought a second opinion from Lisa's boss John Gerathy, who owned a block of land nearby, and on his recommendation bought it. Gerathy, a self-confessed 'frustrated architect', later drew up some rough designs and referred them to his own professional architect. The decision to buy the land was a difficult one because it was a significant financial commitment. Pat and Lisa were forced to sell many of their assets—their home at Campbelltown, the holiday house at Mollymook and an adjoining block of land—to finance the $250 000 land purchase.

Lisa had her doubts about the wisdom of the move and, as with most couples, there were arguments over money. With Pat and Lisa it arose out of differing ingrained philosophies. Pat was a dreamer who worried about the practicalities later and was taught to be charitable to others with his time and money. Lisa was brought up on the principle 'charity begins at home, spend within your means, look after yourself and your family first, then see what's left over for others'.

Some friends and family also wondered if they were getting themselves in too deep, but as always, Pat was far too positive and independent to listen to the doubters. 'People said we couldn't do it and that we wouldn't have enough money,' said Pat. 'But it was our dream, our vision, and we were prepared to work as hard on it as was necessary to make it happen.'

It had truly been a dream home. In fact, Pat's daydreams of his new house helped him endure the most intense pain of the stress fracture during his second Trans America run. 'When the pain got really bad and it was getting me down, I'd think of something pleasant that helped distract me,' he said. 'I imagined what our house would look like down to the most minute detail. I visualised what sort of timber we'd build with, the colours we'd paint with—even what type of nails and screws I'd use. I virtually rebuilt it three or four times and still didn't get it right. I kept putting the back door where the front door should have been!'

But for some time, the dream was a living nightmare. They could only afford to build a large double garage at first, and made slow but steady progress with the rest of the house when they could afford it. Their financial plan had come unstuck because they had budgeted on Pat receiving a new healthy sponsorship contract with Manchester Unity. But there was a change of management and the agreement, which had only been a verbal one, was not kept.

It was a primitive existence, especially with Lisa pregnant with their second child. Lisa's step-mother, June Bullivant, marvels at Lisa's patience and tolerance. 'When they first moved in, the conditions were horrible,' she said. 'I don't know how she managed. She cooked, cleaned, went to work and didn't complain. She made the best of the situation.'

Friends say garage living took its toll on Lisa, who was accustomed to having more orderly and homely environs. She became accustomed to disturbances such as birds darting in through a gap in the ceiling and flying around. But she wasn't prepared to deal with other, larger intruders. Lisa was awoken one night by a flapping sensation. In her initial dazed state, she thought it was Pat. When she realised it was nothing as comforting as her husband but was instead a bat, the tranquillity of the country night air was disturbed by Lisa's scream. 'Lisa absolutely hated creepy, crawly things. That felt like the last straw for her,' said friend Sharon Hutchins.

But, amidst all the drama and stress, there was solace in the little things—the precious family moments that money can't buy and time will never erase. Pat remembers arriving home after another long fourteen-hour day of constant physical exertion that had begun with a 25-kilometre training run at 4.00 a.m. and continued with a day of back-breaking labour as a landscaper. Lisa had also had a forgettable day, with Brooke proving more than the usual handful. 'You take her, I need a break,' said Lisa. The pair adjourned to a comfortable chair by the earth dam, down the back of the house. With his daughter lovingly cradled against him, Pat engaged in a peaceful pastime that was a throwback to his childhood. Just as his father had done, Pat unravelled some of the mysteries of the night sky to his attentive daughter. The child's comprehension amazed him. A world of worries evaporated into the cool night air as they stargazed. Comforted by each other's arms and lulled by exhaustion, they drifted into a deep sleep. When he finally stirred some two hours later, Pat placed a tender kiss on the cherubic face. This is what counts, he told himself. This is what life's all about.

For Pat and Lisa, the dream family was completed with the arrival of another angel on 10 July 1997. Dillon Farmer was named in memory of Lisa's deceased mother, Iris, whose family name was Dillon. They had both been desperate to have a boy and, despite complications with Lisa's heart murmur that forced her to be admitted to hospital for three days, the birth was uncomplicated. 'We had a boy and a girl and everything was perfect,' said Pat. While most parents can't wait for their new-borns to go to sleep, Lisa adored Dillon so much, she couldn't wait for him to wake up. 'Lisa couldn't go past Dillon without tickling him or biting his toes or kissing him or roughing him up. She just couldn't resist him. It wouldn't matter where she was or what was going on. She just loved him so much.'

Conditions were by now slightly more liveable, as they had progressed to the family room inside the house. Life was never busier, as they juggled child-minding, work and training with renovations. Pat and Lisa spent endless nights choosing furnishings, painting and tiling 'like maniacs' until 2.00 a.m., then grabbing three hours' sleep before starting another hectic day. Along the way there were numerous debates that sometimes degenerated into fights about colour schemes, kitchen plans and other final touches. Most times, what Pat wanted, he got. However, Lisa eventually prevailed when it came to the exterior colour of the cement-rendered house. She had fallen in love with a shade of aqua blue she had seen on an office building. Pat approached Dulux and they agreed to replicate the colour. The paint company was so happy with the result that they named it 'Lisa's Dream'.

The Farmer menagerie was also starting to take shape. Friends remember visiting the Farmers when Dillon was one week old and being amused by Pat's comical efforts to chase the chickens out from underneath the family room.

Pat is a man who prides himself on keeping promises. But when it comes to his eldest brother Bernie, it seems there's some room for flexibility. After crossing the Simpson Desert, Pat vowed: 'There is no way I'll ever attempt another desert crossing.' As they flew out of Birdsville, Bernie Farmer scowled back at the daddy of all dunes, Big Red, and muttered quietly and confidently: 'See ya later big fella. I'm glad I'll never see you again.' He was so sure he'd never be back that he souvenired some of its fine red sand.

But alarm bells began sounding less than a year later when Pat rang Bernie at his Canberra home in October 1997 to discuss family plans for Christmas. Pat's parting comment left his big brother stunned. 'Oh and by the way, we're going back to the Simpson Desert in January. See ya.' Pat hung up. Bernie's silence alarmed his wife Deb. 'What's wrong, Bernie?' she asked. 'I'm not sure,' he replied, 'but I think Pat just said something about another Simpson Desert run. I'd better have a talk to that boy and change all that.'

After several phone calls and a face-to-face meeting at Christmas, Bernie was filled with a sense of dread. 'Why go back? There's nothing to achieve,' Bernie told Pat. 'We had a deal. Why are you going back on this?' Pat was as tenacious as ever. 'I wasn't happy with the run last time. I can do a lot better and this time I'm better prepared and better trained.'

When Pat revealed he was planning to race long-time rival Dave Taylor, Bernie hit the roof. 'Bloody Dave Taylor! Why are you running against him? You've got nothing to gain. You'll only make him look good by taking him on. The guy's a buffoon.' After their first encounter, Bernie and Pat respected the desert but thought Taylor might under-estimate the dangers. Bernie was also concerned that if Taylor came to serious harm in the race, Pat's hard-earned and carefully managed public image would suffer irreparable damage.

'I knew Pat was serious, but I didn't know if Dave was,' said Bernie. 'Both Lisa and I thought he was an idiot for wanting to go back. I told her I was trying to talk him out of it but it was fruitless. I know what he's like when he makes his mind up. Eventually I gave up and said: "If you want me there, I'll be there."'

In a challenge reminiscent of the Grant–Rafferty race of 1986, Pat had agreed to race long-time rival runner Dave Taylor of Wollongong across the desert. The race was to finish on Australia Day 1997 and the Australia Day Council agreed to endorse it as one of its official events. Pat was already an Australia Day ambassador and the council agreed to add Taylor to the list. But arguments about the race began at the beginning. Pat insists Taylor challenged him, while Taylor claims it was Pat who extended the challenge. Disputes also arose early in the planning stages over the ground rules for the race. Mindful of his early struggle with the heat the previous time, Pat wanted to start in the evening; Taylor argued the race should begin at 6.30 a.m., the same time as Pat's first crossing. Pat planned to use his specially designed Sportwool clothing again and an ice-vest (designed by the AIS and the CSIRO for Australian athletes at the Atlanta Olympics) to cool his body during rest periods; Taylor disapproved, believing Pat would have an unfair advantage.

Very quickly, the rivalry that had existed between Pat and Dave Taylor, dating back more than a decade, re-emerged. Their duels originated during the Westfield runs and carried on through numerous ultra races ranging from 50-kilometre to six-day events. Records show Pat was the superior runner, beating Taylor in two Westfield runs. Overall he had a win–loss ratio of three to one. Ultra running associates say Dave was more worried about Pat as an opponent than Pat was about Dave. 'The rivalry got more intense from Dave's perspective as Pat achieved greater things in the sport and received more recognition,' said one runner.

Pat admitted he was not keen to return to the Simpson, telling the author in an interview for *ABC Television News* on 3 November 1997: 'I have everything to lose. I hold the record at the moment. I have already done it. I don't need to go back out to the desert to be quite honest with you. I want to beat Dave. I want to beat the elements. I want to win. I want to break my own record. You see my goal is to be the best long distance runner on the face of the earth and in order to do that you have to accept challenges from time to time from different people.'

Taylor denied he was misjudging what both men agreed would be the biggest enemy—the elements. 'I don't underestimate anything,' he said. 'Pat's told me about the desert. I have raced Pat in the past in the heat and I believe the heat is in my favour. All I do when Pat tells me about the desert, I just turn it around and say: "You're more worried about it than me."' When asked what he would do if he were faced with the choice of quitting mid-race if his health was endangered or perish in the desert, Taylor was full of bravado: 'I die. Simple as that. I don't pull out.'

But Pat was working on a methodical plan to beat the heat. He had been put in contact with scientists at the University of Sydney's Exercise and Sports Science Department. He was training on a treadmill in a heat chamber that simulated the temperature and humidity of the desert. It proved to be an invaluable training tool, although Pat wondered at the time if it was doing him more harm than good when he returned home from each session with a dry throat, nausea and a thumping headache. Pat began using it two weeks before he left, training for up to four hours every second day. The concept of heat acclimatisation had been around for many years, but scientists were refining a training technique that helped increase the ability of the body to sweat, hence producing a cooling effect through evaporative mechanisms. Tests on Australia's Olympic athletes at

Atlanta the previous year showed results were best achieved by acclimatising close to the event.

The university's Dr Helen O'Connor was also advising Pat on diet and nutrition. She had worked with a wide array of athletes, including competitors in the gruelling Hawaii Ironman, students at the New South Wales Institute of Sport, the Sydney Swans AFL team and the Canterbury Rugby League Club. 'Pat had a hit and miss approach the first time and I was surprised that he would have gone into such a big event without professional help,' said O'Connor. 'Pat's previous approach of drinking when he was thirsty was flawed because thirst is a sign that your body is already dehydrated.'

O'Connor insisted on devising a food and fluid schedule for Pat to ensure his body was in the 'safe zone' at all times by being properly fuelled and dehydrated. The plan was for him to 'graze' throughout the day on small, easily digested snacks—creamed rice, bananas, tinned baby food, muesli bars and even lollies. He would absorb a lot of his energy from sports drinks—a high-volume carbohydrate drink called Gatorload to be taken before the event and Gatorade to replace lost body salts on the run. They took a highly scientific approach, testing all of the foods while Pat worked out in the heat chamber to see that nothing disagreed with his digestive system. They also began a regime of putting him on the scales every two hours to ensure he wasn't losing too much fluid and weight.

The second Simpson Desert run was a watershed in Pat's career—he had suddenly discovered science. It was an extraordinary about-face for a man who had taken anything but a technical approach to ultra marathons and who viewed doctors and scientists with a healthy slice of cynicism—a trait that still lingers, but in smaller doses.

'They tell me what I can't do,' he said. 'They set parameters for what I can't do but I don't know what my limits are. All they understand is the physical reasons for things to happen to the human body but that doesn't take into account what a powerful weapon the mind can be. I don't get on with doctors because if

I'm not well, they tell me to rest. If I rested every time I didn't feel right, I'd spend most of my life in bed.'

After some early scepticism, Pat embraced the scientific support of Drs Thompson and O'Connor because he realised improvement would only come by addressing the mistakes of the past. 'I think one of Kouros's secrets was that he had a good diet while the rest of us mugs were eating any old garbage,' he said. 'But the Sydney Uni guys were switched on and I began to realise that these were some things that I should have been doing right from the early days.'

Meanwhile, Taylor had approached marketing and advertising expert Wayne Larkin, who agreed to manage his preparation and to help coordinate the event. Larkin also met with Pat and Lisa who agreed the race would be more attractive to a sponsor if the two runners were presented as a package deal. It was Larkin's job to find companies who could 'show them the money'.

Larkin attracted great interest from cable television channel Fox Sports, which was prepared to invest $90 000 to make a one-hour documentary that could be on-sold to television stations around the world. While potential sponsors such as car companies, breweries and sports clothing manufacturers all found some appeal in the idea, especially the notion of a duel, Larkin wasn't flooded with offers. While he remained confident that a sponsor would be found, they were struggling to cover the costs of the event. Any suggestion that Farmer and Taylor would be racing for a lucrative prize quickly disappeared from view.

Pat took time out from his preparations for the Simpson Desert challenge to fulfil a promise to himself and to his Japanese sponsor, Mr Okada. He gave Pat and the Trans Am runners a second and last shot at redemption in the Hong Kong Trailwalker run, assembling his 'Dream Team' comprising Pat, American Bryan Hacker (a last-minute replacement for original team member Steve Maihu) and Trans Am runners Ray Bell and Mike Sandlin. But Mr Okada's mood had turned sombre in recent months. His company was struggling under the pressure of the Japanese recession and was in danger of joining a growing list of economic casualties. As his mood grew ever darker, he expressed concerns that looming financial woes might bring shame upon his family. Pat feared Mr Okada was even contemplating *hara-kiri*, the Japanese term for an 'honourable' death by suicide.

Pat had shared a special relationship with Mr Okada over the years, which extended beyond that of sponsor and athlete and transcended any minor language or cultural barriers. They had developed a great mutual respect. The Japanese businessman's generosity helped Pat to reach out and touch his dreams. Mr Okada says he learned much about the human spirit from watching Pat crash through pain barriers. 'I learned so many things from Pat not in business but in life,' says Mr Okada. 'He ran so many times for charity and I thank Pat for showing me his sense of kindness to others.'

Pat inspired Mr Okada to pursue his 'third life'. His first had been as a banker; his second as chairman of Moonbat; his third saw him return to study for a Masters of Social Welfare at the age of 52. 'I wanted to contribute something back to society. I am still enjoying my third life,' he says.

When Mr Okada rang the Moonbat team as they lined up for the start of Trailwalker on 21 November 1997, his obvious depression had Pat deeply concerned. Today was his birthday, he said, but he no longer had anything to be happy about. 'I would really like it if you would win this race for my birthday,' he told Pat, who covered the mouthpiece while he relayed the conversation to his teammates. 'Don't you dare make promises we can't definitely keep,' said Ray Bell. Pat ignored the advice and boldly replied: 'Don't you worry, Mr Okada. We're going to win this race for you, no risk.' Pat's teammates berated him. The pressure was on. It really was a case of do or die.

The mission was tough. There were 720 teams and almost 3000 runners. The mighty Hong Kong Gurkha regiment, which had dominated the race for sixteen years, was absent because the former British-controlled territory had just returned to Chinese control. But there were still two Gurkha teams from a regiment stationed in Brunei and a potentially greater challenge with the debut of a team of Chinese soldiers, intent on flexing their military muscle. The Moonbat team had the perfect start in the warm and humid conditions, powering away from the Gurkha and Red Army teams over the first 40 kilometres of the Maclehose Trail that snaked around some of the finest scenery in the region. The course then zigzagged through hills and finished with an assault up Hong Kong's highest peak, Tai Mo Shan at 1180 metres—perfect terrain for the Gurkhas, who had the speed and agility of mountain cats.

Adding to the difficulty was the fact the trails were susceptible to natural disasters such as bushfire, landslides and tropical storms that could create mountain torrents capable of washing runners away. Concerned the Chinese might use newly acquired local knowledge to cut corners, Pat scouted ahead to keep tabs on a breakaway runner. Each team comprised four members who all wore electronic wristbands. These registered their passage through nine checkpoints, but teams could not pass through unless they were together . . . symbolically, each team was only as strong as its weakest link.

The test of their strength and unity came when Mike Sandlin suffered a stomach upset. He started vomiting and became delirious. The Moonbat team was in front and just 20 kilometres from the finish with night falling. Sandlin doubted he could continue and urged his colleagues to continue without him. But that would have seen them disqualified. With the torchlights of rival teams signalling their approach, Pat could see the race slipping from their grasp. He had made a promise to himself and Mr Okada and hated breaking a vow. Pat supported Sandlin by putting his arm around his shoulder and they pushed on. When his ill team mate again faltered, he slung him on his back in a fireman's carry—later sharing the load with the other two runners when he weakened.

As they approached one of the final checkpoints and aid stations, Pat dashed ahead to organise food and drinks. Sandlin collapsed in a state of near-exhaustion. His team mates force-fed him on soup, tea and bread, overdosed with salt and sugar, then implored him to start moving with them.

'I can't. I feel like I'm going to throw up,' said Sandlin.

'Well just hurry up and vomit. Just get it out of your system and you'll feel better. Stick your fingers down your throat if you have to,' said Pat. The argument raged for several minutes before Pat threatened drastic action.

'If you can't throw up, I'll stick my fingers down your throat. Just hurry up. They'll be here soon.'

'You stick your fingers in my mouth and I'll bite them off. You're just interested in winning this race. You don't give a damn about the rest of us.'

'You're just a big wooz.'

'I'll show you what kind of wooz I am.'

'Yeah, well you got to catch me if you want to hit me.'

Bell says he was glad it wasn't him on the receiving end of Pat's verbal volley. He and Bryan Hacker played United Nations peacekeepers. Thankfully, Sandlin began to feel better and the tension eased. While the run home was relatively easy, being downhill and flat, they had one further drama. Pat was running ahead of the group wearing a bicycle helmet with a powerful light attached to guide the way. Bell was trailing and heard a crashing noise. Pat had tripped, fallen and struck his head on a granite boulder.

'When I saw him he wasn't moving, he was out to it,' said Bell. 'I didn't know if he was alive or dead. We were all holding our breath, because it looked like he had serious problems. Then he groaned so we knew he was alive and after about 30 seconds he sat up and, still dazed, said: "I'm okay. Let's go, let's go."' Pat was groggy for five minutes but undoubtedly would have been in worse shape if not for the bike helmet. 'I remember hitting the rock really hard,' he said. 'I didn't think of it at the time, but I guess the helmet probably saved my life. I was wobbling around for a few minutes after. The guys were pretty worried but we couldn't afford to waste time.'

Basic instinct drove them home—fear of being overtaken, fear of letting down a team-mate, fear of failure. They crossed the line together fourteen hours and 24 minutes after the start—the winning margin was 31 minutes. Mr Okada had flown in for the finish and greeted them with warm and vigorous two-handed shakes and a smile that seemed to spread across his entire face. There was no monetary prize for the runners. Mr Okada's boosted spirits were enough for them, along with the satisfaction that Moonbat's $90 000 donation had helped the 1997 Trail-walker run raise almost $20 million.

Mr Okada was eternally grateful to his team for the victory. Celebrations went late into the Hong Kong evening with champagne and sake flowing freely along with an endless supply of fine Chinese and Japanese fare. 'They got first prize because they were all strong, brave runners,' said Mr Okada. 'It made me very, very happy that they did this for my birthday. I got a huge new energy from the win. My company was still suffering but I knew we could survive and as it turns out we did.'

'It was a very personal thing for us,' said Pat. 'There was a lot at stake for Mr Okada, including personal and company pride. We did it for him. It was payback time for all the faith he'd shown in us. He's a special man. We knew we couldn't afford to finish second again.'

When Pat returned from Hong Kong, the Simpson Desert Challenge was in serious trouble. The event had run foul of the authorities, particularly South Australian police and National Parks bureaucrats who refused to issue permits. They thought it was a highly risky event and were concerned about their liability and the cost of a possible rescue operation. In desperation, Pat rang a very influential friend—his local Member of Parliament and Olympics Minister Michael Knight. Pat and Lisa had had many official and social encounters with the New South Wales power broker—the Farmers had been Knight's guests at dinner at Parliament House on more than one occasion.

Knight warned Pat his influence might be diminished by state borders and the fact that South Australia was run by a Liberal government, but promised to try. Knight rang the South Australian Environment Minister, Dorothy Kotz. She was in New Zealand on official business but her office agreed to get a message to her. 'It's amazing how quickly people ring back when the Olympics Minister calls,' chuckles Knight. 'Pat wasn't as famous in those days as he is now, so I had to explain to the Minister who he was and what he was about.' They had a trans-Tasman conversation in which Knight basically had to convince Kotz that Pat wasn't just any 'loopy runner' embarking on a suicide mission. He vouched for Pat's credentials, preparation and background. Kotz was reluctant to overrule her department, especially on a health and safety issue, but promised to review the matter.

The Environment Minister rang Knight back a few days later after returning to Adelaide and speaking with departmental officials. 'She was very good about it,' said Knight. 'She finally relented when I told her Pat had given me an iron-clad guarantee that if he was going to die, he would wait until he had crossed over the South Australian border and was in the Northern Territory or Queensland! She had the guts to overrule her department and for that Pat and I will be forever grateful.'

Everyone was aware of the dangers, especially in Pat's camp. At a pre-race meeting weeks before the event, Pat bluntly warned his crew they were going into an area where any of them could possibly die. Kevin Junor, who was studying for his Masters of Education and had conducted a case study on Pat as an elite athlete, was also going to join him as part of his support crew. 'I never had second thoughts but when we all got a letter from National Parks clearly outlining the dangers, it heightened my level of awareness,' he said. 'One day I was contemplating what lay ahead with the run and began thinking what a terrible thing it would be for my family if I didn't come back.'

Junor left a poignant farewell message and will for his wife, Sharon, and three daughters in case he didn't return alive. Recorded just days before his departure, it said in part: 'In case things go wrong girls, I just want to tell you all that I love you very, very much. You're all really, really talented. God has given you great skills. Sharon, honey, we've had some ups and downs in our life, but together we've succeeded. I love you sweetheart.'

Junor had particular cause for concern after doing his calculations on the amount of water that would be required to safely sustain Pat and his crew in extreme heat. Junor strongly believed they needed to take 860 litres of water. The four-wheel-drives were only able to carry 560 litres. He mentioned this to Pat, but was told they couldn't afford to hire another vehicle and would have to make do with what water they had. 'I hope this expedition/race doesn't fail because of the lack of water,' Junor told his family in his farewell message.

Time had also run out for sponsorship. Larkin had been unsuccessful in attracting corporate interest and the agreed imposed deadline for raising the money had passed. This is where the central dispute that caused the duel to be abandoned occurred, just days before the event. Taylor claims he rang Pat shortly before they were due to leave and suggested they still proceed with the race using their own money. He says Pat rejected the offer, but claims he was deceived because Pat failed to mention he had secured an individual sponsorship deal with Western Suburbs Rugby League Club. Taylor says he only learned of this deal through the media, days before the event. Pat's Wests' sponsorship sparked Taylor's withdrawal from the challenge. He was angry at Pat for not offering him half of his sponsorship money. 'There was a lot of shifty stuff going on but basically Pat shafted me,' says Taylor. When asked why he didn't reignite the challenge when he realised Pat had the money, Taylor became evasive. 'Let's just say Pat deceived me about the money and his sponsorship arrangements. He left us in the lurch, once the deadline was expired.'

Pat denies Taylor's assertions and says he told Taylor's manager Wayne Larkin about the Wests' deal at least a month before the race. Larkin confirms Pat's version and says he also told Taylor at the time. 'It was not a last-minute deal,' he said. 'But when

Pat got his sponsorship is irrelevant anyway. It shouldn't have affected whether or not the challenge went ahead.'

The mere mention of each other's name still makes Taylor and Farmer's blood boil, two years after the aborted challenge. When I met with Taylor to discuss his version of events he felt compelled to be accompanied by two physically imposing witnesses—fitness adviser Vito Gaudiosi and proposed Simpson Desert crew member Reg Hitchens. The resentment and hostility still lingers. 'Pat Farmer's lucky to be on the earth today,' said Taylor. 'Twenty-five years I built my name up. Worked hard. It cost me $100 000 out of my own pocket to raise $300 000 for charity. Pat is very lucky he's on this earth today.'

When I asked Taylor if he was inferring he would like to inflict physical violence on Farmer, he repeated his statement: 'Pat Farmer is very lucky he's on this earth today. Okay?' Yet in the next breath Taylor also offered begrudging respect for his rival's achievements. 'I respect him as an athlete but not as a person. He has done some great things for the community, but he can sure sell himself. He's got the gift of the gab. He could sell a Volkswagen to the Pope.'

Dave Taylor is one of the few names that makes Pat see red. 'I didn't have to prove anything. I held the record. I'd love to hammer the guy. He's a mongrel. That idiot frustrates me. He's just all talk. I went out there and was good to my word. I had to put my anger aside and focus on the job. I went out there against Lisa's wishes. I spent that time away from Lisa and we argued like nothing else about the whole thing. I went against everything that she wanted. In light of Lisa's death I'm even more furious about the situation.'

Admittedly these comments were made just days before the first anniversary of Lisa's death, when it was obvious Pat was tense. Crew members say Pat didn't want Taylor's name even mentioned when they finally set out for the Simpson Desert on 21 January 1998. 'That didn't stop us from using Dave Taylor as a bit of a motivational tool against Pat—all light-hearted of course,' said Kevin Junor with a laugh.

When they flew into Oodnadatta, South Australia, Pat, Bernie and sister Annette were upbeat and positive and thinking only of setting a new record—it wasn't a case of 'if' but 'by how much'. They had never been better prepared or better equipped for any event. They had four vehicles and a crew of sixteen. This time Pat had the medical support crew he had lacked the previous time, including physiotherapist and resident joker Ian Austin, Dr David Wilson and registered nurse Amanda Donaldson. The mood was relaxed the night before the race as they enjoyed a swim in the pool at their hotel, 'The Pink Roadhouse', a barbecue with the local police sergeant and a game of street cricket with local children.

It was more emotional the following night as the clock ticked down to the start. Jenny Bolwell, who along with her husband Kevin was a tour leader, shed a few silent tears after Pat spoke of the grave risks, his attendance to his will and his emotional goodbyes to his wife and children before he left Sydney. In the hour before the run, crewmen Austin and Junor joined Pat, Bernie and Annette in a huddle as they all said a prayer for a safe and successful journey.

They had learned much from the many mistakes of the previous crossing. This time Pat began his Simpson Desert assault in the evening—the aim was to get off to a better start in the cooler temperatures. The night provided little respite from the heat, however, with the mercury dropping from 50°C to the low forties. Nature also gave Pat a few subtle reminders on the first night with a nasty sandstorm threatening to blanket him in fine red particles. At one point Pat disappeared behind a tree for a toilet stop. He emerged screaming. 'Where's the torch? I think I got bitten by a scorpion.' It turned out to be nothing more than a 'vicious' bush pricking him in the backside. Sometime later Pat was forced to hurdle a king brown snake that was too curious for his liking. But these were minor obstacles compared with the main enemy, the heat, which would not fully test his preparation until the sun rose.

Meanwhile, Junor had trouble with his primary task of rigidly enforcing Pat's fluid schedule. 'Educating other crew members was difficult because, despite our previous discussions, they slipped back into the old bad habits,' he said. 'We had to keep track of everything he drank and give him drinks every fifteen minutes because he could have easily become dehydrated like last time, then we would have been back to square one.' Pat went through an incredible 148 litres of fluid for the run—and was still dehydrated.

Equally important to the schedule was the monitoring of Pat's weight, which was done by putting him on a set of scales every two hours. Pat's scientific support team had stressed the importance of keeping his body weight fairly constant and had told him the loss of even 2 kilograms would put him in the 'red zone'. At the first weigh-in after two hours of running, Pat was alarmed to see his weight had dropped from 63.5 kilograms to 61.5 kilograms.

'What! That can't be right. The scales are wrong, the scales are wrong. Get a new set of scales.' Pat soon disappeared into the night, leaving Junor with the simple assignment of finding a new weighing device in the middle of the Simpson Desert. 'Thankfully we realised there was nothing wrong with the scales,' said Junor. 'Pat had drunk so much fluid before the run he was over-hydrated and carrying more than his normal weight. He also ran hard for the first few hours so, given all of that, it wasn't surprising his body had some adjustment to make with the weight loss. The situation stabilised at the next weigh-in where we explained all that to Pat and he was fine.'

Pat also had early problems with back pain, which physiotherapist Ian Austin attributed to tight hamstrings and quadriceps in his legs. Some gentle stretching fixed the problem. When Pat stopped for a ten-minute sleep every 20 kilometres, Austin would stretch his taut muscles.

'While he slept I stretched both muscle groups passively,' said Austin. 'He had a great ability to nod off for ten minutes—go out cold—while I worked on him. Then we'd wake him up after ten minutes exactly—not a second later. He'd get up and start running again. I've never stretched anyone while they slept. I guess it made it easy for both of us.'

The heat chamber training ensured Pat coped much better with the 50°C temperatures this time, passing through the first milestone of 100 kilometres on the first morning. It was resourcefully marked in felt pen on an old bright pink sleeping bag that was laid across the track. Pat crossed it then gladly took his first long rest break, totally indulging by cooling down with an ice vest, a more substantial meal of rice custard, peaches and juice and a two-hour sleep. Despite his somewhat weary state, Pat's amazing powers of recovery saw him back on track and ploughing through the afternoon heat. While roaring winds had left his body with sand grazes, Pat made great progress over the first 24 hours. He covered 125 kilometres—putting him 25 kilometres ahead of schedule. Bernie was ecstatic that they had avoided a repeat horror start, but still cautious. 'We want a buffer, we want a buffer,' he said. Because of the unpredictable nature of the Simpson Desert and ultra runs, Pat also never allowed himself to become complacent. He reminded himself and his crew: 'So many things can go wrong. No matter how good I look or how far I am in front of the record, it's not over till it's over; it's not done till it's done.'

His caution was well founded. Rarely did nature give adventurers an armchair ride through such an inhospitable climate. After enduring another day of temperatures in the low fifties, Pat had to push through another sandstorm that irritated his eyes and aggravated his windburn and sunburn. Pat reached Poeppel Corner with its sun-baked salt lake towards the end of the second day. A thunderstorm descended upon the desert, drenching and cooling the runner, then moving on as quickly as it had arrived. But instead of making his continued passage smoother, Pat became bogged down in the sodden earth. He replaced his shoe gaiters with plastic bags but mud still stuck, leaving him feeling like he was running with leg weights. Nonetheless, he emerged from another testing section still more than eight hours ahead of his old record.

'Where's Big Red? How far away is Big Red? How many sand dunes to go?' It was obvious to the support crew that Pat was getting anxious—perhaps even obsessive—about the sand dune they called Big Red. Conquering it was again a major psychological barrier for him. Pat knew it signified the end of the desert and the start of the home stretch.

'It's 7 kilometres by the GPS [a hand-held satellite navigation system] as the crow flies, Pat,' said Kevin Bolwell.

'Tell Kevin I'm not a crow,' said Pat. 'What sort of tour operator is he? We've lost Big Red and I'm going to lose the record because we can't find it.'

Finally, when it loomed, Pat mustered his reserves of energy and produced one last short, superlative effort to reach the summit, surging with an explosive action through the sand. Bernie and Annette trailed behind him—jogging, walking and scrambling. When the breathless trio had all reached the pinnacle, they joined arms and hugged. Their deep emotional bond was strengthened by a shared sense of relief, joy and triumph. The desert conquerors had again beaten the elements and the odds. They looked back at how far they had come. 'We all knew what a desperate struggle it had been last time and we were jubilant that this time we'd done it in style,' said Pat.

Pat rested on the other side, but it was clear the exertion was taking its toll on his battered body. He dropped to the ground and he began to shake uncontrollably. The medical team was concerned enough to check his vital observations, monitoring blood pressure, pulse and body temperature. His temperature was up and his blood pressure down but not alarmingly so. A tense confrontation followed when Bolwell asked Junor to weigh Pat to ensure he wasn't dangerously dehydrated. Junor refused. He knew Pat had lost some weight but believed he had consumed enough fluid to keep out of the red zone.

'The doctor said he should be weighed,' said Bolwell.

'And I said it's not necessary,' replied Junor.

'You're not the doctor. He wants Pat weighed.'

'I'm in charge of the fluid schedule and the scales and I'm saying no.'

The aggravation was partly a product of the crewmen's fatigue. Hackles were starting to rise just a little more now. Over three days, none of the crew had consumed anything more lavish than cold canned food and had slept no more than a few hours. Junor explained to Bernie that, while Pat's weight was down, it wasn't dangerous and he believed the weigh-in would do more harm to Pat's psyche than it would help with a medical diagnosis. Bernie was ever the mental master, at least when it came to Pat, and he concurred.

Their collective judgment proved correct as Pat hit top gear on the 33-kilometre run home. They were so far ahead of schedule that Bernie was forced to hold his charge back. The deal with the Australia Day Council was for Pat to finish on Australia Day, but he was in danger of coming in before midnight. When finally Bernie let go of the reins, Pat was like a brumby. He doubled his average speed to more than 15 kilometres per hour, running the final kilometres into Birdsville proudly bearing a large Australian flag. Pat hit the tissue-thin finishing tape amid a cacophony of car horns, hoots and cheers at 3.36 a.m. on Australia Day. He smashed his old record by eight hours and 56 minutes, lowering the mark to three days, eight hours and 36 minutes. The satisfaction at conquering another demon was enormous. This was one piece of business that was now definitely finished.

9

Running on empty

'Citius, Altius, Fortius'—faster, higher, stronger—is the Olympic motto. 'Bigger, better, braver' is the Farmer creed. By 1996, with many of the world's toughest roads and runs conquered, Pat was starting to run out of challenges. He had always felt the need to find or create an event that was tougher and more testing than the last to fuel his internal drive and sustain interest in the corporate sponsorship and media worlds. His mind was always ticking over, ready to spring surprises on family and friends. They had become accustomed to news of the latest venture, often prefaced by Lisa saying: 'Bloody Pat, guess what he wants to do now?' No matter how crazy and impossible the ideas might appear, supporters had long stopped doubting his ability to achieve anything he set his sights on.

Having twice broken Ron Grant's Simpson Desert record, Pat pondered the Queensland runner's greatest feat of all—his 1983 record for running around Australia: 13 383 kilometres in 217 days. It was widely acknowledged as one of the greatest achievements in endurance sport in Australia's history. But Pat always needed a reason for doing events other than just breaking records. The year 2001 would mark the one-hundredth anniversary of the birth of the Commonwealth of Australia. It was Lisa's idea to tie together the two major events. The prospect of running around the country to unite and inspire Australians immediately appealed to Pat. It would eclipse anything he had ever achieved in the past. But Pat was also mindful that he was drawing towards the end of his career, and envisaged an even grander finale.

It was after hearing of an adventure of Lisa's boss John Gerathy, who had become a good friend to the Farmers, that Pat began to think of the ultimate big picture. Several years before, Gerathy had driven from London to Sydney in a car rally. The proverbial light bulb went on in Pat's head. 'I thought: "Why not do it on foot?",' he recalls. Australia's journey to nationhood was only made possible by the tens of thousands of overseas immigrants. Pat would run from London to Sydney via the countries that had generated the largest immigration waves, spreading the message across the globe of Australia's upcoming birthday and inviting the world to join in the celebrations. He'd then depart from Sydney to run around Australia counter-clock-wise and attempt to break Grant's record. He also planned to include Tasmania, which Grant did not. The epic run was to take over ten months and cover a staggering 22 000 kilometres. It would be almost four times longer than anything Pat had ever run before.

Pat and Lisa, helped by friends David Fookes, Suzie Yates and Carolyn Grant, spent months scrutinising airline and boat schedules of European and Asian countries. They had sessions where they would lay maps out on the table and floor as they investigated the feasibility of running around the world. A preliminary budget estimated the cost of the run at a cool $3 million. As much as they tried to ignore all the noughts, the group faced the reality that they might just be biting off a little more than they could chew. They were also keen not to jeopardise the central feature of the event, the run around Australia.

'We just about had it planned pretty well, but we just couldn't get the budget together for it,' said Pat. 'I know it sounds like a lot of dollars—it was more money than I'll ever see—but it was peanuts when you consider the advertising and promotions budgets of some of the big companies we were pitching at.'

• • •

At 5.15 a.m. every day, Tony Eggleton sets himself a challenge. The 68-year-old Canberra resident sets off from home in his running shoes and heads for nearby Red Hill, in suburban Deakin. It's a grinding, hour-long 7-kilometre run up a steep and winding incline. After conquering the peak, he turns around, runs home, has breakfast and returns for a second, more leisurely, assault at walking pace with his wife. As a lifelong runner, he knows what sort of discipline and tenacity is required for tough physical enterprises.

Eggleton is also one of the shrewdest and most experienced operators in conservative politics in Canberra. As former Federal Director of the Liberal Party, he has had the ear of five Prime Ministers spanning four decades. In his current post of Chief Executive of the National Council for the Centenary of Federation, he is entrusted with driving the day-to-day planning for Australia's one-hundredth birthday bash and ensuring it reflects the appropriate mix of history and grandeur while retaining a sense of relevance to as many Australians as possible.

When his counterpart at the Australia Day Council, John Trevillian, contacted him about a potential project involving Pat Farmer, Eggleton was curious. While he had never met Pat, he had been impressed from afar by his persistence and success during his Trans America and Simpson Desert adventures. Trevillian, who has known Pat for five years and is one of his most ardent supporters, set up a meeting in Canberra with Eggleton in September 1997. 'I was happy to steer him in the right direction,' Trevillian said. 'The meeting with Tony Eggleton was very important because the Centenary of Federation was the perfect link for Pat's run and Eggleton was the power-broker in the Council and he has the confidence of everybody in Canberra. I guess the small role I played was to vouch for him by saying:

"Pat is a truly decent man, a man of integrity and if he says he can do it, he can do it."'

Pat flew to Canberra for the meeting, accompanied by Trevillian and publicist Carolyn Grant. The runner was in full swing, delivering his most passionate sales pitch about the merits of the Around Australia Run, how he would visit every state and territory and speak at schools and daily functions along the way, when Eggleton stopped him. 'Thankyou for coming to Canberra,' he said in his official and distinguished tone. 'I don't need to hear any more. I believe you can do it. I'm going to help you achieve your dream. Tell me what we need to do.'

Eggleton knows disingenuous salesmanship when he sees it, but says he was quickly impressed by Pat's achievements, style, communication skills and dedication to his country.

'From that point on I didn't have any doubts myself that it was worth doing,' he said. 'Pat's modest lines that everyone could do something and he could make his contribution to the centenary by putting one foot in front of the other enthused us. I think Pat's absolute commitment to the project and motivation was also very important. I thought the run would be a very appropriate way of us spreading the message in the early stages of our promotions campaign. I was left feeling that, barring accidents, he would be successful.'

Inevitably, Pat had to jump through various bureaucratic hoops to get federal government approval. First base was a subcommittee of the National Council for the Centenary of Federation, chaired by Phoebe Fraser, daughter of ex-Prime Minister Malcolm Fraser and marketing consultant to CARE Australia.

'I thought it was a terrific idea,' she said. 'It captured my imagination, the idea of one person committing themselves to such a huge undertaking and going around Australia trying to unify the country ahead of our one-hundredth birthday. The challenge with any historical celebration is to make it relevant to people today . . . but Pat has such a down-to-earth quality and his commitment to address functions everywhere gave us a chance to do that by taking the message to the people.'

Fraser went in boots and all to convince the seventeen-member council that it should endorse Pat's Around Australia Run and back it with $250 000 of its precious funding dollars. Pat soon found another, even more powerful, ally in the Council's chairman, Dick Smith. The concept also struck a perfect chord with the businessman and adventurer.

'I also thought it was a fantastic idea. It was very simple in some ways, just a guy spreading his patriotism using his feet and his voice, but I like things that are simple,' he said. 'But I doubted whether the council would accept it because it was quite bureaucratically and politically sensitive and Pat's adventure was quite risky. Twenty per cent of adventures don't succeed. I deliberately didn't lobby other council members because I thought they might not understand if it failed.'

While the Council had yet to formally meet to vote on Pat's proposal, all the signs were positive. But just as the plan was beginning to fall into place, Pat's world fell apart with the tragic loss of his wife Lisa on 7 May 1998. He couldn't bear to contemplate life without her, let alone embarking on the longest run of his life without the most important person in his life. Pat and Lisa had planned to take the children with them on the 14 500 kilometre seven-month journey—sharing together as a family what was to be Pat's last run. In the aftermath of Lisa's death, Pat questioned everything about life—even his self-worth. Nothing was the same any more. Who he was and who he wanted to be had been inexorably changed. Inevitably, in his darkest moments, he doubted his will and ability to fight on and whether his existence would make much difference to humanity. But very quickly he would remind himself, helped by family and friends, that his reason for living was before him, in his children, Brooke and Dillon. They were a life raft in a sea of despair.

'As long as the kids need me, I'll be around for as long as I can,' he said. 'My biggest regret about the whole situation is that . . . it's like I would have easily loved to have my own heart cut out and I die and Lisa to have lived. But I had no choice to do anything noble or no choice to be a good person.'

For the first time in his life, Pat also questioned his faith. 'I was brought up as a Catholic but I have questioned the sense of it all every day since Lisa died,' he said. 'I'm not scared of dying myself and I've never questioned the right to live and die. I'm just not sure now what happens after you die. When I think about things decaying and going away, it's hard to believe that someone who could have so much life could only amount to that. But I need to believe for my kids' sake. I need to have something to hang on to.'

Some family members also questioned their religion. Pat's brother Tony says his faith diminished as a result. 'Pat and Lisa were people who had dedicated their lives to doing so much good for others,' he said. 'You wonder why would you split up a team like that? Why not leave them to go on to their achievements and raise money for charities and everybody benefits by that? That was the thing I couldn't make any sense of.'

In the weeks and months after Lisa's death, the children seemed to cope with the loss of their mother. They appeared contented enough during daytime play, although Brooke would occasionally ask: 'When is Mummy coming home?' Pat would struggle to explain that Mummy had gone to Heaven where she had important business to do. 'I want to go up there,' Brooke would plead. Pat would be almost lost for a reply, as he choked back the emotion. 'Darling, we can't go up there for a long time.'

Everyone thought Dillon was too young to understand what had happened, but Pat found himself questioning that six months after Lisa's death, when his sixteen-month-old son awoke one night in a hysterical state.

'He was screaming his head off like something terrible had happened to him,' said Pat. 'It was weird, so unlike him. He wasn't sick and no matter what my mother or I did we couldn't stop him crying uncontrollably. Up to that time he'd hardly spoken a clear word, but then he said "Mummy" with more force and passion than I can muster now. It was like something happened to him to make him say that. I thought if somehow Lisa could come back and see just one person and let them know she was all right, it would be Dillon because she loved him so much.'

Pat's brave exterior deceived some friends into thinking that he was coping with Lisa's death. But those closest to him knew that it was tearing him up inside. 'It was like he'd lost his right arm,' said former training partner Mark Gladwell. 'I didn't see Pat until some time after the funeral and even then he couldn't talk about Lisa without breaking down.'

Tony Farmer stayed with Pat for a week and says the nights were the worst. 'We'd say good night and retire and he'd be holding Lisa's photo and you could hear him sobbing,' he said. 'It seemed like there was nothing you could do or say to make things any easier for him. The other side of it was that Lisa was the most organised person I've ever met and organised 90 per cent of Pat's life. He left it all up to her and it all ran like clockwork. She was so efficient it was unbelievable. She wasn't just a wife and mother; she really was the other half of Pat. There's no other way to explain it.'

Pat desperately wanted to see Lisa, to touch her. He admits there were days when that urge was almost overwhelming. He would go into Lisa's closet (which he had left untouched since her death) just to smell the lingering fragrance on her clothes. Pat would become cranky and frustrated with friends who told Pat they had dreamed about Lisa. Every night Pat would close his eyes and hope she would come to him. But all he ever saw was black. 'I so wanted to see her in any shape or form but it never happened,' he said. 'I'd say to friends who said they'd had visions of her: "Next time you see her in your dreams tell her to come and visit me."'

Amidst his grief, Pat had to confront some unwelcome realities. The family finances were not in the healthiest state. The debts had been steadily mounting. After a decade of giving to numerous charities and causes, it was time for Pat to receive.

Rotary's Granville club president, Geoff Lynch, and his deputy, Robyn Horn, rallied their troops in quick time.

Pat and Lisa were well known through Rotary. Lisa had been a tireless worker for Rotaract and Rotary, while Pat had been an honorary member for many years. Lynch hit the road and called on clubs in his district over the course of a week.

'I addressed their meetings by saying: "You know who I am and you know who Pat is and he needs our help",' said Lynch. 'I think people were incredulous that he was in dire financial straits. There was genuine shock at his plight. A lot of them thought that because of his profile he must be a multi-millionaire. But they didn't know that most of his charity runs cost him money. People dug deep because of their love for Lisa and the fact that Pat had always been so willing to help others more needy. Within days we had $10 000 for the Farmer Family Assistance Fund and it didn't stop there.'

A lot of the money came from average people in clubs. Known battlers donated up to $150—more than they'd spend on their own family for Christmas presents. Larger organisations, like the Parramatta City Council, donated $5000. Around $45 000 flowed into the fund, which paid for Lisa's funeral and wake, as well as some other outstanding debts. Money still remains that will be used for future family expenses. As well, the Western Suburbs Leagues Club Campbelltown, which had just sponsored Pat's record-breaking Simpson Desert run, organised its own 'Brooke and Dillon Farmer Trust Fund'. It was kicked off at a benefit luncheon at the club on 14 July 1998. Nearly 300 guests paid $100 a head to attend. Leading 2UE breakfast announcer Alan Jones, who had promoted Pat's runs and fundraising ventures, was the compere and motivational speaker.

The occasion was deeply moving for all who attended. Jones encouraged Pat not to lose his will to run and to continue to help others, despite his own tragic loss. With Pat's consent, organiser Fred Borg played a motivational tape that featured Lisa's voice. Katie Melrose, from the Australia Day Council, says the function was one of the most emotional days of her life. 'When they played Lisa's tape, Pat was in tears, as was everybody else in the room,' she said. 'You couldn't help it. It was just so incredibly sad. It was a sea of tears. Everyone cried again when Pat spoke about how much inspiration he drew from Lisa and how giving and supportive his family had been since her death.'

An auction of donated sports memorabilia and other prizes was also held. Items included autographed New South Wales and Australian Rugby League jumpers, a limited edition cricket print, 'Caught Marsh, Bowled Lillee', and racing silks autographed by winning Melbourne Cup jockey Jim Cassidy. In total, the luncheon raised about $120 000.

As well as finding a reason to live, Pat had to search deep within to find a reason to run. The proposed Centenary of Federation event had been Pat and Lisa's dream. But now it was a nightmare whenever he left the children. Pat would head out the door for a training run, but 200 metres down the road, he would be so worried that Brooke or Dillon were crying out for him that he would trudge back home. While his mother Mary was now living with them and bearing much of the domestic burden, the children were still his responsibility. For weeks, he was reluctant to run again. Lisa was his strength, his inspiration. He was missing something and someone who could never be replaced.

While the pain of his loss was still ever-present, gradually some of the fog lifted. Pat's youngest brother Christopher remembers having a heart-to-heart while driving to their sister Annette's place.

'Pat was going through some guilt, saying it was nuts that he'd spent all his time running, trying to reach his goal of being the world's best ultra runner, when he should have been spending time with Lisa,' he recalls. 'But we agreed that if Lisa hadn't wanted him to pursue his goal, she would have told him. We also agreed that Pat was the person he was because of running and stopping running now wasn't going to bring Lisa back. I pointed out that he and Lisa had spent so much time preparing for the Centenary of Federation, how it was Lisa's hard work as well and how important it was going to be sharing an adventure like that as a family. At the end he decided he'd go through with it. I didn't talk him into it, but I think that discussion helped crystallise the issue for him.'

Pat decided that, by fulfilling his commitments to run, he could make the causes a tribute to Lisa. 'I believe she would have wanted me to go ahead with it,' he said. 'I thought that through the Centenary of Federation run I could carry with me around the nation everything Lisa stood for and, even though she couldn't be there us in person, I had no doubt she'd be beside me every step of the way.' Sixteenth-century English poet John Heywood once wrote: 'Nothing is impossible to a willing heart.' There was no doubt that Pat's heart, as wounded as it was, was still willing.

When Pat promptly notified the Centenary of Federation Council of his decision to proceed with the run, some of its members were astonished. The council held its quarterly meeting on 12 June 1998 and finally formally voted on the proposal. It drew together a wide array of distinguished Australians, including the Most Reverend Anglican Archbishop Peter Hollingworth, historian Professor Geoffrey Blainey, former Director of the National Gallery Betty Churcher and lead singer with rock band Rose Tattoo, Angry Anderson. They were a disparate and wily collection of people, but all bonded by the patriotic cause. The proposal to back Pat Farmer sparked lively debate. While generally the Council was impressed with Pat's statement that he was more determined than ever to complete the run after Lisa's death, some members thought the whole concept a surprising and curious project for them to be involved with.

There were all sorts of questions in the mind of the council. Was it achievable? Were they putting too many eggs in one financial basket? What if something went wrong and Pat didn't make it? Would it be a disaster if the council's first big promotional venture failed? But the doubters were in the minority and ultimately, says Eggleton, it wasn't such a difficult task to sell the Council on the idea. 'I think everyone saw the merits of it and saw it as a way—and a very unique way—of getting a focus a year or two before the Centenary that we probably couldn't get in any other shape or form,' said Eggleton.

While Pat had originally wanted to leave in May 2000 and finish on 1 January 2001, the Council was keen for Pat to start his run one year earlier. It wanted to use a 1999 event as the vanguard for its promotions campaign and didn't want to overlap with the 2000 Sydney Olympics. There was also the problem of drafting an appropriate contract. But this was such an unusual, and in the eyes of some still risky, contract for the Commonwealth to be signing that it was sent off to the big guns in the federal Attorney-General's Office for expert advice. They came back with some ridiculous requests of Pat. The worst was that he should have his appendix removed before he left on the run, even though, as far as he knew, it was perfectly healthy. 'I just laughed when I was asked and said there was no way I would do that for anybody,' Pat said. A crisis clause was also added to the contract in the unthinkable circumstance of Pat dying mid-journey. The Centenary of Federation run would be completed no matter what. The contingency plan was to form a relay of runners around the country, comprising famous Australians and school and club athletes, who would complete the task if necessary.

Pat had another running commitment to fulfil—to the Autism Association. He had agreed to a second run up Sydney's AMP Tower (formerly Centrepoint Tower) after previously falling short of his fundraising and world targets. This was to be much tougher. Instead of 33 382 steps in five hours, Pat would attempt to run up 100 000 steps in 24 hours and fundraise $100 000. But a haphazard training routine (which mainly consisted of infrequent sessions at home on a Stairmaster treadmill as well as the occasional training run inside AMP Tower) left him ill-prepared for such a gruelling event. He argued with friends and family about whether he should proceed with it. His former training partner, Mark Gladwell, suggested he should at least postpone it. 'I knew he just hadn't done the training for it and

I told him this was the one time no one would think any less of him if he didn't honour a commitment,' he said.

But, as always, Pat felt compelled to keep his promise. There were other, more profound, reasons too. 'I just needed to feel some self-worth,' he explains. 'I needed to match the emotional and psychological pain I was feeling over Lisa's death with physical pain. I wanted a reason for hurting that I could explain. I needed to ache with my body because I could understand that, instead of aching with my heart and my head.'

It seemed the event was jinxed. It had been postponed a year before when AMP withdrew a sponsorship offer. Sydney Water later picked up the baton, but it too was having second thoughts when it became immersed in the water contamination scare that saw the city's tap water rendered unsafe by unacceptable levels of cryptosporidium and giardia. In the midst of a public relations nightmare, Sydney Water feared the event would be seen as a cynical attempt to divert attention from its woes, even though the agreement with Pat had been signed before the health crisis.

'There was a lot of drama leading up to the event,' said the Autism Association's Business Development director, Kel Beckett. 'I'd go to meetings at Sydney Water's headquarters and I'd have to wade through a huge media contingent that was camped outside just trying to doorstop anyone from Sydney Water about the health scare. I was really worried Sydney Water was going to pull the plug on the sponsorship deal, but thankfully they bit the bullet and stuck with us.'

When Pat attacked the start of the 24-hour event at 7.30 a.m. on 30 September at a fearless pace, friends and family feared he was on a mission of self-destruction. Some saw it as bravery; others thought it was stupidity and argued with Pat about his strategy. Some, like manager David Fookes, threatened to walk away if he didn't moderate his pace. Pat smashed the world record for vertical running after eight hours, and kept hammering away, but then he heeded their message. However the damage was already done to Pat's body—he had depleted much of his energy reserves.

Sheer guts and willpower fuelled the assault on the next 50 000 steps. He climbed hard and had minimal rest—never any more than 40 minutes. Many of those present were moved to tears by the extreme pain Pat inflicted upon himself and the courage he displayed in coping with it. In the early hours of 1 October, friend and Trans Am sponsor Mr Okada arrived to lend him support. He ran several circuits of the 1100-stair tower with Pat. At one point, Mr Okada insisted Pat needed to take salt because of his profuse sweating. Not wishing to insult him, Pat swallowed the pure salt sachets offered to him. They stayed down for only a few minutes, before Pat vomited them back up over the steel stairwell.

Observers describe the event as a spiritual and supernatural experience, such was the inexplicable nature of the forces driving an utterly exhausted Pat Farmer up each flight of stairs. John Gibson, an AMP employee who was a volunteer helper for the event, says the event changed his perspective on life. In a letter to the Autism Association, he wrote: 'I couldn't help thinking that any pain I had ever felt, whether physical or heartache, was meaningless compared to the torture this man seemed to be going through. There is one thing for sure though, I will never complain about having a hard day again. Any right I ever had to complain about anything was taken from me. I was left speechless and tiny, overwhelmed by the size of this man's compassion. Pat ran 101 934 stairs. I believe he said: "I love you" to his wife, on every one of them.'

Utterly spent, Pat was not in the condition or mood to join in the champagne celebrations at his world record. A friend rested a comforting hand on his shoulder as he sat slumped in a chair. 'It's still not right, is it Pat?' 'It's just not the same without Lisa anymore,' he replied. 'Nothing is the same.'

While the record was in the bag, the money was not. Instead of his $100 000 target, Pat raised $40 000, despite public appeals for donations in television and radio interviews done before, during and after the event. Beckett says the disappointing total was a reflection of various organisational and sponsorship problems. None of Sydney Water's $45 000 sponsorship money went to the Autism Association. Half was eaten up in fees and running costs by sports and event managers Grand Slam International, while the other half was paid to Pat to enable him to give up landscaping and prepare for the event. But Pat's fundraising still had a genuine practical benefit for autistic children. It covered the cost of replacing an old and dangerous playground at the Forestville School in Sydney for autistic children with a modern facility that enhanced their sensory perception—a skill vital for their development.

Any of Pat's disappointment over the fundraising venture was buffered by the knowledge that he had made an enormous contribution to the world community. The second tower run pushed Pat's charity contributions to over $2 million—a benchmark reached by few other individual athletes in Australia.

• • •

Only one sport rivals ultra marathon running for loneliness—long-distance swimming. When Pat had the opportunity to join with long-time friend Susie Maroney in a team event on Australia Day 1999, he leapt at the chance to share the experience of an endurance event. Both had been Australia Day Ambassadors and had undertaken gruelling challenges on past Australia Days—Susie had swum from Newcastle to Sydney; Pat had run across the Simpson Desert.

The pair joined ultra marathon cyclist Gerry Tatrai, a six-time winner of the Race Across America cycle race, in an event to celebrate Australia Day and the fiftieth anniversary of the Snowy Mountains Scheme. They swam, cycled and ran a total of 160 kilometres in tag team fashion over fifteen hours. The trio escorted a scroll bearing the names of all the men and women who worked on the Snowy Mountains Hydro Electric Scheme and visited numerous towns in the region, where they gave motivational talks to school children. 'It was something special to finally be able to do an event with Pat,' says Susie. 'While we were doing something that hadn't been done before, the Snowy Challenge was more of a fun thing than what we're both used to.'

Pat and Susie first met at an Australia Day lunch in 1992. They have been more than friends ever since. Pat and Susie are soulmates—bonded by the unusual and punishing nature of their solo sports. They have found solace and motivation in comparing experiences and always support each other before and during major swims and runs. 'Pat is such a positive person who's so passionate about what he does,' she said. 'You can't help but let some of it rub off on you. He's helped to inspire me during tough swims.'

One of Susie's most famous events was her attempt to swim from Cuba to America in June 1997. She rang him before she flew to Havana, seeking fresh guidance about how to endure the endless painful hours. His advice was simple: distract your mind with happy thoughts and just take it hour by hour.

'I remember during the first night of the swim I was really struggling and I got this very timely message from Pat,' Susie recalls. 'I had been vomiting and wasn't feeling very well. Pat had somehow managed to ring through to the boat and spoke to my Mum. She came out while I was having a break in the water and said: "Pat Farmer just rang to say he was thinking of you. He said hang in there and don't give up." Getting a message from Australia gave me a lift but I got a double lift knowing it came from Pat and that he knew exactly the sort of pain and torment I was experiencing.'

From the start of 1999, Pat channelled most of his energies into preparations for the Centenary of Federation Run. Frustration mounted as Pat and his promotions company, Avviso, chased major sponsorship dollars for the run. The budget was $1 million and while the Council for the Centenary of Federation was giving $250 000, they still needed some major corporate dollars to make his latest dream a reality. Originally they had sought three more major sponsors at $250 000 each, but had suffered numerous rejections from some of Australia's biggest companies. 'Sorry, but we've committed a large slice of our promotions budget to the

Sydney Olympics' was the common reply. While disappointing, it was mind-boggling stuff to Pat's friends and family. Here was the boy from Granville competing for sponsorship money with *the biggest sporting show on earth!* 'I guess it was a measure of how far I'd come, but that was no consolation when it came to getting the dollars to put my show on the road,' said Pat.

With time rapidly running out, Pat and one of his biggest allies and promoters, Carolyn Grant from Avviso Public Relations, were getting very anxious about sponsorship. Grant had invested a great deal of her personal and company time and money in backing the event. They were still over $200 000 short and a deal with Chrysler to provide two vehicles was yet to be finalised (eventually it was). After knocking their heads against the wall of corporate Australia for two years and pitching to over 100 companies, the financial jigsaw was incomplete. A constant roundabout of phone calls, meetings, proposals and more meetings had secured backing from nine organisations, but Farmer and Grant faced the prospect of being forced to take out substantial personal loans.

Their final break came in a timely yet roundabout fashion. In 1995, fifteen-year-old Sydney schoolgirl Lisa Ormrod had returned home from school one day, totally inspired and brimming with motivation. Her school had received a guest visitor that day who had used his experiences to connect with his teenage audience. Her father Kevin knew his daughter was highly pragmatic and held a cynical view of the world. She easily saw through facades and he wondered what sort of person could have such an impact. He thought nothing more of it until February 1999 when, as marketing and communications manager for GIO Financial Services, he took more notice than usual of a document addressed to him from an athlete seeking sponsorship. That athlete was Pat Farmer, the person who four years earlier had moved his daughter by his words and deeds.

'I was totally impressed with Pat before I even saw that document but the Centenary of Federation Run was also a perfect promotional vehicle for GIO because here was an ordinary Australian doing extraordinary things, while we were about

helping ordinary Australians achieve extraordinary financial positions,' he said. 'I arranged a meeting with Pat and Carolyn Grant
and emerged from that convinced this was ideal for our company.
Pat personified so many wonderful human qualities that are so
often abstract and it was a chance to put something back into
the community.'

Just like Pat Farmer, Kevin Ormrod wouldn't take no for an
answer. Three times he put up a proposal to his immediate
superior to sponsor the event. Three times he was rejected,
although each time he detected a chink in his boss' objections.
He was finally successful at the fourth attempt. Despite having
precious little time to gear up for a major promotions campaign,
GIO agreed to fill the final sponsorship void just weeks before
Pat was due to embark on his journey around the nation.

• • •

Part of the inspiration for Pat's Centenary of Federation Run
came after Lisa read of the exploits 100 years ago of Australian
Donald Mackay, the 'Last of the Explorers'. With Federation
looming, 28-year-old Mackay attempted to ride around Australia
by bicycle, spurred by his insatiable thirst for adventure. He was
also intent on breaking the cycling record that was set by Arthur
Richardson while Mackay was part-way through his journey.
Mackay, an amateur cyclist and gold prospector, left Brisbane in
July 1899, hitching his two wheels to a similar record attempt
of two professional cyclists, brothers Alec and Frank White who
had pedalled from Adelaide. They cycled north, stopping at night
but also resting some days when locals in various towns tempted
them with too much hospitality, either in the form of food, drink
or entertainment such as ghastly cockfights.

Mackay was a larger-than-life character who displayed numerous tattoos (he later became a walking picture gallery with almost
every square inch of his skin covered with body art). He also
attracted fascinating company during his journey, such as Harry
Redford, who had performed the greatest known cattle rustle in

the history of the world—lifting a thousand head of stock from western Queensland. Acquitted of the crime in 1873 by a jury impressed with the magnitude of his feat, his story was romanticised in the classic Australian novel, *Robbery Under Arms*. Mackay and his fellow cyclists rode along dirt tracks, sand tracks, railway tracks and once over 'a sleeping Chinaman', who was camouflaged by darkness as he attempted to smuggle himself into Queensland.

The trio endured severe dysentery and nearly died of dehydration and starvation. Their lives were also in peril when they were attacked by a group of spear-throwing Aborigines in the Northern Territory. Ultimately it was a broken crankshaft that ended Frank White's trip, while chronic dysentery stopped Alec White in his tracks. But Mackay pushed on through all adversity, breaking a string of cycling records on his way to a complete victory. Mackay arrived back in Brisbane after covering 17 700 kilometres in 240 days—a new around-Australia record by three days. He later led important explorations to the Northern Territory, Papua (as it was then called) and the South Pacific.* In the 1930s he was awarded the Order of the British Empire (OBE) and Commander of the British Empire (CBE) and, according to *Who's Who* won 'deserved recognition as the last Australian explorer'. Donald Mackay died in 1958, aged 88.

But Pat knew from his modern inspiration, friend and fellow ultra runner Ron Grant, that he would not have to dodge hostile Aborigines or cattle rustlers during his adventure of 1999. Despite the fact that Pat had twice broken his Simpson Desert record and was endeavouring to break one of his last major records, the pair share a healthy respect and friendship. Grant was generous with his advice and encouragement. 'I don't mind my record being broken, as long as Pat acknowledges I was first,' he said with a laugh, just a month before Pat's departure. 'It's been sixteen years since I set the record. That's long enough. I was always about doing things first anyway.'

* Clune, F., 1942, *Last of the Australian Explorers*, Angus & Robertson, Sydney pp. 120–72.

Grant calls himself and Farmer 'adventurers', and offers this insight into what makes them both tick. 'We're not really racers,' he said. 'We would probably have more in common with Sir Edmund Hillary than we do with blokes who line up for the average marathon or ultra run. We go out looking for adventures. We like the extreme endurance. We like the unknown—can we make it and can it be done? It's the extreme conditions. If Pat or I had been born 150 years ago we would have been the explorers, we would have been the Burkes and Wills. Mind you, we probably would also have been dead out there in the desert.'

Grant warned Farmer that boredom and loneliness would be the toughest aspects of the run, as well as the constant wear and tear on the body. He was resigned to the fact that Pat would soon own his around-Australia mark—and a host of his inter-city records as well. 'Pat's a decent bloke. He's out there trying to have a fair go. He's not trying to pretend,' Grant said.

But Grant didn't afford the same generous words or assistance to another runner embarking on a similar attempt, Gary Parsons, whom Grant had once coached and mentored. The pair had a falling out, seemingly over trivial issues, although Parsons believes Grant became jealous once he broke two of his records. Parsons left Brisbane on 25 April, Anzac Day—five weeks ahead of Pat—with a mission statement to raise funds and awareness for Legacy. Parsons had impressive credentials. The 49-year-old grandfather had twice broken the world track record for 1000 miles (set by Tony Rafferty at Pat's 1989 Granville Challenge). He was aiming to run 500 kilometres further than Pat by averaging 75 kilometres a day compared with Pat's target of 70 kilometres a day.

'It will be interesting to see how we go,' Parsons said. 'We'll both be on the Internet and we'll both be looking up each other's sites and checking out how many kilometres we've both done each month. But that's part of the game, part of the sport. It adds excitement—makes you get up every morning and get going.'

Pat was clearly annoyed and angered by the Parsons venture when questioned about it before his departure, especially his attempts to outbid him in what had become a pre-run auction. Pat also believed Parsons was riding on the coat-tails of the publicity he had generated for his own event. Both questioned each other's ability to meet their targets.

'If he wanted a race he'd start with me at the starter's grid and we'd treat it as a real race,' he said. 'I'm blowed if I can see how he can say he's going to run 15 000 kilometres because we're both supposed to be running the exact route Ron Grant ran, except we're adding in Tasmania. If he was fair dinkum about taking me on he would have contacted me and said: "Hey Pat, you think you're pretty good, how about we make this a contest?"'

Despite Pat's ambition to finish the run with a new record for running around Australia, he was adamant he wouldn't be checking up on Parsons' progress ahead of him. He couldn't adjust his schedule, he said, because it was pre-set before he left with speaking engagements in towns every night. 'I'm not interested in the guy,' he snapped. 'I've got too much to be concerned about with my own event. If Parsons can do more each day than me, then he'll break the record and good luck to him.'

Pat's life leading up to the Centenary of Federation Run was a crazy whirlwind of meetings, functions, media and public commitments. In between, he juggled a less-than-satisfactory training schedule with work as a landscape gardener with his brother and family life. Despite every minute of the day being accounted for, he was typically also ever-ready to lend support in various ways to friends in times of their own crises.

He went to help one friend sift through the charred remains of their house that had just burnt down; he was on hand to lend emotional support to another friend whose son had become addicted to pain-killers after injuring his knees while serving in the Gulf War. Always, his touchstone to reality was the quality time he had with Brooke and Dillon. He was more appreciative than ever of the precious gift of life and took delight in everyday things like taking them both to learn-to-swim classes or Brooke to weekly dance classes. He was also continuing to climb the steep learning curve of a single parent, helped immeasurably by his mother Mary. 'Even though he can't spend as much time with the kids as he and they would like, Pat is very patient and caring with them,' said Mary Farmer.

As always, Pat was trying to bite off plenty and chew like mad. He was trying to finish aspects of his and Lisa's dream home, despite the fact that he would soon be vacating it for seven months. The kitchen was finally being installed and Pat had contracted his brother Tony to pave the driveway and edge the garden beds. Pat mucked in, mixing concrete and trowelling garden edges in between taking phone calls about the Centenary of Federation run. Why bother with home improvements when life was already crazy enough?

'This is a house for the rest of my life, which I hope to pass on to my kids,' Pat explained. 'I'm worried if I stop work on the house, things will never get done. I could have stopped after Lisa died, but I didn't. I wanted to go forward. I make three hours of phone calls chasing sponsors for the run and I have nothing to show for it. With labouring if I do three hours' work, I've got a tangible result to show for it. I'm the sort of person who feels he has to be going forward.'

But Pat wasn't moving forward as fast or as often as he'd like when it came to training for the Centenary of Federation Run. It was impossible to train specifically for a 14 500-kilometre event. He tried to run every day, with sessions that varied between 15 and 70 kilometres. But, as always, the toughest aspect of the run would be mental. It was impossible to prepare the body for the shock of running upwards of 70 kilometres a day every day for 216 days. But in many respects, Pat couldn't wait to hit the open road and do what he knew he did best. He would run to fulfil himself and inspire others with his deeds by day and words by night. Pat found reassurance in the knowledge that, no matter how tough it got, he would be carried through by his vast experience and public support coupled with his never-say-die attitude, fierce patriotism and memories of Lisa.

Lisa's enormous impact on Pat in both life and death came into sharp public focus when he was the subject of the top-rating Nine

Network program *This Is Your Life*. The program was recorded on 30 March before Pat left and aired nationally on 15 July when he was in the Northern Territory. Host Mike Munro ambushed Pat after the runner was talked into recording a bogus television ad for the Centenary of Federation in a Sydney park. There was no feigned incredulity by the subject, as is often the case. 'Out of the 60-plus people we've done, Pat was the most genuinely put out and embarrassed,' says Munro. 'He believed there were far more worthwhile people than him. Even though the cameras were rolling, he was initially reluctant to be part of it and at one point I thought I'd have to do a real sales job on him.'

This Is Your Life was recorded later that evening before a studio audience of 200 family and friends. Midway through the show, producers paid tribute to Lisa by playing one of the motivational audio tapes she had previously compiled for Pat. It was set to music and overlaid with photographs and home videos of Lisa. While it was done with the consent of Pat's family, Pat had some misgivings about it. Mike Munro quickly points out the use of Lisa's voice wasn't his idea and says he felt uncomfortable watching Pat have to sit through it.

'I thought we were milking it too much,' he said. The scene was highly emotional for Pat as well as for viewers. Munro says he cried when he later watched the show, as did his boss, Nine's Chief Executive David Leckie, known as one of the hardest men in the ruthless world of television. The taping of *This Is Your Life* was especially painful for Lisa's parents, Barry and June Bullivant. 'It was like the day of the funeral all over again,' says Mrs Bullivant.

As well as celebrating Pat's achievements, *This Is Your Life* provided the Farmers with a rare family reunion, with Pat's sister Catherine being flown to Sydney from Tasmania. Munro says it was his favourite show of the year. 'I love doing the unsung heroes and that show had real warmth and emotion,' he said. 'Pat Farmer is an extraordinary Australian. There are very few Aussies with not only a heart the size of his, but also the will to go on helping others when they've had such a tragic loss.' At one point during the recording of the show, Pat's elder brother Michael whispered to sister Annette: 'Fancy all this fuss. A Farmer on *This Is Your Life.*' The show touched a chord with the public. It was the highest-rating episode of 1999, with an estimated national audience of almost three million viewers.

Pat had a series of send-offs before embarking on his Centenary of Federation run. There was an official launch on 30 April in the city where he grew up, Parramatta. Mayor C. Paul Garrard calls Pat 'Mr Parramatta' because of his willingness to act as roving sports ambassador. Pat was presented with the keys to the city—according to Garrard, the first time it had been done in his 25 years on the council. Earlier in the day, 'Mr Parramatta' had returned from a media launch at the Town Hall to find a $60 parking fine on his car windscreen. 'I can't believe they gave me a ticket! What's the good of getting the keys to the city if they don't let you park there?' Pat wondered. He contemplated asking Mayor Garrard to waive the fine at the launch that night, but then reconsidered. 'It would have cost them a bit more than $60 to put this launch on,' he mused.

Pat was also special guest at a Centenary of Federation dinner in Parliament House, Canberra, two nights before he left. Political and business heavyweights were amongst the guests including Prime Minister John Howard, Opposition Leader Kim Beazley, transport magnate Lindsay Fox and media magnate James Packer. There was also a preview of a national television advertisement for the Centenary, starring Pat. He was swamped by well-wishers at his table, as the esteemed audience finally seemed to grasp the enormity of his undertaking. Pat felt like reality was slapping at him as well, as he began to think seriously for the first time about the road ahead. He began to feel the weight of expectation, which was now beginning to gather a momentum of its own. This was to be the greatest journey of his life. Pat knew he would encounter unbelievable amounts of emotional and physical torment. The finish line was too far away to think about. But, as in life, it was the journey and the experiences along the way that counted most.

10

The last great adventure

The atmosphere in the national capital on the morning of Monday, 31 May 1999 was thick with low, grey rain clouds and history. Canberra was abuzz with the landmark deal between the Howard government and the Democrats over the Goods and Services Tax (GST), although confusion reigned over what tax would be levied on food. But as he arrived at Parliament House to start writing his own page in history, Pat was clear about his mission and the importance of it. Here was a perfect outlet for his own fervent patriotism and a way of touching and inspiring ordinary lives. He felt excited and challenged, tinged with a sense of apprehension and fear at the enormity of the task and the fear of failure. Pat still had so many unresolved issues and questions about Lisa's death in his mind. He would have quality time with himself, and plenty of it. He hoped he would find some answers on a quiet stretch of road. He desperately hoped he would feel closer to Lisa.

The agreement by Prime Minister John Howard to send Pat on his way was of enormous significance for Pat. Politics aside, he felt that the mere presence of the nation's leader elevated the stature of the event. After more than a decade of battling perceptions that he was crazy or foolhardy, he felt that finally here was the recognition and respect he had craved for himself and his sport. The snapshot of a smiling Pat with his mother Mary and children Brooke and Dillon, together with the Prime Minister in front of Parliament House, was definitely one for the front of the next family album.

Pat's children were to accompany him on the entire journey around Australia. That was what Lisa would have wanted. As well, he couldn't cope with the thought of not seeing them for seven months. 'I need my kids desperately,' he said proudly. 'I need to know I can see their faces and they can see mine. I could never do this run otherwise.' Mary Farmer had the job of keeping Brooke and Dillon happy and healthy—a task that many considered to be almost as difficult and tiring as Pat's. Mary was more apprehensive than most. 'It will be very difficult for the children because they'll want to be with their Dad and because of our schedule they'll be in a different bed every night,' she said.

Once again the Farmer family was making sacrifices that seemed above and beyond the call of family duty. Eldest brother Bernie had sold his Canberra cleaning business and was leaving his family to spend the entire seven months on the road as crew manager, although his 18-year-old son Danny had been recruited as a crewman and cameraman. As well as Pat's 19-year-old niece Kristy Walsh, the road crew that began the epic included loyal friends Ken Fuz and Nigel Simmons as drivers of the two Chrysler Voyager support vehicles. Simmons was a handy man to have in case of emergency, having been security guard for two Australian Prime Ministers. As well, three of Pat's siblings had plans to drop in and out as relieving crew members at various stages, and his sister Annette had timed the sale of her own house so she could house-sit for Pat in his seven-month absence.

A short official farewell ceremony took place in front of Parliament House. Speeches were made by the Federal Minister for the Centenary of Federation, Peter McGauran, and council member and rocker Angry Anderson. 'If I've ever met anybody in my life that has the heart, the big heart to run around our big and wonderful country, then Mr Farmer has that heart,' said Anderson. John Howard expressed his thanks and admiration for Pat, saying the run was a spectacularly Australian way of beginning the public face of the celebrations of the Centenary of Australia's nationhood. He asked Pat to be his emissary in inviting Australians to participate in the nation's one-hundredth birthday and presented him with a scroll that he would escort for the entire journey.

Signed by the Prime Minister, the scroll read:

> All the people of Australia are invited to celebrate the Centenary of the Federation of our nation in 2001. I hope that, whatever your heritage and backgrounds, you will join the governments and local communities of Australia in commemorating the 100th birthday of our great nation. It is a time to reflect on the past, take pride in the present and look to the future with confidence. A very proud Australian, Pat Farmer, is linking symbolically all States and Territories as he undertakes this ultra-marathon run for the Centenary. It is this kind of courage and determination that built our great nation. I am delighted to have Pat Farmer as my special emissary in delivering this message to you.

An emotional Pat labelled it as one of the greatest days of his life. 'The first step that I take and the last step that I take on this journey will be for my wife Lisa, who planned this together with me and I'm sure will be with me every other step of the way. And every other step that I take in between those two will be for my God and my love of this country.' His last great adventure took him north from Parliament House through Canberra's peak-hour traffic, accompanied by about 40 runners and a convoy of police cars and vintage vehicles. Pat was relaxed as he waved to the spectators and school children who lined the route. 'See you when you get back, Pat,' yelled one youngster. Pat even conducted an interview on a mobile phone for a radio station while running out of the national capital.

As expected, the first 48 hours were a real shock to the system. While Pat's aim was to run an average of 70 kilometres a day over seven months, the first two days—from Canberra to Goulburn to Mittagong—involved churning out around 90 kilometres each day. The second day carried the added challenge of crossing over the Great Dividing Range where the hills seemed endless. Pat got an early taste of the public enthusiasm for his feat when curious spectators and supporters braved near-freezing temperatures to cheer him on. He had braced himself as best he could for the sharp aches and pains that would dog him in the early stages. His knees were the first problem area, followed soon by an inflamed Achilles tendon in his right leg—an old injury from pounding a few too many thousand kilometres over the years.

The Achilles injury caused a good deal of concern, given the intensity of the pain and the fact it was so restricting so early in the run. Pat's support network swung into action. Physiotherapist friend Ian Austin drove 300 kilometres south from Penrith to spend two days treating Pat's injuries. Ideally, Austin would have spent the entire seven-month run as Pat's personal physio, but couldn't leave his private practice or his wife and five children. But he had arranged, through the Australian Physiotherapists' Association, for Pat to receive regular free treatment from practitioners in different towns. The injuries settled down after massage, ultrasound treatment and painkillers. The moral support of his family was also to the fore. Younger brother Tony rang Bernie and, as always, tried to add some levity to the situation. 'Tell Pat to stop whingeing,' Tony said. 'Tell him to remember the time when he cut his foot with a chainsaw at work and he should have had stitches. He just stuck some Band-Aids on it, threw his sock and shoe back on and kept working. Remind him of that and he'll be all right.'

'My family just believe in me so much,' said Pat. 'It's that sort of logic that will be a major help on this run because they've seen me go through so much that they know whatever the current problem might be, it isn't worth worrying about. Sometimes you get so caught up in what's gone wrong now that you forget what you have run through before. It's like my family know me better than I know myself sometimes. I put my trust in them and that's why I can't help but succeed. The first two weeks were always going to be tough, but I'm quite confident if I can get through that, the rest of the run is a done deal.'

As predicted, the first fortnight wasn't fun for anyone, as Pat and his crew adjusted to the surreal and contradictory world of confined living on the open road. Pat was irritable as he came to grips with the expected—injuries and fatigue—and the unexpected—detours that added more kilometres, an unsatisfactory diet and the demands of functions. The added extras to the run—the public speaking commitments—were an unwelcome chore in the early stages, as his body struggled with the physical demands. While the public were embracing his exploits and patriotism, their expectations were sometimes a little excessive. When Pat began to run late for a series of civic functions on the New South Wales north coast, he was forced to cancel an unscheduled school visit that a local official had tried to squeeze in. The official had a dig at Pat over the cancellation, prompting him to bite back. 'I'm not a train,' Pat said. 'I don't arrive at the station at a certain time. I have bad days with pains, cramps and toilet stops. That's what makes me human.'

Pat received some timely advice and welcome support after he crossed his third border, into Queensland. Ron Grant drove more than 100 kilometres from his home at Caboolture, north of Brisbane, to welcome Pat to the Sunshine State and, in keeping with the historic nature of the run, presented him with a bottle of wine from Queensland's oldest winery. Grant had been troubled when told of Pat's heavy functions timetable.

'He's got to be careful in taking on all this extra stuff because he needs his recovery time at the end of the day,' he said. 'All I wanted to do at night was put my feet up and have a decent feed, a beer and a good sleep. Pat's got a job to do out there and records are getting harder by the year. If someone is going to break my record, it might as well be Pat. He's a great ambassador for the sport.'

The pair was due to run together into Nambour Agricultural show, close to Grant's home town, but on Ron's advice, Pat bypassed the function. Pat had enormous respect and regard for Grant—an emotion that quickly mounted with each new kilometre he conquered throughout the run. 'He's a typical Aussie, down to earth, but he's achieved great things,' Pat said. 'But he can still be approached and spoken to by anybody. Age certainly isn't a barrier between us [Grant is 21 years older] but I feel I can speak with Ron about anything and he'd understand.'

By the end of the first month, Pat had covered over 2100 kilometres and was halfway up the Queensland coast. But it had taken an early physical and emotional toll on the runner and his support crew. Inevitable cracks had opened up in Team Farmer. For the younger members of the road crew, nephew Danny and niece Kristy, the novelty and adventure of the 'trip of a lifetime' had quickly worn off. As well as missing their teenage sweethearts back home, they weren't handling Pat's demands and outbursts as well as the older, wiser crew members. They had been warned life on the road would be no picnic, with everything revolving around one person, but the lows were far outweighing the highs. 'It's a big ask for teenagers to do this job,' acknowledged Bernie. 'I've said to Pat: "I know when you and I were eighteen what we'd rather be doing."' No one had been spared the brunt of Pat's anger as he grappled with long, tiring days and nights and the frustration of a crew that wasn't yet as organised and efficient as he wanted. He'd even lost his cool with his mother, Mary, one night, but sheepishly apologised the next day. 'You can't change the way he is,' said a philosophical Mary Farmer. 'You have your good and bad days—but I can't remember when the last good day was.' 'Ours is yet to come, Gran,' added Kristy.

Caring for Brooke and Dillon was, as expected, proving to be exhausting. They occupied one car with Mary, Kristy and a driver (a position that was shared by a variety of family and friends who flew in and out of the crew). They also towed a caravan and would regularly leapfrog the other vehicle containing Bernie, Danny and driver Ken Fuz, who always trailed behind Pat at a steady 7–10 kilometres per hour. The children were often restless in the car and had to be occupied by frequent stops and boisterous play. Nights were difficult, with Brooke and Dillon settling late and waking often. Any semblance of routine was further disrupted by the fact that almost every night Pat and the crew stayed at a different motel, hotel or in the private homes of willing Rotary club members. Sleep deprivation also added to the crew's irritability.

'You don't care that you keep Gran and I awake at night, do you Brooke,' said Kristy one day. 'No, I don't care,' replied the high-spirited-four-year old. After a thoughtful pause, she added: 'Yeah, I really do care.' In a bid to create a more settled environment for the children, the crew occasionally sent them and Mary well ahead of Pat and set them up in a motel for a few days at a time. While they missed not seeing their father every day, the option at least gave them some stability.

Pat readily admits he was difficult to live with. 'I think the crew know I'm a different person away from the run and I do have feelings of compassion towards them and understanding for them,' he said. 'But it's a tough job and somebody's got to do it and it calls for tough circumstances and tough decisions from time to time and that's all there is to it.' He hoped they would learn and grow from the experience and not see the time as a wasted exercise.

'It's like anything in life that's really tough, whether it be sport or whatever. When it all seems so hard and hopeless you can't imagine anything ever being good again because you hurt so much. Anyone who has competed in a tough event would have experienced that. But there's a finish line to everything and once it's over, the pain and discomfort quickly fade and you think to yourself: "What was I whingeing about?"' Danny and Kristy left the road crew after a month. Neither rejoined the run at any stage.

Pat and Bernie were also at odds with Sydney organisers of the event over several issues. The Sunshine State wasn't living up to its name and Pat had been nagging his Sydney promotions company, Avviso, to organise sponsorship with the manufacturers of a waterproof jacket. Little progress had been made and Pat had one of his now-trademark dummy spits. 'You don't see the urgency,' he told them on the mobile phone. 'You don't think it matters when I get this gear because I'm out here for seven months. You're 2000 kilometres away and you've got no idea what it's like out on the road. I'm getting drenched for eight hours a day. I might get damned pneumonia and not be on the road in a month and then this whole thing is finished.' Pat promptly rang the company himself. Wet weather gear arrived a few days later.

Bernie was also critical of the gruelling schedule of functions set by Centenary of Federation organisers that locked them into set distances each day (sometimes up to 90 kilometres), regardless of how Pat was feeling. Often he would set off in darkness before 5.00 a.m. and finish in darkness after 5.00 p.m., and have half an hour to recover for a dinner-time speaking function. His head wouldn't hit the pillow until after 10.30 p.m., only to rise again at 4.00 a.m. No one was immune to fatigue, which compounded with each passing week. Some days were worse than others. 'You know you're really tired when you put zinc cream on your toothbrush and you piss on your leg and I've done both this morning,' said Bernie on one of the bad days. In the first month, Pat had only one night off, with some of the functions being so poorly organised that Bernie was left wondering whether the promotions exercise was more trouble than it was worth.

One classic example was on 29 June as Pat ran between Marlborough and St Lawrence in central Queensland. Checks with Centenary of Federation organisers had confirmed there was no function planned for that evening and Pat was relishing the rare reward of an early night, especially after another tough 80-kilometre day, where he had battled incessant rain and a stomach upset. All that changed when crew member James Merritt returned from a reconnaissance of St Lawrence, 5 kilometres off the main Bruce Highway. He showed Ken and Danny a flyer that was posted all around the town advertising a free sausage sizzle that night with guest speaker Pat Farmer. 'I'm not telling Pat about it. Someone else can,' said Danny. 'Me neither,' said Ken. 'I guess I'd better break the news,' said James. To everyone's surprise, Pat took the news calmly, and called for his Walkman and one of his motivational tapes. He ignored cramping stomach pains to 'run his butt off' to make it into town on time.

St Lawrence offers a typical story of the decline of regional and rural Australia. Its glory days, when the town had a thriving population that supported six hotels, and a meatworks and railways maintenance yard that served Central Queensland, were gone. Just over 100 residents remained. The town was punch-drunk from all the blows from economic rationalism, but the survivors weren't going down without a fight. New projects like a tourist caravan park had given new life and new hope. Three-quarters of the town rolled up to hear Pat's patriotic and inspirational message.

'Americans make a big deal about their history and what a great place it is, but they had a Civil War where there were more people killed than in all the other American wars combined. We were able to form a nation with barely a drop of blood being shed. It doesn't matter where you came from originally; all that matters now is that you're an Australian. There's something special about this land. I feel it out there every day on the road. I get busted to pieces by this country every day. It's the wet weather, the roads, the distance, the roasting hot days. Cynics say one person can't make a difference, but I'm telling you they can and I'm proving to you that they do by my actions.' The captivation in the eyes of his audience and their reactions when polled afterwards left no mistake that the message had left a lasting impression.

Neville Hunt, 70, a tourist from Leeton in New South Wales said: 'He's the most inspirational speaker I've ever heard. I used to think I'd done a lot for my country but he makes me wonder what more I can do to be a better Australian and to make Australia a better place.'

And from Mike McArthur, St Lawrence's Mayor: 'I don't believe I've met anybody who speaks with the same patriotic passion as Pat does. The important thing is that kids who are here tonight will never forget that speech. In years to come they'll say they met Pat Farmer and they'll be able to say why he was here.'

Kristy Baker, 18, of St Lawrence, said: 'I've always wanted to have my own motel, that's a dream of mine. But it's going to take a long time. Just like Pat, it's taken him a long time to get to where he is but he's made it and it makes me think: "Yeah, I can make my dreams come true too."'

As he embarked on another taxing 80-kilometre haul the next day, Pat was humbled by the experience. 'I'm embarrassed that I kick up a stink about the speaking engagements and the extra towns I have to run into when I see what an impact my message and actions have on people like that,' he said. 'Sometimes when I'm out on the road and I'm cold and wet and lonely, I think to myself: "Who really gives a bugger about what I'm doing?" But then you attend functions like that and you start to think you're really something special and it's an important episode in people's lives. Breaking Ron Grant's record is important but the message is the priority.' Uplifting encounters like St Lawrence helped carry Pat through the tougher times on his epic journey around Australia.

The public was receptive to Pat's message, with support coming from various quarters. On one occasion, Pat complained on air to a Sydney radio station that the mornings were getting so cold he'd have to buy a scarf and beanie. Within minutes, the switchboard was jammed with calls from ladies offering to knit them for him. There were always plenty of morale-boosting encounters out on the road as well. Passing vehicles would honk their horns with such regularity that Pat's arm would soon tire from waving back. Pat carried a 'Flag of Wishes' for supporters to sign throughout the journey. By the time he finished, every square centimetre was covered on twenty large flags. Motorists would regularly stop and attempt to make donations. Pat would thank them for their generosity, but tell them he wasn't collecting for charity on this run. Often they were insistent and would suggest Pat buy a treat for himself and his crew.

Others would stop to take photos or chat while the fitter ones spent time running alongside Pat. Self-employed electrician Graham Steer spent two hours pounding out some tough kilometres with Pat in driving rain, south of Mackay. His son Matt, 10, joined them for almost an hour. Steer, 34, of Victoria, was celebrating a second shot at life after winning his battle with non-Hodgkin's lymphoma. He felt pretty lucky after losing two cousins, about his age, to cancer and was taking his wife and three young children on a three-month holiday. Steer was a keen runner and endurance canoeist and knew about the loneliness of the distance runner.

'It's good to have someone to have a yak to while you're out there,' said Steer. 'Hopefully I'll give Pat a bit of incentive to keep going. After what I went through with chemotherapy, I can relate to Pat talking about the bad days and the low points. If you have something to fight for—like Pat has his kids and I had my family—it makes it easier. Pat embodies the best qualities of Australia. I admire anyone who can set his or her goals and achieve them. I think that's what most Australians are all about.'

While Pat enjoyed the human contact on the road, he jealously guarded his privacy for the first few minutes of each day. As he stepped on to the black ribbon of tar in the darkness at 5.00 a.m., his first thoughts were with his beloved wife Lisa. Pat would walk off alone, having rejected offers the previous day by willing joggers to join him at the start. 'I just like to spend that short period as quiet time with myself,' said Pat. 'It's not happy or sad memories of Lisa—just a memory, a thought, a prayer. It's just time thinking of somebody that I love even though they're not here.' The hurt of his loss still burned deep inside, but the daily aches and pains encountered on the road were a welcome distraction.

'There's not a step I don't take without thinking about her and reflecting on the different journeys that she has been by my side. As I expected, this is proving to be the toughest running event I have ever done. The only thing I draw strength from is the fact I've had an extremely difficult last twelve months and I realise if I can go through that and survive without Lisa by my side, then I can do anything.'

Pat carried a large framed photo of Lisa in his luggage, which he would unpack and faithfully place beside his bed every night. Just having his children by his side brought him closer to Lisa—he saw so much of his wife in them, especially in Brooke. He savoured their special moments, which provided a welcome release from his daily toil. Moments such as dancing with Brooke to a favourite song, Van Morrison's 'Have I Told You Lately?'. Melancholic but grateful for remaining treasures, he would hold his daughter tightly and whisper in her ear why this song was special, telling her how he used to love singing and dancing to the tribute tune with Mummy. Although Brooke was just a child, Pat felt she understood what these moments meant. What was important was that they both had someone to hug.

Pat was paying tribute to Lisa in other ways, offering his own finely tuned body to hopefully help save lives. Pat was a very mobile human guinea pig, with several medical and scientific experiments being conducted during the seven-month run. In a world first, Pat became the first person to display his heartbeat live on the Internet. He tested the 'Biolog', a new wireless heart monitoring system that had already been used on the Russian Mir space station and by a team of Australian climbers during an assault on Mount Everest.

In Pat's case, information about his heart rate and rhythm was fed on to the Internet via a mobile phone stored in a bumbag. Heading the project's data research team was Gold Coast doctor Geoff Cornish, who first studied medicine in a World War II German concentration camp, in between digging much of the tunnel system made famous in the Steve Macqueen movie *The Great Escape*. (Cornish had been scheduled to be the eighth person through the tunnel. He surrendered his spot and accepted an offer from a British doctor in the camp to teach him medicine.

The airman who took Cornish's place was shot and killed during the escape.)

'The Biolog had already been released to the world when we got Pat involved, but this was a chance to perfect it,' said Dr Cornish, a leading cardiac rehabilitation expert. 'It allows us to send a patients' ECG back to a major hospital where a cardiologist can determine what's happening with their heart. The tests with Pat proved two things: that when you get to a supreme level of fitness, the human heart can tolerate with equanimity an incredible amount of pain and punishment; and secondly that, with tele-medicine, distance is no barrier.' With both Lisa and his father Frank having died of heart attacks, this was an experiment very close to Pat's own heart.

Where he once shunned science and technology, Pat now embraced it wholeheartedly. His crew was equipped with the latest communications equipment, including a portable satellite navigation device (GPS—Global Positioning System) that had all been provided as part of a sponsorship deal with Dick Smith Electronics. Through his own Internet site, Pat was making ultra running a spectator sport, where people could follow his progress from the comfort of their schools, homes or offices. Personally dictated diaries, stories, postcards, photos, audio grabs and emails in fact made it more interactive than many other live sports.

Pat also had had his customary pre-run briefing with dietician Helen O'Connor, although by now he had a good understanding of correct nutrition. Pat tried to maintain his vegetarian diet but occasionally ate meat or fish after being warned about the importance of maintaining his iron levels and protein intake.

'There was a danger of Pat becoming anaemic because of the tremendous stress on his body over seven months,' said O'Connor. 'And that could have seriously jeopardised the run in several ways. Aside from the possibility he would get too sick and weak to run, poor nutritional habits could have led to excessive weight loss and susceptibility to injury. It was important that we maintained a balanced diet all the way and were proactive to ensure problems didn't develop.'

A study by the Queensland University of Technology measured Pat's energy requirements and found he needed between 25 000 and 27 000 kilojoules a day and more than 6 litres of fluid a day just to keep going. That's equivalent to eating 11.5 kilograms of apples or 5 kilograms of tinned tuna, and almost three times the average person's nutritional requirement.*

Typically, Pat would have several slices of toast and porridge cooked by his devoted mother Mary before he started a day's running at 4.30–5.00 a.m. He would regularly snack on fruit, nuts, sandwiches and occasionally lollies before eating something more substantial, such as freshly cooked pancakes, around 9.00 a.m. A midday lunch often saw Pat consume a large bowl of noodles and salad sandwiches, before dinner of fish or pasta with vegetables. Remarkably, Pat's appetite was only occasionally affected by the constant stench and sight of road kill. Pat viewed that as just another occupational hazard, as long as vehicles kept their distance from him. One food that was not part of his staple diet was prunes, despite numerous media reports to the contrary. The rumour had begun when Pat's publicity machine sent out a pre-run media release, in an attempt to whet the media's insatiable appetite for weird and wacky trivia. The release had predicted that Pat would consume 81 375 grams of prunes during the seven-month run. Thankfully for his crew, Pat barely touched a dried plum throughout the entire event.

One of Bernie's roles was to keep Pat's taste buds entertained. The trick was to keep one step ahead of his cravings for a variety of foods before Pat would throw a curve ball in the crew's direction, like asking for soya milk while they were running through prime dairy cattle country. It was often a mind game with Pat and food. Crew members had to be discreet about eating junk food because often what Pat saw someone eat, he'd also want, if only to relieve the monotony. He was also fastidious about the crew's hygiene with food preparation. They had to

---

* Hill, R.J. and Davies, P.S.W., 2000 'Energy expenditure during two weeks of an ultra endurance run around Australia', unpublished.

ensure his water bottles weren't confused with anyone else's. Once, Pat saw a packet of biscuits lying on the floor of the car. He promptly threw them away. 'You'll end up giving me one by the end of the day and I can't afford to get sick.'

When Pat departed Townsville in Queensland on 7 July and headed west for the Northern Territory, he had broken through his first psychological barrier. In his mind he had divided the event into four major stages: the run up the east coast, across the Top End, the run down the west coast, and the final eastwards stage home, which included Tasmania. His spirits were also lifted by the arrival of his brother and close friend Tony, who spent just over two weeks as part of the crew through the Top End. While the nightly speaking engagements were now less onerous, unsolicited daytime speeches increased across northern Australia, with Pat proving to be something of a roving tourist attraction.

Word spread along the bush telegraph that Pat Farmer was on the road. Coach drivers would usually ask him to stop while they took a hat around for donations. Pat's counter-offer was: 'I'll stop but I don't want money. Just give me the microphone.' After he spoke for anywhere between five and 25 minutes, Pat's captive but spellbound audience would cheer and clap. One tourist coach stopped ahead of him and its passengers alighted and formed a guard of honour either side of the road for Pat to run through. 'They wanted to pay tribute to me, but I've got to pay tribute to Australians like that. It was an incredible thing for them to do. It really blew me away,' he said.

By the time he reached Darwin on 8 August, Pat was accelerating into history. He was running further and faster than originally planned and was more than a week ahead of his original schedule. He had broken the record for Brisbane to the Northern Territory border and at the same time broken Grant's Queensland long-run record by almost six days, running 2649 kilometres in 33 days, four hours and 25 minutes. As well, he had wiped nine days off Grant's Brisbane to Darwin record. In fact, it was no longer Grant's records he was breaking. Rival runner

Gary Parsons, who'd left a month before Pat, had broken most of the records by between three and six days. Contrary to Pat's pre-run assertion that he didn't care about Parsons and wouldn't be keeping tabs on him, Pat and Bernie had been watching his progress on the Queenslander's Website. 'We're not worried about him, but we're not silly,' said Bernie. 'We're not going to go all this way and not know what new records we're after and not make sure we break them.' But it seemed Pat had Gary's every move covered. Pat was exceeding his own predicted standard of 70 kilometres a day and was averaging 79 kilometres a day, compared with Parsons' 73 kilometres. He broke Parsons' first three records by two to five days.

But putting a damper on affairs were fears about the health of Pat's mother, Mary. She had barely recovered from a bad case of the flu in Queensland when the crew became further concerned. The road ahead involved many long weeks in remote sections of the Northern Territory and Western Australia with no access to proper medical care. They would often be camping out, with no guarantee of ready access to an airstrip. Pat and Bernie used their contact with Dr Cornish, of the Biolog project, to ensure Mary was sent ahead to Darwin and given a thorough medical examination at the main hospital, mainly as a precaution. She received a clean bill of health, which proved an enormous relief to everyone.

The Northern Territory provided Pat with two of the highlights of the entire run. Between Tennant Creek and Katherine, Pat ran through the town of Elliott. There was nothing remarkable about it—it was the typical one-school, one-pub town. But it was the welcoming party of 30 barefoot local school children who ran the final 5 kilometres with him into Elliott that brought home to him the spirit of a nation that he was trying to promote. Their excitement at his arrival and their constant barrage of questions helped recharge his batteries. Pat was touched by their boundless enthusiasm.

'They had smiles that started at one ear and finished at the other,' he said. 'They were typical kids. This was something a bit out of the ordinary for them and they thought it was fantastic. This was always a run for the people. It wasn't just Pat Farmer involved.'

At the end of the day, Pat and his crew stopped at a veritable oasis in the desert that they'd been directed to by one of the local teachers. The large inland lake 10 kilometres off the beaten track was a well-kept local secret. It was a magnet at dusk for all manner of wildlife seeking relief after another sun-baked day. Pelicans, cockatoos and kangaroos flocked there to bathe and drink. The backdrop was a stunning purple-red sky. 'This place was amazing in the middle of what looked like a typically arid part of the Territory,' Pat said. 'It just showed to me it doesn't matter where you are, there's Paradise around the corner if you know where to look.' This slice of Paradise obviously came at a price. It was owned by media magnate Kerry Packer, Australia's richest man.

Pat received a surprise visitor two weeks later as he dodged road trains along the Stuart Highway while heading south from Darwin back towards Katherine. As the sun climbed above the horizon to bake another day in the Territory, Pat spotted a lone runner heading towards him. 'Are you running around Australia, mate?' the stranger yelled. 'Yeah, I'm running the other way around Australia,' Pat replied. Pat's mind then emerged from its confused state, as he realised the runner was fellow adventurer Dick Smith, who crossed the road to hug Pat. Smith, also Chair of the National Council for the Centenary of Federation, had flown to Katherine in his private jet for a surprise visit.

'I went there just to see Pat,' said Smith. 'It was all secretly organised with hardly anyone in Pat's crew even knowing. He had absolutely no idea. His mouth hit the ground when he saw me and when the penny dropped for Pat he burst into laughter. I had always planned to drop in on him, but it was even more important to pay tribute to him on the road because of the fantastic job he was doing.'

'The fact that Dick flew all the way up from Sydney made me feel very, very privileged,' said Pat. 'I knew he was a very busy man and it made me realise that I wasn't alone. I thought I might be forgotten in the big cities after I left, but it showed they still cared very much about my welfare and the progress of the run.'

Smith, who considers himself a fit 56-year-old, jogged for a kilometre with Pat—and admits even that tested him. 'And to think that he was running more than 80 kilometres at that speed every day—that's two marathons for 217 days. You stand there thinking: "This is impossible, he can't possibly do it",' said Smith. 'Pat is an exceptional Australian, but a typical and un-assuming Australian. A lot of our sports heroes are portrayed as different and the public think they could never be like that. But Pat has such a common touch with his speech and his demeanour that admirers can think: "I can do that." And that's very important.'

Pat's Pied Piper appeal was again to the fore as the pair ran down the highway. A busload of local schoolchildren stopped to join them. They ran gleefully along the bitumen road with the two national heroes. Inevitably they were impressed with Farmer's current deeds rather than Smith's past aviation adventures. It was the same story later that day when Pat and Dick were special guests of the School of the Air. Dick readily admits Pat was the main attraction.

'All the kids we spoke to that day just loved it,' said Smith. 'I'm sure they found it very motivating listening to Pat and hopefully they thought: "Maybe I can do something like this, or something equally challenging one day." The best thing about this run is that it takes an important message to the little country towns which often get neglected.'

11

Homeward bound

The impending dawn of a new millennium had sparked an unprecedented burst of activity among adventurers in Australia. As well as Pat Farmer's and Gary Parsons' record-breaking runs around the country, a host of other ultra athletes were trying to pound and sweat their way into the history books. The evergreen Cliff Young was also attempting to break Grant's Around Australia record for the second time. He left Wollongong on 22 February 1999 and headed north to Queensland. Cliffy showed that, even at the age of 78, he was not a spent force as an endurance runner, making it almost to Mackay in North Queensland. But he was afflicted by a carcinoma in his eye that threatened to leave him blind if he did not have immediate surgery. He reluctantly stepped off the road but two family friends (also members of his crew), 25-year-old twins Paula and Bridget Powers, fulfilled a promise to complete the journey. They ran and cycled an average of 100 kilometres a day to the finish.

The 'tortoise' of the ultra marathon scene, partially blind Adelaide runner Johnny Moyle, was determined to run further rather than faster. Moyle left Darwin on 22 March 1999 in a bid to break the world long-run record of 17 071 kilometres, set by American Robert Sweetgall in 1993. While running fewer kilometres per day than Farmer or Parsons, he achieved his aim in May 2000, running 19 500 kilometres—400 kilometres farther than Parsons would eventually run. Foreigners had also been attracted by the lure of Australian records. French ultra runner Serge Girard, a former Trans America starter, set a new Perth–Sydney record of 46 days 23 hours and fifteen minutes, knocking seventeen days off the old mark set by ultra runner and Trans Am race organiser Jesse Riley. And an eight-man team of British Army and civilian cyclists took the two-wheel approach, breaking the record for cycling around Australia. Using a tag-team tactic that saw at least one rider on the road at any given time, they completed the 14 257 kilometre circuit in nineteen days, nine hours and fifteen minutes, breaking the old record by two and a half days.

Pat Farmer continued to set record times in his journey across the Top End. He broke Ron Grant's Queensland long-run record by six days; wiped nine days off the Brisbane to Darwin record; and five days from Grant's Northern Territory continuous long-run record. This ordinary man who was proving it was possible to do extraordinary things simply by putting one foot in front of the other was devouring the milestones. He was on the verge of reaching the halfway mark of the 14 500-kilometre journey in remote Western Australia. The night before, Pat was in a down mood, weary from another day's footslog and again questioning whether the world remembered or cared about Pat Farmer and his mission. Personal motivator Bernie read him a faxed message of congratulations from Prime Minister John Howard, which he had been intending to save for the following day. The letter paid tribute to Pat for his courage and determination in spreading the Centenary of Federation message and fostering national spirit. Big brother also had the knack of knowing what to say and when to say it. 'No other ultra runner in Australia, not Cliff Young or Yiannis Kouros, has captured people's imagination or tapped into our patriotism the way you have,' said Bernie. The words, both spoken and written, were just the tonic for the time, drawing a smile from Pat's weatherbeaten face. Event organisers made some fuss over the halfway milestone the next day, but Pat refused to indulge his emotions too much—there were still over 7200 kilometres to go.

The run across northern Australia would prove to be the most testing time of the entire journey. There were few crowds to spur him on, although it helped when the entire population of the remote township of Elliott's Crossing—four—turned out to give him their support. The lure was always a black bitumen line leading to an ever-receding horizon. Bed was a thin mattress in the caravan or sometimes the back seat of the crew car. Modern luxuries were a distant memory; basic provisions like fresh milk were occasionally difficult to find.

The event was proving to be a roller coaster ride in every way—physically, emotionally and mentally. Pat's body was bruised and blistered, his mind somewhat battered and jaded from constantly pushing himself through the down periods and the down days. He had also developed another injury to his foot. A vital tendon had been strained by the constant pounding and was giving him enormous grief, particularly during the last 40 kilometres of each day's running.

While peak temperatures in the north regularly hovered around 35°C, that generally wasn't a problem. Pat didn't mind running in the heat and never had. It was the flat monotonous stretches of unwavering road where there was little environmental distraction that presented the greatest challenges. Marathon runners talk of hitting a physical and psychological wall during races. Pat hit numerous walls, some thicker than others. 'One of the things that played on my mind a lot was a dull pain that was there all the time in my legs,' he said. 'It wasn't pain from a specific injury, it was just severe muscle fatigue and soreness.'

As always, it was the little things that played most on his mind—the sun-dried and split lip that bled when he bit into food, not having proper shower or toilet facilities during seemingly endless days of running in remote locations, and the flies that constantly loitered, forcing him to eat and drink under a fly-net. (Pat's caring, sharing nature meant he was happy to introduce newfound friends to brother Bernie by opening the car door and shooing the flies inside.) There were never days when he felt like he couldn't continue—the passion for the cause, personal pride and his internal drive saw to that. Some days were just a hell of a struggle. The schedule, too, was relentless. Whereas Ron Grant allowed himself easy days where he ran just 25 kilometres, Pat's timetable of speaking engagements and functions allowed little scope for relaxation. His obsessional personality would not permit him to slacken off, no matter how far he was ahead of schedule.

When he encountered the bad days (about once every two or three weeks), Pat used several coping strategies—techniques that he believes are just as useful to anybody in everyday life. He rarely allowed himself to be over-awed by the vastness of the task and the continent he was challenging. He would break the run into bite-sized pieces. There were the huge chunks—the four large stages on each side of Australia; then the morsels, which were one day's running at a time; and finally, when the going really got tough, he would simply take it 10 kilometres or 5 kilometres or even 1 kilometre at a time and try to set his focus no further than the next drink stop. He tried to occupy himself with happy, pleasant thoughts—priceless things his children had said and done the day before, precious memories of Lisa, or childhood reminiscences. When those were exhausted or their impact wore off, he reminded himself he had been through worse pain or greater boredom at some stage in his life and survived.

'It's a lesson I think everyone can relate to, whether it's a bad day in sport, at work or at home with the kids,' he said. 'You have a bad day and if you push forward you'll be rewarded with a good day or days. As well, you learn a lot about yourself and life from coping with adversity. I think it also helps that I accept pain as an inevitable companion. I've found over the years, it's much easier to deal with if you don't fight it.'

At his lowest ebb—and there were many of those—Pat prayed to God or listened on his Walkman to motivational tapes made by Lisa over the years. He drew strength, comfort and inspiration from both these things. Listening to Lisa's voice invariably pro-voked a flood of memories and a torrent of tears. In life, he ran for Lisa. In death, he ran in her memory. But he was at his best when things were toughest. They were also the times when he felt closest to God. Pat thrived on adversity. It was a strangely welcome bedfellow, as it forced him to dig deepest. He found no challenge in the comfort zone of normality: he had lived most of his life in peaks and troughs. While many people crave equilibrium, Pat shunned it.

But life on the road exacted a mental toll from Pat. After the first month of toil, the constraints on his daily life left him feeling like he was a prisoner, albeit of his own volition. He had certain freedoms, but he was not in control of his life.

'It's a funny scenario. It's not so bad some days and other days are terrible,' he said. 'It's like I have a seven-month prison term. Like everything in life, there is a finish line or an end to something and I have to stick it out until then. When I do, I'll be a free man. Then I'll be able to taste life for everything that it is and to share the moments with my kids and the successes of what I've been through, but until then it's prison life day after day where very little changes.'

It was while away from the city hustle and bustle, when he had more time with his own thoughts, that Pat sensed a spiritual side to the event. There were so many difficult days when running 80–90 kilometres was a chore. But when the going got hardest, he could feel a wind at his back. It was like a helping hand, gently pushing him along. He wasn't sure if it was Lisa's spirit or a greater force, but it seemed very real to Pat. It was a sensation shared by crew member James Merritt. 'It was funny. I was running along with Pat one day and I said to him: "It's like somebody else is controlling this run and we're just following their path."'

However, there were plenty of good days, when Pat couldn't abide the thought of doing anything else. The days when the kilometres just rolled by as mind and body worked in synch. Often, these were the times when he felt at one with the environment, when the colours of the sunrise seemed more vibrant, when the wildlife was at its most exuberant and captivating and Pat found himself absorbed by the flight pattern of every bird in the sky and the contour of every leaf and branch on passing trees. He couldn't imagine living a mundane existence or being stuck behind an office desk.

Also uplifting was the enormous public support he received along the road, at functions and through the media. It fed his imperfect ego and helped him to believe that his run was making a difference to ordinary people's lives.

'At the end of the day, it's the people and the experiences we share that matter most,' Pat said. 'What counts is the hospitality they extend to me and the encouragement they offer, because it makes me feel special and in return hopefully I have an influence on them. That's my best trophy. It isn't a piece of paper that says I'm a world record holder or something I can stick up on the mantelpiece. As far as Lisa and I were ever concerned, those things were just good for starting fires and holding up books.'

Pat drew strength and comfort from the regular stream of emails he received on his Internet site. Friends, fans and complete strangers of different ages from around Australia and around the world logged on to 'The Pat Farmer Run Around Australia' site and sent messages of support. There were countless emails from people whom he had helped and inspired. Few were more touching than this, from a woman named Wendy.

'Hi Pat & the crew too. You continue to be a real inspiration to me. I am coping with the recent death of my daughter and every day, I get on line and see how you're doing and then I immediately feel that I too can cope with the day ahead. Thank-you, keep it up—you're all pretty darn amazing.'

Pat had also achieved cult hero status among 21 Year 5 students at Macgregor Primary School in Canberra. Teacher Heather Swift used Pat's story and his Centenary of Federation run to reduce schoolyard bullying and invoke a greater sense of community spirit in an underprivileged suburb riddled with a range of modern social ills. The children watched Farmer's *This*

Is Your Life story, followed his progress on the Internet, sent him emails and brought newspaper clippings to school. Mrs Swift said the project had a stunning impact, with her students soon talking about and displaying 'Pat Farmer deeds'—acts of kindness and consideration to classmates.

'The kids really fell in love with Pat,' says Mrs Swift. 'The whole thing really bonded us together, although I have to say they were more interested in Pat as a person than the Centenary of Federation issue. The children will remember the experience for the rest of their lives. It really made a difference to them as people. I'm noticing it this year with behavioural issues with this class that I didn't have last year.'

The injection of fresh blood in the crew also made a difference. More than 30 family and friends spent time on the road as crew members throughout the run, flying in and out on a regular basis. They would stay between a fortnight and two months, depending on their personal circumstances, and were paid between $60 and $100 to work what was usually an eighteen-hour day. Only Pat's mother Mary and brother Bernie stayed for the entire run. 'It was good to get a fresh face, some new enthusiasm, because it was a bit boring sitting in a car all day, following Pat along at less than 10 kilometres per hour,' said Bernie. 'I had days when I was grumpy and Pat and I wouldn't talk to each other for hours, but it always evened out. If I thought I was having a bad day, I just looked at Mum. She was the only cook and had to care for two young kids day and night—sometimes with a migraine—and I drew inspiration from that. She never ceased to amaze me and everyone else.'

Pat and his crew raced the clock to reach Broome on the coast of Western Australia on 3 September, to honour a commitment to meet with Aboriginal leader Pat Dodson at a local festival. The self-imposed deadline had been a positive influence, as it had given Pat another intermediate goal and helped him to pick up his pace and daily average kilometres when it would have been easy to relax and enjoy the scenery. While Broome was another unscheduled stopover, Pat didn't really mind this time because the coastal town had always held an allure for him. He and Lisa had tossed up whether to honeymoon there in 1993, but instead opted for Lord Howe Island. It was one of many regrets after Lisa's death that they never found the time to travel there.

Pat and his party were hailed as outback heroes by hundreds of locals and tourists who lined the road into Broome. They were guests of honour at a local Shinju Festival that paid tribute to the town's diverse and exotic cultural heritage, and later took part in a flag-raising ceremony to commemorate the day when the Australian flag was first raised 98 years before. Broome marked the end of the 'second stage'—the run across northern Australia. For a brief moment, Pat took the 'half-empty glass' approach and saw it as having reached the furthest point from home. But, as always, his optimistic side immediately kicked in and he realised that every step from here was a step closer to home.

Pat Farmer and Pat Dodson had a private meeting in Broome, where they spoke of their shared vision of national reconciliation and a more harmonious Australia. The day's highlight, and a lasting memory of the trip, was a simple Australian pastime— playing at the beach with his children. He gazed at the Indian Ocean. It didn't seem that long since he had cast a farewell look at the Pacific Ocean. Rarely did clear, blue water look so appealing. Certainly the soothing saltwater massage on his bare feet was a welcome indulgence. The cool water cleansed his soul and his dust-stained body after weeks of basic living conditions.

The trip was proving to be a richly rewarding parenting experience. Pat treasured almost every minute with Brooke and Dillon, especially after they'd been separated for a few days. When he stopped for meal breaks, they would be all over him. One or both of the children slept in his bed most nights when they were together. When Pat awoke, they were the first things he'd see. He would study their angelic faces, listen to and watch them breathing and, in the peace of the early morning darkness, everything seemed so perfect. He also noticed how quickly they were growing up. Brooke especially continued to astound her father with some of the things she said.

On one occasion, some tourists produced a video camera so they could add Pat's run to their 'guess what we saw?' travel stories. Brooke proudly told them: 'My Dad's Pat Farmer and he's running around Australia. I'm Brooke Farmer and my brother Dillon is in the car.' 'Are you famous?' the female traveller inquired. After a brief thoughtful pause, Brooke responded: 'Mmm, just a little bit.'

'It was just amazing how much they matured during the trip, especially Brooke,' said Pat. 'It was obviously stimulating for the kids seeing so many unusual and different places and the people we met along the way. Brooke would come out with all these smart, intellectual words that would just blow me away. And she developed into a little lady with a real self-confidence. I think a big part of that was the influence of Mum, who did a fantastic job, and the fact that Brooke was mixing with adults most of the time who treated her like a grown-up.'

Dillon was always keen to get in the thick of whatever play was on offer, even if it was something as potentially hazardous as boomerang throwing. The pastime became a regular feature of the crew's rest stops, especially when wide, open spaces beckoned. Bernie became the master exponent of a boomerang presented to Pat by Aboriginal dance troupe Doonooch after they had performed at his official Sydney run launch. The two-year-old boy was mesmerised as the v-shaped stick circled and swooped high over their heads at the end of another hot Western Australian day. It was little wonder that he failed to take evasive action when it slipped through the hands of the newest thrower and clobbered Dillon, who was standing behind them. A piercing child's scream filled the country air just moments after the boomerang split his top lip, the gush of blood sparking a mini-medical emergency. Thankfully it didn't require stitching and Dillon was soon happily occupied by a different form of play that didn't involve boomerangs.

Pat's campaign gathered more momentum as he travelled down the Western Australian coast. He could focus more on what he did best—putting one foot in front of the other. There weren't as many evening functions and other distractions. Caravanning and camping out agreed with him—it was a comforting reminder of his childhood. It helped when he could grab a few extra hours' sleep each night. Remarkably, he had managed to get this far on an average of four to five hours' nightly sleep. Pat would usually be on the road by 4.30 a.m. and put the bulk of the day's running (over 50 kilometres) behind him by 10.30 a.m.

He was now sixteen days ahead of schedule, but refused to let up. It helped to have specific and significant events in major towns and cities to aim for, even if they did impose ambitious weekly kilometre goals upon Pat and his crew. They had agreed to another tough target—running more than 2400 kilometres from Broome to Perth in 29 days, which would put them further in credit. After discussion with the Sydney- and Canberra-based event organisers, Bernie and Pat would calculate what was achievable. Pat was always keen to oblige and would then lock himself into a target date. But there were many days of hard, grinding kilometres when they realised they had bitten off more than they had the energy to chew and almost regretted their insatiable appetite for challenges.

Such was the case as they belted down the west coast to reach Perth in time for the last day of the Royal Show. Pat received the traditional enthusiastic welcome as he ran around the main ring at the showgrounds, sandwiched between equestrian events and the sheep dog trials. After a series of functions and a meeting with federal Opposition Leader Kim Beazley, Pat was finally eastward-bound again, in the right direction to get home. Three sides of the continent had been conquered in 125 days, and the kilometres, hours and days were now passing quicker than anyone could have expected. But the extra effort came at a price to his body, leaving him feeling even more sore, tired and listless than he had been before.

Certainly Pat was proving too fleet-footed for scientists from the University of Sydney, who had been chasing him around the country. Because he was so far ahead of schedule, their local researchers missed collecting blood samples from him in Darwin and Perth. The scientific aspect of the run—which Bernie had at times considered an unwanted imposition—was the only thing which was unravelling. The added demands of keeping dietary sheets and waiting around to supply blood and urine samples had proved too onerous. Insufficient data resulted in some of the studies being cancelled.

One of the true highlights of the trip was breaking Ron Grant's and Gary Parsons' 10 000-kilometre records near Moorine Rock on the road between Perth and Coolgardie. There was nothing remarkable about the setting—a pub, a general store and a few crows. The stationary crew vehicle marked the point. Pat jogged past it at his usual pace and stopped for refreshments. He had knocked a massive 33 days off Grant's old record and almost six days off Parsons' record. 'There was just Pat and the crew and the local store owner for that milestone,' said Bernie. 'We gave ourselves a pat on the back, had a quick break and were on our way again.'

Western Australia proved an easier conquest than expected, even crossing the monotonous ribbon of tar across the Nullarbor Plain. Pat and Bernie had feared it would be one of the most difficult legs of the run. Each morning, they braced themselves for a really tough day, but it never came. But running through hundreds of kilometres of flat landscape created other problems. The even surface required little variation in Pat's stride, which meant he was using the same muscles in a repetitious way. His knees, calves and quadriceps began to ache more than usual from overuse. He often woke up 'feeling like a cripple'. But Pat proved what a remarkable piece of work the human body is. 'People thought I'd just break down completely during the run, but thankfully it didn't happen,' he said. 'You might think because you run ten times as far, you feel ten times worse, but that's not the case. There's no doubt I had lots of aches and pains, but the human body adapts.' Certainly he was thankful for the daily attention of physiotherapist Karen Mooibroek from the Western Australian Institute of Sport, who joined the crew for much of the eastwards trek.

The support he received from family, friends and the public continued to be the backbone of the run. There was an added surprise when Pat's Japanese benefactor, Toshihiko Okada of Moonbat, dropped in on him in Western Australia to experience life on the road first hand. He had been in Australia on business but made a special trip to provide moral support to his friend. Mr Okada was running with Pat when one of the few unsavoury incidents occurred that soured the trip. Pat was running along the highway towards the mining town of Kalgoorlie when a car carrying several teenagers approached from behind. Pat felt them before he saw them, as one of the passengers threw a half full bottle of sports drink at him. 'I thought the car had hit me, the force felt so great,' he said. The missile struck him in the lower back; its combined weight and velocity knocked him off balance, leaving him temporarily felled by the side of the road. 'It really hurt and took the wind out of me. I was pretty gun-shy for the next few days and ran with the traffic coming towards me.' While a large red welt appeared, Pat's pride was more wounded than his body. Pat's crew members were more angry and concerned about the incident. But there was an overwhelming feeling in the camp, that nothing or no one could stop him.

The self-appointed torchbearer of unity and nationalism received one of his best civic receptions as Australia prepared to go to the polls on the divisive issue of the republic. Pat arose at 5.00 a.m. on Saturday, 6 November to run the final 30 kilometres into Adelaide and was joined by a large entourage of local runners and a police escort for the last few kilometres into the city. Before a curious and admiring crowd in Rundle Street Mall, Pat said it was none of his business how they voted in the republic poll, but that they should reflect on how lucky they were just to have the freedom of choice.

This was the easiest day of the entire odyssey—just 42 kilometres—but there were plenty of other things to occupy Pat and the crew. After lodging their votes and fulfilling numerous media and community obligations, they collected new running shoes from a sports store, dropped off old support vehicles for servicing and made a dash for the airport to catch a flight to Hobart where Pat was to begin his journey around the Apple Isle. He lingered too long in the welcome comfort of the Qantas lounge and, before he knew it, was being informed that he was holding up the aircraft which was ready for departure. Embarrassment followed as cabin crew announced, 'Pat Farmer is now boarding the plane.' But the on-board reception made all of Pat's support crew feel like celebrities, especially Pat's mother Mary. Another announcement informed passengers it was her birthday and she was presented with a bottle of champagne—all highly embarrassing to Mary who by nature felt uncomfortable when others fussed over her.

For Pat, there was the added thrill of a bird's-eye view of the landing from the cockpit. That was exceeded by the captain's disclosure that his one life ambition was to ride a bicycle from Adelaide to Darwin and how Pat had inspired him to chase his dream. 'It just proves that ordinary, everyday people want to take on these challenges,' Pat said. 'It made me feel 10 feet tall because here was a guy with a job that many people would envy and he was saying he envied me.' The day ended with a family birthday dinner for Mary and a guest appearance at Hobart television studios in one of the last episodes of the Nine Network's long-running *Hey, Hey It's Saturday*.

Tasmania proved to be one of the most enjoyable legs of the entire run. The cooler, changeable weather and rich, green countryside with its historic buildings provided welcome relief from the searing heat of the mainland—although there were days they could have done without, when they endured near-freezing temperatures and hailstorms. Adding new spark to the crew was the presence of Pat's eldest sister, Catherine, a teacher of mentally handicapped children, her husband Ric Cape and their son

David. While Brooke and Dillon were being cared for by Mary at the Capes' home, Pat was briefly playing surrogate father to two baby Tasmanian devils, found pining precariously by the side of the road for their mother, who had been killed by a car. The orphans were later delivered to a lodge that cared for injured wildlife.

Pat also had the rare distinction of bringing the business of the Tasmanian government to a grinding halt. Premier Jim Bacon, an avowed sports lover, was so appreciative that Pat was one ultra runner who 'acknowledged that Tasmania was part of Australia' by including it in his run that he wanted to personally thank him. By agreement with the Opposition, the Premier took the highly unusual step of asking the Speaker to suspend Parliament so he could be guaranteed to be free of official duties. After receiving an ovation from MPs in the chamber, Pat and his crew were honoured at a state reception. MPs joked among themselves about the irony of Parliament being stopped for a runner, but genuinely marvelled at his feat.

Tasmania was also the closest Pat ever came to encountering his rival, Gary Parsons, who by now had completed his 14 399 kilometre loop around mainland Australia. Parsons, who had begun his run a month ahead of Pat, had endured his own trials and tribulations. He was hospitalised for several hours in Adelaide after becoming dehydrated from a vomiting bug. As well, his only son, Julian, 23, had been hospitalised after breaking his back during a cliff-diving mishap in Darwin. Parsons was more than 2000 kilometres away in Albany, Western Australia at the time. He says he cried himself dry, agonising over whether to abandon his record attempt. At his son's insistence, he continued on after learning he had not suffered spinal damage. Parsons flew into Tasmania two days behind Pat, but the closest they ever came to each other was about 160 kilometres with Pat tracking up the west coast as Parsons set out from Hobart.

By now Parsons had changed his original publicly stated goal of running 15 250 kilometres and had decided to run past the finish line to attempt an assault on the world long-run record of 17 071 kilometres. But it did pose a new dilemma: should Team Farmer adjust its objectives and keep chasing Parsons? Pat's publicist and confidante Carolyn Grant says there was very brief discussion about whether to extend the run, but the notion was quickly dismissed. 'I thought the other attempt was a joke,' said Pat. 'I could never take Gary Parsons seriously because he was never sticking to any plan. One minute he was trying to set one record, and then when I beat him, he changed it around to do something else.'

'This was more than just a run, it was an event—a national event,' says Carolyn. 'While records were important, Pat didn't want people outside the event, like Gary Parsons, setting the agenda and we thought it would be silly to just keep on running for the sake of one extra record.'

It seemed to Pat that life on the road was hurtling forward at a great rate of knots on his inexorable journey into history. He was now three weeks ahead of schedule, but this caused further consternation in the Farmer camp. With the decision made not to chase Parsons, the next issue was whether there was any point in filling in time by 'going bush' in New South Wales until 1 January, when it would gain him no new records? Carolyn and her organising team were also becomingly increasingly concerned about the potential problems of finishing on 1 January. Sydney's Millennium celebrations had grown beyond original expectations and left an air of unpredictability hanging over the harbour city. Emergency and infrastructure resources would be stretched to the absolute limit with more than one million people expected to join the city's New Year's Eve party. Pat was reluctant to change his original plan, fearing a premature finish would damage his credibility—a commodity he jealously guarded. It was only when sponsors agreed to the change, that the date was moved from 1 January to 12 December. The bonus for Pat was they would be home for a very special family Christmas.

Pat returned to the mainland after twelve days and struck out from Adelaide by road, this time with his thoughts very much on home. He could imagine the familiar feel and warmth of a house alive with comfort and memories and tried to visualise in greater detail the homecoming and reception at the finish line in Sydney's Centennial Park. He thought of pastimes he would enjoy with his family; of the joy of not being too sore or exhausted to kick a ball with his kids; of implementing some of the countless home improvement ideas he had daydreamed about during the long days on the road; and of the freedom he would have to do whatever he pleased.

Yet being surrounded by those memories at home would force him to attend to his innermost feelings. Strangely enough, contemplating life after the run left him scared and anxious, primarily because it would mean confronting life without Lisa. He had used the event and its planning stages as a means to disguise his heartache. By keeping himself constantly busy and focusing totally on the Centenary of Federation Run, he could partition off his grief. While outwardly he had appeared to be coping, he had not dealt properly with his loss. As well, he fretted over his employment prospects when he returned to Sydney. This event was his endurance swansong and he would have a void to fill after retiring from ultra marathon running. He still wanted to inspire, motivate and help others. There was much talk of promotional work with various event sponsors, but nothing in writing and Pat knew from experience that talk was cheap and promises easily forgotten. While he had never shirked a hard day's labour, he wasn't keen to return to landscaping with his brother. Pat always needed to feel he was moving forward with his life.

But he moved quickly towards one record that really counted. On 21 November in the tiny town of Keith, 230 kilometres east of Adelaide, he finally eclipsed Ron Grant's Australian long-run record of 13 383 kilometres. Grant had run the distance in 217 days. Pat shattered the record by running the distance in 174 days—breaking it by an incredible 43 days. The cynics in the ultra marathon world said Grant's was a soft record, but none of the cynics had tried to beat it. As significant as it was to them, again neither Pat nor Bernie would indulge in too much celebration—their focus still had to be on the only finish line that counted, Centennial Park in Sydney.

This was becoming more difficult when there was plenty of back-slapping at functions and ceremonies on the home run. With twelve days left to run, Pat and his crew arrived in Melbourne for another colourful civic reception, where hundreds of flag-waving children awaited his arrival. As was often the case over the final weeks, they were ahead of schedule and Pat had to cool his heels three times in the run to the Victorian Parliament—the last time just 500 metres from the end. They were due to meet new Victorian Premier Steve Bracks. Pat and Bernie were sorry they would not meet Jeff Kennett, who was licking his wounds after voters cut short his political career. 'It was nothing to do with politics,' said Bernie. 'We could just relate to a guy who achieved what he said he would. He had got things done and lifted Victoria out of trouble.' In the end there was double disappointment, with Mr Bracks unable to leave a Cabinet meeting.

The run from Melbourne to Sydney felt like 'a stroll in the park', with Pat running stronger than at any other stage of his life. He was like a thoroughbred that had caught a sniff of the finish and couldn't be held back, despite all that had gone before. Even though heel and hip injuries continued to plague him, the run was gathering momentum. As he galloped north, the memories came flooding back from the old Westfield races. This was where it had all begun fifteen years earlier when a starry-eyed colt had tried to bolt along the track, learning the lessons the hard way. He thought about the paths ultra marathon running had led him down; about the pain and the ecstasy and those who had suffered with him in the bad times and revelled in the good. He felt there were no more challenges left in the world of ultra running. It was fitting that he was heading to the end of his career on these familiar roads and that he should be doing it in such style.

While the finish line in Sydney had always loomed foremost in his mind, the welcome he received when he returned to the national capital on 8 December was the greatest reception of his life. Pat received a full police escort from the ACT border for the final run back to the point where the epic journey had started just over six months earlier. Thousands of people lined the final few kilometres, sometimes eight or ten deep. Local radio station FM 104.7 tracked his progress, broadcasting live updates during its breakfast show. A spectacular jump by flag-bearing parachutists heralded his arrival. Hundreds of people formed a guard of honour at the road entry to Parliament House, waving flags and banners. 'I was really surprised by the reception. I felt like the Queen coming to Australia,' said Pat. 'It was the greatest feeling to have so many people out there cheering for me, especially considering it was such an obscure sport as ultra running.'

Pat approached a finishing banner held by Macgregor Primary School children Nathan Coleman and Emma Wannell, who were given the honour after winning their class 'kindness raffle'. A beaming, jubilant and proud Pat Farmer ran through the finishing tape and was greeted and hugged by well-wishers. The man who had surrendered his records to Pat, Ron Grant, was as warm as any of them. The Prime Minister rushed to the finish and extended a handshake. In a spontaneous display of emotion, Pat accepted his hand and converted it into a hug. 'Thankyou Mr Howard for all your support,' said Pat. The Prime Minister patted him on the back and returned the thanks. Canberra political hacks couldn't remember the last time they had seen Mr Howard being hugged by a sweaty sportsman.

Pat choked back the tears as he told the ceremony, attended by politicians from all sides, that giving your best in any endeavour was as worthy as any Olympic gold medal. 'If you do that, and you believe in yourself, this country will prosper,' he said. Later that day, in scenes that exceeded anything the Farmers dared dream of in their younger years, Pat, Bernie and Mary were feted by the federal Parliament.

There was lunch with the Prime Minister and afternoon tea with the Opposition Leader. But the greatest honour was when Mr Howard personally invited the Farmers to be his distinguished guests in the House of Representatives chamber—an extremely rare privilege, extended only to the Queen and US President Bill Clinton. 'It was a tremendous honour for my family, although I wish my Dad and Lisa could have been there,' he said. 'It just goes to show that in this country ordinary people can achieve great things and be recognised for it.'

Both Mr Howard and Mr Beazley lavished praise on the Farmers, which was recorded in the official Parliamentary *Hansard*.

'We admire what you have done, Pat. It is a great inspiration to us all. You are a wonderful resonant example of what it is to be an Australian, and we thank you for your contribution to this country,' said the Prime Minister.

'Having seen Brooke and Dillon on the run, I am not sure they fully understand your achievement,' the Opposition Leader said. 'Nevertheless, they will be able to look back on your welcome to this Parliament and the welcome that you have had around the country as matters of great pride and great family achievement.'

Bipartisanship was then dispensed with as Parliament moved on to Question Time with Mr Beazley trying to ambush the Prime Minister with a question about the GST. As was the case when Pat had started his epic journey, the national capital was still abuzz with tax talk. Life had turned full circle.

Pat was reflective as he ran his 300-kilometre 'victory lap' from Canberra to Sydney, As always, the nostalgic journey in his mind helped distract him from the pain and sheer exhaustion of his current travels. He had always envisaged his legs would feel like wings on the run home. It had been a romantic notion, for instead they felt more like sand bags. They were long days in rain, wind and heat, but it helped him focus on surviving the run. Pat was incredibly weary and wished the event was over. He couldn't help but feel like the run was complete, but he knew he still had to see it through to the last step. 'Even if something had happened to him—short of getting hit by a truck—it wouldn't have mattered,' said Bernie. 'We had come so far that nothing was insurmountable. I knew if he had to, he would have crawled to the finish on his hands and knees.'

On the second-last day of this most incredible adventure, Pat received yet another hero's welcome at Parramatta after running 99 kilometres, one of the longest days of the run. Finally, reality began to sink in that he was tantalisingly close to home. Lord Mayor Paul Garrard joined with more than a hundred guests in lauding the Granville boy's deeds. Just when Pat thought he could unwind for the rest of the day, a Channel Ten television news crew that had arrived late asked him if he could re-enact his final run into Parramatta. Ever obliging to the media, Pat ran another 2 kilometres. 'That's show business,' he said. 'Besides, the media had been fantastic to me all along the way.' Pat ended the day with one more speech at a conference for one of his major sponsors, GIO Financial Services.

The last day of the last great adventure, 12 December 1999, began in low-key fashion. There was no entourage, just Pat Farmer, father, ambling awkwardly down Parramatta's streets holding the hands of his two children. His departure was delayed from its scheduled 9.00 a.m. start while he chatted to 50 spectators and signed autographs. 'I bet you won't wash that,' said a bystander to an elderly lady whose shirt had received the Farmer moniker. 'No way,' came the reply. Pat made time to thank the police officers who formed his escort 'because I probably won't get time later', before hitting the road for the final 30-kilometre run through Sydney's western suburbs to Centennial Park in Sydney's inner east.

His mind was a jumble of emotions on the journey home. He was relieved this was the finish but sad that his running career was coming to a close. It had been his *raison d'être* for almost half of his life and he knew a difficult transition lay in the months and years ahead. He reflected on the sacrifices his family and friends had made to make the dream come true. He especially thought of the absolute devotion of his mother Mary.

As happened whenever he had a police escort, Pat found himself running faster than he wanted to. He tried to catch up to the flashing blue light several times to tell the rider to slow down, but each time Pat accelerated to convey the message, the motorcyclist sped up. Eventually he gave up and enjoyed the sensation of running at speed again. Pat had spent 195 days racing the clock, in what often proved to be a losing battle to get to a town, school or function on time. This day he won, arriving at Centennial Park almost one and a half hours early for his own homecoming. What else does a guy who's run 14 968 kilometres do, but run another 18 kilometres? It seemed cruel, suddenly moving the finish line he had dreamed of for three years, but he had no choice. Pat took it all in his stride, heading towards Sydney airport with some local runners before turning back. Finally he passed through the park's ornate wrought iron gates.

Pat swept down one last hill to Federation Valley, the place where the Commonwealth of Australia was born at a ceremony in 1901, triumphantly bearing one of the symbols that had driven him relentlessly, the Australian flag. A school band began playing 'I Still Call Australia Home'. At the first distant sighting, more than 700 friends, family, fans and supporters began clapping and hooting. The cheers built to a crescendo as he loomed larger, eventually drowning out the strains of 'Waltzing Matilda'. 'Good on you, Pat,' boomed Master of Ceremonies Dick Smith from the stage. A passage was cleared to form one last guard of honour as he ripped through a large football final-style paper banner. Finally he took the last steps across the finish line he had dreamed of. It was a special moment and one to savour in his heart and mind with the woman who had shared his dream.

After being crowned with a victory wreath and lauded in a series of speeches by dignitaries, there was the chance to make the most important victory speech of his life.

'I'd like to think that through my steps I've symbolised the Australian spirit of having a go—that an ordinary person can do extraordinary things if they just set their mind to it and they never, ever give up,' he said. 'We need to have dreams and goals greater than life itself so that we can pass them on to our children for the betterment of this country. Thankyou all very, very much for being a part of this event and making it what it is . . . and to Lisa—thankyou.'

While Pat was receiving all the accolades, he was quick to pass them on to his support team and crew, above all his mother Mary.

'Mum looked after the crew and I as well as she looked after the kids,' said Pat. 'She was invariably the last one to bed, but she was like clockwork when it came to waking at 4.00 a.m. or 4.30 and organising breakfast. She's always been an endless supply of devotion and support and she did much more on this trip than anybody should have been expected to do. And she always does it without complaining. She might look like she's frail, but she's as tough as nails.'

After spending 195 days on the road and clocking up 14 986 kilometres or more than 20 million individual steps (which involved using fourteen pairs of shoes)—and talking to more than 200 community and school groups, Pat was looking forward to a hot bath and a chocolate milkshake. But that would have to wait. A queue of over 300 people sought his autograph on anything they could lay their hands on—t-shirts, posters, caps. He spent over two hours patiently signing for friends and supporters, in between fulfilling media requests for interviews and photographs. When the crowd finally dispersed, someone asked Pat what he was going to do. 'I'm going home to spend time with my kids and my family and I'm going to get my life back,' he said.

Despite being the most publicised, scrutinised and documented of any foot journey around Australia, the world body, the International Association of Ultra Runners (IAU) had still not ratified Pat Farmer's records at the time of this book going to print. While acknowledging Pat has an excellent reputation, the IAU says it has 'insufficient documentation' to officially recognise the records.

12

·

A new life

Getting your life back when you've been public property for seven months isn't as simple as it sounds. Sponsor and media commitments, coupled with a host of debriefing issues, meant Pat Farmer didn't walk through the door of his home until more than a day after the completion of the run. The Sydney finish had been an anti-climax compared with the reception he had received in Canberra. He felt flat and down for several days—as much a product of coming off an all-time high as it was due to his state of complete physical and mental exhaustion.

The sponsors and promoters of the Centenary of Federation run deemed the event a complete success. Pat had broken eleven records, finished three weeks ahead of schedule and completed the task on budget. But he did surrender the world long-run record. Queenslander Gary Parsons held it briefly after running 19 030 kilometres, but that was exceeded by South Australian John Moyle, who ran 19 500 kilometres. Just hours after Pat had crossed the Sydney finish line, he was doing a victory lap at a conference for one of his sponsors, GIO Financial Services. Over 400 delegates had been following Pat's progress, not just for six and a half months, but also throughout the final day via video clips that were beamed through to the conference. Marketing and communications manager Kevin Ormrod witnessed the scene. 'Pat was introduced to the conference and ran through the crowd and I have never in my entire life seen or heard such a sustained standing ovation. A lot of these people had been cynical at the start, but by now they were totally swept up by Pat's achievements. I hope that accolade went a long way towards off-setting all the pain and drama Pat had endured for the previous six months.'

GIO had commissioned research to establish whether it had received value for money from the sponsorship. The conclusion was that the company had received almost the exact same value it would had it taken out paid advertising in the media. Coupled with the fact that the company received extra goodwill in the marketplace by being associated with a high sporting achiever like Pat, and his numerous personal appearances and motivational talks at company functions around the country, it added up to a good deal. 'There's a healthy degree of cynicism about sponsorships in the corporate world,' said Ormrod. 'They're often regarded as wasted dollars. But that was far from the case with Pat. The company saw it as a very, very successful venture.'

More importantly, Pat had fulfilled his promise to spread the message of the Centenary of Federation far and wide throughout the nation. Tracking research done by the Federation's National Council showed there was a huge surge in the public's recognition of the Centenary of Federation logo and awareness of the fact Australia was preparing to celebrate 100 years of nationhood. Fifty per cent of people surveyed were aware of Pat's promotional work. Recognition was higher in rural regions, peaking at 60 per cent. The National Council had also run an awareness campaign, trying to rectify the widespread ignorance about the identity of Australia's first Prime Minister (Edmund Barton). A survey showed that by the time the run was over, more people knew the answer. But an even higher percentage of respondents knew who Pat Farmer was. The first board meeting of the National Council after the completion of the run was held on 18 February 2000 in Launceston. Council members were effusive in their praise and appreciation for Pat's achievements. Outgoing chairman Dick Smith presented Pat with a framed replica of the scroll he had carried bearing Prime Minister John Howard's message.

Pat lost 5 kilograms on the run and it took several weeks before he returned to his normal weight. A Christmas feast with his family helped. Being home for the festive season was an unexpected bonus. Again he took pleasure from the simple things—decorating a tree with his children, buying them presents and watching their delight when they opened them, and playing backyard cricket. Pat had no desire to lace up his running shoes for more than three months. Physically, he was almost incapable. The heel and hip injuries that had dogged him for the final month of the run did not repair quickly. University of Sydney researcher Dr Martin Thompson was keen to perform follow-up tests on Pat to compare with pre-run data for his physiology studies. Pat tried running on the treadmill a week after his return, but lasted no more than 90 seconds. 'He pulled up lame. He was too broken down,' said Dr Thompson.

Such is the self-belief and ambition of the man, that before he embarked on the Centenary of Federation run, Pat contemplated using the six-and-a-half month journey as a 'training exercise'. Figuring he would be in peak fitness by the finish, Pat thought he would try to make the Olympic team by competing in the Australian selection trial for the marathon in April 2000. Originally, he planned to use every second day on the road to do some specific training for the marathon, which would involve running some of his 80 kilometres at almost twice his average speed. It sounded simple enough to Pat. Perhaps it was just as well Dr Thompson brought him back to earth. 'I quickly convinced him to get the notion out of his head by warning Pat that he stood a good chance of getting injured during the Centenary of Federation Run,' he said. 'It was highly likely had he tried to do both he would have stood a good chance of achieving neither. Running 15 000 kilometres isn't the sort of preparation you'd use for a marathon.'

But he put retirement on hold for one last, important run. A near-capacity crowd gave Pat a rousing reception on a final victory lap around the Sydney Cricket Ground during the lunch break of the opening day of the third test between Australia and India. Pat and his mother Mary were the guests of cricket-loving Prime Minister John Howard. Before the start of play, they rubbed shoulders with a range of well-known Australians including singer Kamahl, former Prime Minister Bob Hawke and the head of the Catholic Church in Australia, Cardinal Clancy, which was the highlight for Mary. The best was yet to come for Pat, though, who received a surprise invitation to enter the inner sanctum of the Australian cricket team. Batsman Justin Langer, who had long been fascinated by Pat Farmer's life story and philosophy, spontaneously organised for him to talk to the players in the dressing room during a rain delay.

The setting was informal, the speech came from the heart. It was one elite sportsman sharing his winning formula with his peers. He told the Australian side he was able to continually push himself towards distant goals because he could clearly picture the finish line at every stage of the day, particularly when his body was telling him to quit. He also spoke about the importance of believing in one's ability to achieve great deeds. While it was the type of address Pat Farmer had given many times before, it struck a chord with the Australian team, especially Langer. 'Like any great achiever he has this look in his eyes—a steely determination—which said to me he really meant what he was talking about and it wasn't just hollow words,' says Langer.

Despite a prolific run-scoring record, the SCG had been a bogey ground for the 29-year-old. The Test number three batsman had never hit a century in any form of cricket there and was desperate to do so. When his innings began later that day, he looked far from a man on his way to 100. 'The first 50 I hit them like an absolute busted arse,' says Langer frankly. 'But I remembered Pat saying about hanging in there and how the good times followed the bad. His words and deeds really helped me with my mindset during my innings. There were a couple of times when I felt tired and thought to myself: "I'm tired! How must Pat have felt running 15 000 kilometres?"'

When he finally walked off the SCG after seven hours at the crease, he had 223 runs beside his name—a defining innings that set up Australia's sixth consecutive test victory. His good form continued three months later on a tour to New Zealand where Langer topped the batting averages and established himself as the hottest batsman in the world at the time. Langer has since set his sights on one day running a marathon—but not an ultra marathon. Wicket-keeper Adam Gilchrist and captain Steve Waugh were two others who drew inspiration from Pat Farmer's speech.

'I thought he was a great Australian before I met him and probably a largely unsung hero,' says Waugh. 'I admired his single-mindedness, his dedication and his will to achieve things. His message was very relevant to cricket. He reinforced that it's one step at a time and if you keep doing the right things and putting the work in, you'll make it to your goals. It's great to have different sportspeople in the change rooms talking about their sport, you do learn a lot from each other. Pat Farmer is a guy to look up to and he would inspire anyone.'

Waugh also identifies with Pat's humanitarian side, having devoted much of his own time while on cricket tours to helping the sick and underprivileged, most notably leprosy sufferers in India. 'As a sportsperson you're in a position to help other people, especially charities and kids,' he says. 'I think it's really important. You have an obligation to do that and Pat certainly does it well. He doesn't seek any publicity from it, so it's got to be a positive if you're helping other people out.'

Pat also weaved his spell over the New South Wales Rugby Union team before the start of the Super 12 season. The highly-fancied Waratahs have been tagged the perennial under-achievers in the strongest provincial Rugby competition in the world which features teams from Australia, New Zealand and South Africa. Coach Ian Kennedy recruited Pat to address his side at training two days before they were due to play a pre-season match against reigning Super 12 champions, the Canterbury Crusaders from New Zealand.

'Our team motto for the season was: "Never give up", so Pat was the perfect person to explain the full meaning of that,' says Waratahs captain Jason Little. 'His dedication and commitment are incredible. When you look at what Australians have achieved in the face of adversity, it's hard to go past some of Pat's achievements. We complain about a lot of very minor things but to hear his stories about running most of the way across America with a stress fracture just amazed us because most of us wouldn't even get out of bed in that situation.'

The Waratahs' motto was fully tested against Canterbury. The match was played in atrocious weather conditions and at one stage, New South Wales was defending grimly on its own line for fifteen minutes while the Crusaders launched one attacking raid after another. Displaying typical Aussie bravery, the Waratahs held the line. Pat Farmer watched from the grandstand, and was transfixed despite the torrential downpour. He derived almost as much pride and satisfaction as the Waratah players from their 16–3 victory. 'The big thing we all carried into that match from Pat's speech was the value of mental toughness,' says Little. 'There are a lot of sportspeople of similar ability but the six inches between the ears is what makes all the difference.' Unfortunately the Waratahs could not consistently tap into their reserves of physical courage and mental toughness throughout the Super 12 season. They finished a disappointing ninth.

The acceptance as an equal by his sporting peers has been very important to Pat, after years of craving recognition and respect in a sport that was generally afforded oddball status. 'It's so nice to be able to pass the knowledge and experience I've gained from ultra running on to other sportspeople and receive the recognition from them as well,' he says. 'They're asking me for the answers from what I do, to help them with what they do. That makes me feel very good about myself.'

But there are many people outside the world of sport who continue to be inspired and motivated by Pat Farmer. One of them was Paul Rudd, a senior television executive with the Nine Network. As Executive Producer of Special Events and Millennium Events, Rudd commissioned the making of a documentary on Pat's Centenary of Federation run. Thirty-four-year-old Rudd had dedicated a decade of his life to scale the ladder in the most cut-throat and pressurised television workplace in Australia. He had devoted the last three years towards planning Channel Nine's 30-hour live coverage of the Millennium celebrations around the globe. Yet, in September 1999, he took a leap into the great unknown by quitting his job to preserve his health and his young family. Rudd believes he was on the verge of a physical breakdown. He was later diagnosed as suffering from Chronic Fatigue Syndrome.

'I knew it was a life-altering decision I was taking and that the economic impact on my family could have been enormous, but thought: "There's more to life than grinding away at the coalface",' says Rudd. 'I drew strength from all that Pat had done—his courage and sheer determination to do what *he* wants to do and his dedication to his family. I had to do what was right for me and Pat gave me the courage to take the tough decision.'

After a complete six-month break from work, Rudd's health showed a dramatic improvement. He returned to television, albeit with a totally different outlook on life.

The awards and honours have flowed Pat's way following his record-breaking run. He was nominated for Australian of the Year, a prize that went to leading Australian scientist Sir Gustav Nossal. But Pat did receive an Australia Day award from the Prime Minister, recognising his outstanding achievements. He was also nominated as an Olympic torch-bearer, running one of the final legs into Sydney through his childhood suburb of Granville.

While Pat has been thrilled and humbled by the honours, he laments the fact that Lisa is not alive to share the rewards of a mission that was a shared dream. His quest around Australia was partly about finding answers to so many of the questions that had muddied his mind after her death. But there were no blinding flashes of realisation on his odyssey. The countless hours alone with his thoughts helped him to deal with the questions and why they had troubled him so, but the answers were never as clear-cut as he had hoped they would be. One desire was achieved: the run brought him closer to Lisa.

'I think I did end up feeling closer to her,' he says. 'Before that the overwhelming feeling was that of being distraught but now there is a greater sense of acceptance. I accepted that she wasn't here but I accepted that she was here through Brooke and Dillon. The time on the road certainly helped to clarify my thoughts on that.'

The one revelation that visited Pat answered for him the question that everyone asks themself: what is the meaning of life? He delved deep into his faith and pondered the Bible's teachings about the loss Mary felt over the crucifixion of her only son Jesus. He came to the realisation that the greatest pain any parent could endure would be to lose a child. As an extension of that, he recognised that life was all about the creation of new life.

'I figured the greatest thing you are able to do is to give the gift of life and later in life be able to look into your child's eyes and for them to be proud of you and to have learnt from you and to leave something behind,' he says. 'At the time I just got this incredible message and it just cleared my mind up entirely. It helped me to deal with everything else.'

But Pat still misses Lisa more than ever. He still hasn't let go and struggles to imagine a day when he will. He has never taken off his wedding band. Lisa's wardrobe remains as it was before her death. Pat can still picture the way she looked while wearing certain clothes. He still polishes her shoes regularly. Could he ever love again? 'Nobody knows what the future holds but I just can't see it,' he says. 'The kids are very fulfilling for me and that's all I need.' Every night since the death of his wife, Pat has gone to sleep hoping Lisa would come to him in his dreams. She never has and he accepts that she probably never will.

So he keeps himself occupied up to eighteen hours a day,

every day. It helps take his focus away from the pain and dulls it at other times. He has used part of the proceeds from his payment for the run, and much of his time, to add improvements and finishing touches to the dream home. He continues to do things as Lisa would have wanted. Pat has brought into play his landscaping experience to create a pond and fountain specially dedicated to his wife. The main feature is a sculpture of a mermaid with a child's face—that of his daughter Brooke. He has also had a swimming pool built, reconstructed fences, built gardens and finished painting inside the house. 'While I'm busy, I'm happy.'

Brooke and Dillon continue to be his main priority. His daughter started school in January 2000, and has revelled in the stimulation it has provided—something that has thrilled her father no end, considering school days were not the best days of his life. Unavoidably Pat has become involved in the everyday school duties expected of parents—working bees, school fetes and selling raffle tickets. Brooke picked up where she left off with dance classes, returning with a new air of self-confidence.

Dillon continues to be his own little man—happiest when he's with his Dad, working away with his own toy shovel or hammer; canoeing in the earth dam on their property; or helping to build home-made kites. It's part of the circle of life, Pat bonding with his children by spending the type of quality time that shaped his formative years.

Mary Farmer still plays the role of devoted mother and grandmother, and lives with her son to assist with day-to-day child care. Lisa's parents, Barry and June Bullivant, have relished spending time with Brooke and Dillon again. Barry has been a great source of advice for Pat in dealing with the high-spirited Brooke. But the Bullivant family has also struggled to deal with its grief. Barry was bedridden for a month after suffering a breakdown after his daughter's death. Wife June spent much of 1999 recovering from a stroke that afflicted her in the aftermath of the tragedy. Other family members have used counselling and anti-depressants to cope.

Lisa's parents have a box in which they have preserved photos, videos, dresses, magazines and other memorabilia of their only daughter. They do not look at it, and have found they are unable to confront the memories. They have stored all the items away for the future and will hand the box over to Brooke and Dillon when they are older.

Another tragedy loomed in 1999 when Lisa's older brother Craig was diagnosed with leukaemia. It was an enormously stressful time for all of the Bullivants. But it appears he has won his battle for life. He emerged from three months of chemotherapy and radiotherapy, wryly telling his father: 'Hi Dad, I'm back from the dead.'

So what does the future hold for Pat Farmer? For now, he appears to be at peace with his decision to close the curtain on his sixteen-year running career. 'I think I'm very fortunate in that I have gone beyond whatever my expectations were as far as the sport is concerned, although I have to say I wouldn't be keen for my kids to get into ultra running because it can be a tough and crappy sport at times,' he says. Some friends can't envisage Pat not pounding out the kilometres on some long and lonely road and predict that the around-the-world run will happen one day. But the practicalities of raising two children as a single father make further forays into the record books unlikely—at least for the foreseeable future.

Pat will continue to have a public profile in the short term, through his promotional work with the Centenary of Federation through to 2001. No matter what he does, there's no doubt it will be done with 100 per cent effort. 'I'll always continue to set very, very high expectations of myself and I don't think I'll ever achieve those,' he says. 'I'll never be content because I set higher standards for myself than anyone else does.'

A career in politics even appeals to him—several parties have already made overtures. Like many Australians, Pat has long been critical of the quality and ethics of politicians but is honest enough to admit that it's easier to throw stones from the outside. 'I probably would be prepared to get involved in politics and while I see faults in all parties the only way you can possibly be successful would have to be with a mainstream party. Unfortunately in this country that's the way it is,' he says. He says if he chose that career path, it would happen sooner rather than later.

His oratorical skills are in demand as a motivational speaker on the charity and corporate circuits. But, as always, the picture Pat Farmer sees in his mind is far more expansive. He thinks he stumbled on to something on the dusty trails and in the timber halls of a country preparing to celebrate becoming 100 years young—a willingness in people to believe in themselves and Australia, a keenness to express their passion and pride for a place most still believe is one of the luckiest countries in the world. All they need is someone or something to help them to believe that they as ordinary individuals and Australia as a people can achieve extraordinary things. Pat Farmer feels his work is not over. He believes he still has a role to play in galvanising patriotism and engendering self-belief in a nation's people that nothing is impossible if they have a dream—if they set their heart, mind and soul to making it come true and prepare to put one foot in front of the other.

Index